BOOKS BY ROBERT S. KANE

Africa A to Z
South America A to Z
Asia A to Z
Canada A to Z
South Pacific A to Z

SOUTH PACIFIC A TO Z

SOUTH PACIFIC

A to Z

Australia, New Zealand
The Tropic Isles of Fiji
New Caledonia, The Samoas
Tahiti, Tonga—and Hawaii

ROBERT S. KANE

Photographs by the author
Maps by Louise E. Jefferson

Doubleday & Company, Inc., Garden City, New York

"At the Play," by C. J. Dennis from *The Sentimental Bloke*, reprinted by permission of Angus & Robertson Ltd.

DU
15
K3

Contents

MAPS

Foreword

This is a book of islands.

Or, actually, a book of selected islands—the most representative, the most accessible, and the most developed for visitors, of the South Pacific, that unfathomably tremendous stretch of land and water which is surely the most romanticized and stereotyped portion of our planet.

One of the islands is so large that it constitutes a continent, others are but pinpricks on the map. They are places of diversity and of beauty, but they are, as well, infinitely more complex than they are given credit for being by many of us who live in the Northern Hemisphere.

Here, the magic words South Pacific conjure up visions of beauteous maidens in grass skirts, of coconuts plopping from the tops of palm trees onto deserted white-sand beaches, of semi-alcoholic beachcombers at waterfront bars, of Captain Bligh as personified either by Charles Laughton or Marlon Brando (depending upon the generation of the conjurer), of sarong-clad Dorothy Lamour with a ukulele in one arm and a bronzed Jon Hall in the other (if one is sufficiently mature), of Mr. Michener's lusty Bloody Mary and Mr. Maugham's provocative Sadie Thompson.

The more geographically adept might go a bit farther, when thinking of the South Pacific, and in the mind's eye see a beer-drinking, steak-consuming Australian, cavorting to the strains of "Waltzing Matilda," a rakish slouch-hat shielding him from the sun, immense herds of sheep in the background; or, perhaps, Sir Edmund Hillary climbing a New Zealand Alp in preparation for his ascent of Everest. There might even be a vague history-class memory of Captain Cook darting about on expeditions of discovery, and it could be that there would be visions of the brilliant Polynesian paintings of Paul Gauguin.

I doubt, though, if there would be a good deal more. Most of us who live on the top side of the equator more or less unconsciously dismiss the lower half of the globe from our considerations, unless crises or disaster call it to our attention in the headlines or on the television screens. Happily, the South Pacific, since World War II when it was a major theater of operations, has been about as peaceful a chunk of earth as one could expect in an imperfect world.

But it has not been asleep. While most of us have been otherwise occupied, the South Pacific has been rather quietly bringing itself into touch with the times. In the pages that follow, there has been an attempt to capsulize the situation for the prospective traveler, armchair or otherwise, to paint a picture—most certainly including lovely grass-skirted ladies, Australian sheep stations and New Zealand climbers and, for that matter, the bars, waterfront and otherwise. As in the earlier *A to Z* books, there is orientation based upon on-the-spot sampling, on the ever-so-vital practicalities of transport, accommodation, food, shops, after-dark amusement, and the chief daytime occupation of the pleasure traveler, sightseeing. And there is, as well, a bit of background— political, historical, geographical, social, economic—which, hopefully, will help dispel at least some of the clichés which the South Pacific peoples so patiently endure, life in their countries embracing a good deal more than beachcombing and beer-drinking.

Examples? I want you to read on, so I cite but a few. Australia will surprise with the excellence not so much of its lager but of its wines, not to mention the excitement and sophistication of its handsome cities—Sydney has become one of the world's great ones—and the cosmopolitan ambiance so largely the result of the contributions made by about a million recently arrived continental European immigrants. New Zealand, on the other hand, is most appealing beyond the towns, with incredibly lovely snowy peaks, fiords, and forests. Western Samoa is not only more than fourteen times as large as American Samoa, but the one newly sovereign nation which chooses not to join the United Nations. Its neighbor, long-neglected U.S.-governed Samoa, is being transformed into a model Pacific territory by means of an ingenious crash-development program which includes, of all things, an incredibly bold educational television system. The tiny Kingdom of Tonga—not heard from since its late Queen was a hit at Queen Elizabeth II's coronation in London—has built its first hotel, making possible regular tourist visits, in contrast to those of only occasional travelers. Britain's beauteous Crown Colony of Fiji—more heavily East Indian in populace that Fijian—has developed to the point where it is about ready to strike out on its own. France's New Caledonia is booming with bauxite. Also French Tahiti replaces the bauxite with tourists, so many of them that huge jets bring in several planeloads each day.

Still, the transition has not been so abrupt or all-encompassing as to wipe out the traditional. The post-World War II style and excitement of burgeoning Australia have not changed the casual, informal, friendly approach of that country's people, nor the eternal allure of its "Outback" and its Great Barrier Reef. New Zealand remains in many ways more quaintly British Colonial than far younger ex-colonies of the Crown. The delightful Fijians, in their neat villages, welcome newcomers with the traditional toast of *yaqona,* to the accompaniment of centuries-old ritual. New Caledonia, despite its disproportionately large European population, is as Melanesian as it always was—just down the road and over the hill. The Western Samoan Parliament meets in a thatched house of classic Polynesian design, and the American Samoan, TV in his village classroom notwithstanding, continues to excel as host at feasts as old as his culture. Even the Tahitian, somewhat bewildered by the hordes of temporary visitors in his midst, remains as gracious, as quick to smile, and as just-plain-good-looking as he was in Gauguin's day. Everywhere the pace of life has an even, pleasant cadence, and, with the partial exception of New Zealand, with its relative lack of spontaneity and verve, there is an agreeably lighthearted partiality for the joy of festivity, however inconsequential the occasion.

Will the jet change it all? Conceivably. But one hopes, and not without optimism, that all hell will freeze over before the Aussie refrains from a chat with the stranger from abroad at his side, in a pub. Surely it will be a long time before Tahitian eyes fail to twinkle, or Fijians dispose of their *meke* dances, or Samoans lose their skill as architects, or New Zealanders become unenthusiastic over their Alps, or Tongans replace the pomp of their monarchial system. The South Pacific populations have withstood the elements, great wars, the occasionally dubious imports of the explorers and colonists and missionaries and traders. They remain the easiest to know of an increasingly small planet's peoples. Rather than fear the consequences of the jet's penetration of their territory, we must welcome and exploit it, hopeful that the interchange it makes possible will dissipate the gap that engulfs the Top Half from Down Under.

Robert S. Kane

Introducing the South Pacific

THANK YOU, CAPTAIN COOK!

The key name in this book is Cook: James Cook, Captain, Royal Navy. For the South Pacific is really Cook's Pacific. By the time he was forty, some two centuries ago, he had surveyed the eastern coast of Canada, and was off to the *new* New World, the Americas being relatively old hat at the time. What he did not discover in the South Pacific, he rediscovered. What had been sighted from the decks of ships in earlier decades, he went ashore to see. What the rest of the world had been curious about—but not *seriously* curious—he investigated and charted and chronicled.

Cook was not completely alone, of course. There were other bold wanderers after new horizons. But it was Cook who both literally and figuratively put the South Pacific on the map and brought it to the Northern Hemisphere's attention. The Australians are so grateful to him that they had the English house in which he was born transported to Melbourne stone by stone, and re-erected in a public park. (You may visit it today.) The British named an island group for him. (You may fly to it, and cruise ships stop there as well.) The New Zealanders call their highest peak after him (you may stay in a luxury hotel at its base) as well as the strait that separates their North and South Islands. And Cook Inlet, on which is situated the city of Anchorage in America's forty-ninth state, is testimony to the incredible range of his Pacific exploits; he discovered it in 1778.

The Cook explorations were the starting point for colonization and development which is detailed, country by country, in the chapters following. Australia, long populated by smallish groups of nomadic aborigines, began modern life as a prison. New Zealand, to which the Maoris had paddled in their great canoes from what is now French Polynesia a millennium ago, was later settled by hand-picked cross-sections of British communities. The tropical islands became targets, about simultaneously, for prim and proper Christian missionaries, ruthless traders, the fleets of the imperialistic powers (that of the United States included), and motley assortments of occasional visitors who ranged from disreputable beachcombers to greats like Gauguin and Stevenson.

The relative inaccessibility of the South Pacific, coupled with the ingredients of the romantic (who could ask for more than azure seas, white beaches, palm trees, cannibals, wrecked ships, and beautiful women?) combined to create an alluring image for the rest of the world. But tourism was later in coming than has been the case in any other major area, sub-Sahara Africa possibly excepted.

Only since World War II has there been any concerted effort at luring the casual traveler. But once started, there has been no stopping it. Airlines like Australia's Qantas have made transportation effortless, with almost all of the major destinations now served by jets, and the minor ones within air minutes of larger jetports. The great shipping companies concentrate now on passengers as well as freight, moving them about in air-conditioned luxury both on regular services and special cruises. And at the receiving end there has been all manner of activity. Governments, both sovereign and colonial, have set up professionally staffed tourist departments. Modern, air-conditioned hotels now are a feature in every one of the destinations included in this book— and they are being supplemented with additional facilities. Travel agencies on the scene work with those aboard to coordinate local arrangements for visitors.

Getting about is made easy by the tremendous choice of package tours taking one throughout the area, by local exploratory junkets of as little as half a day, by the availability of self-drive and chauffeured cars. Most important of all, perhaps, is the time gap. Board a Qantas jet at New York's Kennedy Airport and you can be in Fiji twenty hours later, and Sydney three hours after that. (Fiji borders the International Date Line; one loses a day going east, gains it going west.) Tiny American Samoa has one of the most splendid jet-equipped airports in the world. Even obscure Tonga, to whom the airplane is about as new as the air conditioner, is now linked with nearby Fiji by rapid daily flights. And so it goes. The essence of the South Pacific is now open-sesame to the contemporary traveler. He will not be regarded as quite the curiosity that Cook was. But, on the other hand, he is not likely to meet the fate of that pioneering tourist, Cook having been killed by decidedly inhospitable Hawaiians in 1779.

THE SOUTH PACIFIC AND PATA

The blue-and-white insignia you'll see displayed at various establishments as you journey through the South Pacific is that of PATA, the Pacific Area Travel Association, a non-profit association of government tourist departments (including those of the United States and its State of Hawaii, and of Canada), airlines, steamship lines, hotels, travel agencies, shops, and other organizations with Pacific interests. Headquartered in San Francisco, PATA exists solely to develop Pacific tourism and make it more pleasant for the traveler. Through its annual conferences and workshops (held each year at a different Pacific point) and by means of research and promotion programs, it works to lessen the traveler's burden through intensive campaigning for lower fares and increased amenities. And it shares with Pacific countries its conviction that travel is an approach to peace, helping improve economic, international, and cultural relations among peoples. At its 1966 conference in New Delhi, an American—John W. Black, the crackerjack director of the United States Travel Service —was elected president. From its headquarters (442 Post Street, San Francisco) it disseminates gratis material on all member countries, and, at a charge of one dollar, it will send you its Explorer Kit, containing among other things a color map of the area, an outline map for itinerary planning, and a log book for your trip.

FIRST STEP: OBTAINING A PASSPORT

For every South Pacific destination in this book (the en route stop-off point of Hawaii and American Samoa naturally excepted) U.S. citizens must be in possession of a valid passport. The United States Government deserves kudos for the ease and rapidity with which they are issued. To obtain a first passport one needs a birth certificate (or a notarized affidavit of birth vouched for by a relative or long-time friend), ten dollars, and two passport-size photos (front view, three inches by three inches, on a white background, without retouching but with smile—if you like to smile). The passport is valid for three years but can be renewed for two additional years at the bargain rate of five dollars.

To obtain a passport after you've already had one, the procedure is the same as applying for a new one, except that your expired passport will take the place of a birth certificate or notarized affidavit. Applications must be made in person (not even your travel agent can do this for you) at the Department of State Passport Offices in New York, Miami, San Francisco, Washington, Boston, Seattle, Los Angeles, Chicago, or New Orleans, or in other cities at the office of the clerk of a federal court. Allow ten days or two weeks but don't be surprised if the postman surprises you with even earlier delivery. And don't hesitate to request extra-quick service if you feel it necessary.

INOCULATIONS AND HEALTH

Your principal requisite in this department is a valid smallpox vaccination; it must be not less than eight days nor more than three years old, and must be validated by one's local board of health, or a regional office of the United States Public Health Service. Have it inscribed on the yellow form known as the "International Certificates of Vaccination as Approved by the World Health Organization"; these are issued by the U. S. Public Health Service, often via airlines, steamship companies, and travel agencies. A physician's letterhead will suffice, instead, but the yellow forms are passport-size and I find it convenient to staple mine in the inside back cover of my passport. Note that the smallpox vaccination is a requisite for re-entry into the United States, and is also required by most South Pacific countries. *Requirements, country by country, are in the chapters following.* Though not required, I suggest you also get immunizations for typhoid-paratyphoid, tetanus, and polio. The smallpox injection is a one-shot affair but others may require as many as three visits, with about a week or ten days between each, so allow about a month to six weeks for this pre-trip jollity, so that by the time you depart you'll have recovered from whatever unpleasant reactions might result from the shots.

If you are combining a visit through Asia with your South Pacific journey, you'll want cholera shots as well, and possibly yellow fever ones, too. Most South Pacific countries understandably require that you be immunized against these diseases if coming from an area where they are prevalent.

Keeping fit as you travel need be no problem whatsoever. Australia, New Zealand, and of course Hawaii are drink-the-water-everywhere places; elsewhere the best water rule is: If there's a carafe of the stuff in your hotel room, don't drink from taps. By sticking to the better places, in the islands, you preclude any need to worry over salads and the like. At alfresco feasts in islands like Tahiti, the Samoas, and Fiji, live dangerously and sample everything, exercising discretion with doubtful-appearing novelties. Be as merry as you like everywhere, of course, but eat and drink in moderation, get a good night's sleep every night (sightseeing can be enervating), and you'll not come in contact with Tahitian Tummy, the Wellington Wobbles, Suva Shakes, or whatever it is you'd like to name the indispositions which can befall one in *any* new place in *any* country.

THE VISA RITUAL

The South Pacific is among the least bothersome of world areas as regards visas. However, you still need to go through the red-tape absurdities involved in getting those rubber stamps affixed to your passport (that's all visas are) in a number of cases. *Country-by-country requirements for tourist visas are indicated in the chapters following,* but let me indicate, at this point, that before even embarking on the visa routine you will need your validated vaccination certificate and proof of onward transportation to the next destination on your itinerary. Should the actual ticket not be in your hand (and chances are it won't be ready until just before departure) ask your travel agent, or the carrier from whom you're purchasing your ticket, for a letter certifying that the ticket is being prepared for you. Have available also a supply of the photos you ordered for your passport; some countries ask for them on visa applications.

If your trip is *purely* of a business nature, you will probably have no resort but to apply for a *business* visa. But if you can call yourself a tourist—*by any stretch of the imagination,* and still sleep nights—apply for a *tourist* visa, in which case life will be much easier for you, and the red tape throughout considerably lessened. Although passports must be applied for in person, visas can usually be obtained by a third party, so that your travel agent can be helpful, in this respect, making the rounds for you, with your passport. (American Express, in New York, has a special visa section and gets them at almost lightning-like speed for its clients.) Even if you do the work yourself—and you won't need visas for a number of South Pacific countries—check with your travel agent for the latest changes in regulations, and for visa application forms; travel agents specializing in the South Pacific should have supplies of them. Happily, all of the countries in this book generally issue tourist visas while one waits, without requiring return pick-up visits to consulates. The one exception is Western Samoa; it can take as long as a month for a visa to come through for that country.

CLIMATE: GO WHEN YOU CAN

An area as vast as the South Pacific, with both tropical, subtropical, and temperate zones, cannot, of course, be ideal at all times. Pick out winter for a Round the South Pacific journey, and you've summer in southern Australia and New Zealand—an ideal time. But to the north you may run into some rain. Pick the driest months in the tropical islands, and you'll find cooler or wetter weather elsewhere. The point is, go when you can. In so vast an area, the law of averages tends to be with you, somehow or other seeing to it that you'll get more than your share of pleasant weather. *Details of climate, country by country, are in the chapters following.* Remember, though, that rainy seasons in the islands are not necessarily periods of incessant downpour. Sometimes it may rain for but a bit of each day; very often rains tend to fall at night, while you're sleeping. Sometimes entire days will be fair. I repeat: Go when you can.

PACKING: LIGHTLY, PLEASE

Easier said than done, I know. But please: Easy does it. Even cruise passengers on ships, unconcerned with imposed baggage-weight maximums, are happier with a relatively selective wardrobe, for they may supplement their casual wardrobes at ports of call along the way at places like Tahiti, New Caledonia, and Hawaii and, particularly in Australia, pick up just about anything they like in the clothing line, knowing that it will be fine style and quality, and reasonably priced.

The air traveler, of course, has to live with the weight factor. Not his own, of course. (Although I have flown small airlines that *do* weigh passengers.) But his baggage's. Unless he wants to be charged overweight (and there is nothing the traveler more dislikes paying) he must stay within limits: forty-four pounds economy class; sixty-six first class. Because he'll want to pick up souvenirs en route, he does well to pack *under* the limit, to allow for additions to his bags. He knows that wash-and-wear garments are the easiest to care for, and he should be advised that throughout the South Pacific he can count on quick, and generally good quality, laundry service (overnight, or frequently, at a surcharge, back in time for dinner if handed in before breakfast). The man knows that ties and shirts will vary what otherwise might be a monotonous wardrobe, and the woman traveler is so beset with magazine and newspaper advice on how to accessorize for variety, that I'll not venture into that area.

It should be apparent (but it is not, always) that the Round the South Pacific traveler is rarely in any one place long enough for the locals to get bored with his (or her) clothes, even if, on occasion, repetition becomes necessary. It should be realized, too, that most people on the scene are aware that travelers cannot take along all they possess on a globe-girdling journey. Still, quantities will vary with the individual. There are times when packers cannot possibly resist including that extra blouse or sports shirt, even if they know they'll probably have no need for them. Ship passengers will want beach-type garb for daytime pool and deck activity, and those traveling first class, and on luxury cruises, will require evening wear (including dinner jackets for men). Ashore, in South Pacific countries, formal wear is not needed, unless, of course, one knows in advance that special occasions will make such clothes necessary. Men generally wear jackets and ties in Australian and New Zealand cities, and after dark at most, but not all, of the islands and resorts in this book; there are some, of course, where evening dress is completely casual. Women should know that the level of style is high in the major Australian cities, that in-town daytime wear usually calls for gloves and stockings (even in summer), and that evenings on the town—better restaurants, nightspots, the theater—are as dressy as they would be in comparable

American and European cities. Hats for women, except as a precaution against the sun in hot spots, are not generally a requisite. Shorts and slacks are worn by women only at beach areas and resorts throughout the South Pacific; excursions into town call for skirts.

A basic woman's wardrobe—and here I am grateful for the expert suggestions of Qantas Airways' much-traveled Joyce Chivers—would include the following:

A lightweight coat, a lightweight wool travel suit, several blouses that can be worn with suit skirts (possibly including one jersey shell); at least one extra-full skirt for active sightseeing; two cocktail or late-afternoon ensembles, in either cotton, linen, or uncrushable silk; a wool dress for cooler places; cotton shift-type dresses (they require no undergarments), and casual playclothes for the islands and resorts; sockettes to take the place of stockings in the islands and resorts, two swimsuits, each in its own plastic bag for packing when wet; a lightweight jersey-type stole for coolish evenings in the islands and resorts and/or a cardigan sweater usable for the same purpose; playshoes (preferably rubber-sole sneakers which are essential for walking on coral reefs), a pair of rubber thongs (easily procurable en route); a pair of low-heeled walking shoes preferably with closed toes, two pairs of dressier shoes; several changes of lingerie and stockings. (Bear in mind that Hawaii, Tahiti, and New Caledonia are excellent sources of local casual wear, quantities of which prove irresistible to distaff visitors; if they're early stops on your itinerary, save space in your luggage for what you're bound to buy on these islands; straw sunhats need not be packed; amusing locally-made ones are available on all the islands. About hairdoes: Keep them relatively simple, allowing for easy management as there is a dearth of high-style hairdressers between Honolulu and Sydney. Tip: Carry along a wig for evening wear.

A basic man's wardrobe—and here my own experience guides me—should include a dark (gray or navy blue) summer-weight dacron-and-wool suit which is suitable for both day and evening city wear; a cotton-and-dacron sports jacket; a pair of gray dacron-

and-wool summer-weight slacks, for wear with the sports jacket and with sports shirts, of which there should be about four; a supply of long-sleeved shirts (the quantity depending upon whether they are drip-dry to be washed by the wearer, or for the laundry, which in any case is always quick) which may be worn with ties or, if desired, as sports shirts in cooler places; a good choice of ties, there being no better or lighter-in-weight variety adders; a pair or two of tan, chino-type wash-and-wear slacks; a pair of wash-and-wear pajamas (wash them before breakfast, they're dry at bedtime); a raincoat with a detachable wool liner which will serve also as topcoat (if there will be really cool weather), *and* as bathrobe; socks, underwear, and handkerchiefs; a hat, if you wear one (straw beach hats are everywhere obtainable), two pairs of shoes (one might well be loafers); a pair of rubber thongs (obtainable everywhere en route); two swimsuits, each in its own plastic bag, for packing when wet; a thin long-sleeved sweater (cashmere or pseudo-cashmere is ideal), and of course, a toilet kit. If the itinerary will include Australia and New Zealand in winter, add a winter-weight suit or sports jacket and slacks.

Now, I have saved until last the matter of walking shorts. Men throughout the Pacific *do* wear shorts, but they are generally shorter than those made in the United States, and *nowhere are they worn with ankle socks*. In the islands and tropical northern Australia, men wear either knee-length white or tan socks with their shorts, and—if going to business—a short-sleeved white shirt with or without necktie. For more casual wear, men wear shorts and sandals or rubber thongs *without any socks*. An additional point: Shorts can be purchased ready-made in all of the islands, as well as in Australia where they are exceptionally well tailored. Or, island tailors will make them up inexpensively and quickly. Knee-length white socks (known as golf hose and needing no garters) are also everywhere available, at modest prices. So, gentlemen, I implore you: If you're modest about exposing that portion of your limbs beneath the knees, wear high socks; otherwise, none at all. There may be valid reasons why some traveling Americans

are considered odd and/or pathetic, but this need not be one of
them.

Both men and women will want sunglasses (two pair are not at
all a bad idea, particularly if they have prescription lenses), an
extra pair of eyeglasses and a copy of the prescription, some Band-
Aids, a roll of Scotch tape (it has innumerable uses on a trip),
a small envelope of paper clips and rubber bands—also very
handy to have along, several plastic bags for wrapping small purchases from markets which do not wrap things (many hotel laun-
dries encase laundered shirts in these; save them!), a few packs of
Chiclets and/or Life Savers for the occasional small aircraft
whose crews do not serve them on takeoff or landing; a supply of
Wash 'n Dris, or similar pre-moistened disposable washcloths; a
half-dozen of the very cheapest ballpoint pens (they are lost occasionally when filling out landing cards, customs forms, and the
like); a pocket-size flashlight; a generous supply of printed or en-
graved personal or business cards; a sturdy shoe-polishing cloth;
a plastic bottle of aspirin; an anti-diarrhea preparation (just in
case); a pocket or purse notebook; names, addresses, and phone
numbers (both business and residential when possible) of friends
and friends of friends to contact (ideally, they should be written
in advance of your arrival); and, I suggest in all modesty, this
book! Men will find well-known toilet requisites easily replenish-
able everywhere. But women, except in Australia and the major
New Zealand cities, do well to take supplies of favorite special
preparations, for use in the islands. A single bar of soap is all
that is necessary; almost all hotels provide it, and small bars may
always be filched from aircraft washrooms along the way.

Luggage? The lighter the better. I have experimented with a
number of designs and materials, but I always end up with the
suitcases of solid color (or plaid) canvas (preferably water-
proofed); they are made in a number of sizes and shapes with
zipper closures. A two-suiter weighs as little as three or four
pounds and the design is such that there always seems to be
space for one more addition. I've tried a number of makes but
Grasshopper seems to stand up the best, in my experience. (Weigh

before you buy: Many luggage shops and department stores now have scales.) The light weight of these bags is in part due to their lack of heavy interior compartments, flaps and the like. They are unencumbered with gimmicky interiors, with the exception of pockets along two or three sides. To compartmentalize smaller items of clothing I use plastic bags—one for shirts, another for socks, another for ties (rolled up), another for underwear, etc. Women may classify similarly with their apparel.

Unpack creasable clothes the moment you check into a hotel. If your bathroom has a shower, and you have some wrinkles you'd like removed but the valet service is closed for the day, hang them on a bathroom hook or shower rod, turn on the shower full strength, close the bathroom door and window (if any), and let your garments steam for a while (not forgetting to turn off the shower after seven or eight minutes). Unless they have been packed for an eternity, you'll find them reasonably wearable.

PHOTOGRAPHY

Snap away! Wherever you go in the South Pacific, no matter how obscure the village of a tropical isle or congested the neighborhood of an urban area, there are splendid picture possibilities. If you're at all interested in photography, I suggest taking two cameras, one for black and white film, the other for color. Or, possibly, one for still shots, the other for movies. If you like, pick up at least one of your cameras at a duty-free airport shop. You'll find them in Honolulu, Pago Pago, Nadi, Sydney, and Auckland. *Film availability is discussed, country by country, in the chapters following.* Generally speaking, though, I advise taking a generous quantity with you, for it's more expensive in the South Pacific than in the United States, and color film is not available everywhere. If you've a great deal in your luggage, partially open the packages and write your name on them, thereby indicating to customs officials that the film is for your own use, and not for resale.

Other points: (1) Tuck a little sack or two of Silica Gel (or a similar preparation obtainable from photo-supply shops) in your camera case or gadget bag to fight the moisture, in those areas where you'll come in contact with it. (2) Airmail exposed color film home only if you're to be away three months or more—and then at your own risk, for even if you insure the film and get reimbursed if it's lost, you'll have to go back to where you snapped the photos to duplicate them. Most color film purchased abroad is packed with cloth mailing bags, each with address label attached. It goes directly to a processing laboratory, from which it is mailed to any address you note on the label. Remember that Kodak color film purchased abroad includes processing in the price, so don't lose the special mailing bag accompanying it; it's what indicates to the processing plant that you've already paid for its services. Exposed black-and-white film—much less sensitive than color—can be kept with you for a longer period, ideally in a plastic bag or airtight container. (3) Remember that the air-conditioned hotel room is as good for your exposed color film as it is for you; leave the air conditioner on while you're out during the day and if a maid turns it off, turn it right back on! (4) I have found that Kodak Plus-X is ideal as an all around black and white film, and Kodachrome II is my favorite for color, although I have had good results with Ektachrome, which sometimes is more readily available in the South Pacific. Much of the Kodak film on sale in the South Pacific is made in Australia or Britain, but it is identical with its American counterparts and can be processed in the United States. (5) Children everywhere—the South Pacific is no exception, heaven knows—are quite mad to be photographed, but their elders may prefer that you ask before you snap; in most places they'll agree. In the Samoas, where village and country houses very sensibly have wall-less façades in fair weather, the passerby can observe a good deal of intimate family life. But before recording it on film, it is good manners to ask permission. Guides are helpful in such instances, and can often pave the way for shots. Sometimes, though, they consider themselves experts at selecting locales for pictures, which may or may not be the case. Give them a polite hearing, but snap what *you* like when *you* see it, remembering that you may not find a similar setting for a later picture, or that, even if you do, the light may be less good. And don't worry about having to use a complicated camera. My longtime favorite is a Japanese Canon. But the new Kodak Instamatics are so simple to load and operate, and produce such excellent results, that I sometimes wonder why I bother with my 35-millimeter.

CUSTOMS

In the South Pacific: Like death and taxes, customs inspectors will always be with us, both abroad and at home. Despite the continuing efforts of organizations like the Pacific Area Travel Association, the global International Union of Official Travel Organizations, and government travel departments, to ease travel barriers, customs counters continue to be regarded by virtually every nation as signposts of sovereignty. The result is that we continue to be considered smugglers, or worse, until proven otherwise—and not only in the South Pacific. Generally, though, customs in this area of the world is relatively painless. Australia, which should know better, has us fill out rather absurdly long forms before we land or dock, and their inspectors—while polite as can be—are so concerned that we may be carriers of hoof-and-mouth disease that we must indicate our most recent encounters with livestock. (It is rather disconcerting, landing at Sydney Airport in the wee hours, to be asked when you last set foot in a barn.) Still, the Aussies are simplifying their red tape, bless them, and most of their neighbors are relatively free of eccentricities in this regard. Everywhere, though, one does well to regard customs inspectors with the respect they expect as officials of their governments; to speak only when spoken to (other than a good morning or good evening), to have necessary documents in hand, and to be candid as regards cameras, tape recorders, transistor radios, cigarettes, and liquor. A carton or two of cigarettes and a bottle of liquor are usually allowable, and, as earlier indicated, there's no problem on film for personal use, particularly if (when there are prodigious amounts) each packet is partially opened.

Returning to the United States: In a woefully misguided effort to stem the balance of payments problem, the United States Government, as from October 1, 1965, allows U.S. residents to return home from trips abroad—not more often than once in thirty days—with one hundred dollars' worth of purchases, duty free. This figure is based on the *retail* rate of the merchandise, *not* the wholesale rate, as was the case.

In addition, however, Americans may ship home, *duty free,* without having to declare them, and not counting as part of the hundred-dollar allowance, gift parcels not exceeding ten dollars in value; send as many as you like from wherever you like, but not more than one parcel per day to the same recipient. Mark each parcel, "GIFT—TOURIST PURCHASE—VALUE UNDER TEN DOLLARS."

As part of the hundred-dollar duty-free allowance, adults (over twenty-one) may bring back with them (but not have shipped) *one quart* of liquor. Also duty free—and this is worth remembering—are antiques, duly certified to have been made before 1830 (except those made in China, which are *verboten*), *paintings* and *sculpture* of any date, if certified as original works of art.

One more point. And a very important one for South Pacific travelers: *The duty-free allowance is doubled—to two hundred dollars for purchases made in American Samoa* (as well as those made in U.S.-governed Guam and the American Virgin Islands). Also, adult travelers returning from American Samoa (and the other two U.S. territories) may bring back a full gallon (five-fifths) of liquor duty free, instead of a quart. Bear this in mind when planning your South Pacific shopping budget. Remember, too, that you still may make purchases in other countries visited in the course of your journey—up to one hundred dollars' worth elsewhere—leaving you a full additional hundred dollars for purchases made in American Samoa, the grand total coming to two hundred dollars.

Note, too, that with the exception of the aforementioned less-than-ten-dollar gift parcels which you may ship home, all purchases must be carried with you to qualify for duty-free status; if it's so bulky you have to ship it, forget about saving the duty. However, the duty may be not as steep as you imagine. On certain articles, liquor for example, it can still be worthwhile to buy at duty-free shops abroad. Write the U. S. Bureau of Customs, Washington, D.C. for detailed information. And if the Federal Government threatens to make duty-free allowances even more stingy, which is, sadly, a possibility, write in protest to the President, your Senator, and your Congressman, as well as to the travel editor of your local newspaper. I have reason to believe that articles like mine in *Cue* magazine and those of my fellow members of the Society of American Travel Writers, in their publications, together with the protests to Congress and the President of letter-writing citizens were in part responsible for this most recent reduction in duty-free allowances being as relatively unsevere as it is.

YOUR SOUTH PACIFIC HOSTS

The South Pacific is a quite superb hodgepodge, racially, ethnically, culturally. Indeed, it is but religion (Christianity) which most of its residents share. Following on the heels of the explorers, mariners, and traders, and sometimes arriving concurrently with them, the missionaries were indisputably dedicated and more often than not braver than they are given credit for being. Many lost their lives, for cannibalism, so often unfairly considered a practice in Africa, where it probably was never indulged in to any appreciable degree, was definitely a part of certain Pacific islanders' cultures.

But the missionaries cannot be given straight A's. They did

their best to stomp out the islanders' great skill as dancers, often forbade them from wearing flowers on their persons, and were zealots in completely forbidding activity of any sort other than churchgoing on the Sabbath. Fortunately, they were not successful as regards dance and floral decor. Sundays, though, on many islands, remains as Blue Law as one can imagine, the pious Tonga Royal Family having enacted rigidly enforced bans against Sunday levity in the little kingdom's constitution.

The islanders' clothing, in recent years so copied abroad, is largely of missionary derivation, and that includes both the long muumuus of the women as well as the skirted garments (called *pareus* in Tahiti, *sules* in Fiji, *lava-lavas* in the Samoas) of the men.

Credit the missionaries, besides, with the introduction of Western-style education, setting down island languages on paper, translating the Bible into scores upon scores of island dialects and languages, teaching Western-style sanitation, offering Western-style health and medical services, making Sunday church attendance the major social (as well as spiritual) event of every week, and—perhaps most felicitously—introducing Christian hymns which, combined with the islanders' own fine music, results in some of the world's loveliest choral singing.

Aside from the European-origin Australians, New Zealanders, and Hawaiians, the minority of Europeans resident on other islands, and smallish, close-knit Chinese business communities on many islands, one may divide the Islanders thusly: *Polynesians* (meaning "of many islands")—handsome, smooth-haired with skins of golden brown, and features not unlike those of the Malays of Southeast Asia; *Melanesians,* sturdily built, good-looking, dark-skinned Negroid peoples; and *Micronesians,* who are an attractive racial blend of Polynesian, Melanesian, and Malay. (Still another group, anthropologically unique in the world, are the aborigines of Australia, a minority of which are pastoral nomads whose technology has never advanced beyond the boomerang and the spear of their ancient ancestors.)

One carries this terminology from the ethnic to the geographic.

Polynesia, roughly speaking, is a great triangle of islands with New Zealand, Hawaii, and Easter Island as the points delineating it. It is represented in this book by Tahiti, the Samoas, Tonga, by the Maori of New Zealand, and the tiny Hawaiian and larger part-Hawaiian populace of our fiftieth state. Melanesia ("black islands" in Greek) extends from Fiji to New Guinea, including New Caledonia. (Fijians, more so than Caledonians and New Guineans, are heavily Polynesian-blended, thanks to centuries of proximity to their Polynesian neighbors.) Micronesia (meaning "small islands") is that area east of the Philippines and to the north of New Guinea. None of its islands are included in this book (tourism has yet to arrive in this region) but it includes the far-reaching U. S. Pacific Trust Territory, whose component parts include the Carolines, the Marshalls, and the Marianas; the U.S. possessions Guam and Wake Island; and assorted other islands, atolls, and reefs. Many of these were World War II battle sites and known to thousands of Americans, myself but one of them.

The ancient Polynesians, and other Pacific peoples as well, adapted themselves to their environment realistically and skillfully. They evolved a culture which, though it embraced polygamy and cannibalism, also included brilliant mastery of the arts of ship-building and navigation (canoes with from one hundred to three hundred passengers paddled as far as twenty-five hundred miles through the Pacific, the millennium-old migration from near Tahiti to New Zealand being the all-time classic), of wood-carving and weaving (crafts still far from extinct), of music and dance (don't let commercial "Hawaiian" luaus keep you away from the real thing), of architecture (Samoan *fales* are classic examples of handcrafted dwellings at once supremely functional and aesthetically pleasing); of a cuisine which if not subtle to Western palates, is practical, economical, and nourishing (it is described in later chapters), and perhaps most important, of a happy philosophy and attitude toward life which has long been the envy of the outsider, and perhaps always will be.

Tattooed faces, ancient polytheistic religions, communal living, non-Western attitudes toward the sanctity of marriage, interisland

and intertribal wars of old, a predilection for feasting and grog, even what many Westerners disdainfully term lack of industry and drive—all these, one cannot deny, are (or were) parts of the Pacific islands' way of life. But who is the outsider to criticize them? How ambitious need one be in a warm, bountiful climate where food, clothing, shelter, and the necessary tools of life (all derived from the coconut) quite literally fall from trees? On small, isolated islands, half a planet away from the great land masses, what was the need for a monied economy? And with months each year which are either very wet or very hot, how could islanders be expected to have the impetus for the kind of activity which temperate-zone life induces? And as for impartiality toward drink, love-making ("moral" or otherwise), warfare, and the cruelty and torture which are its concomitants—how dare the West even suggest criticism? Cannibalism is not to our taste, most certainly, but is it any more to be deplored than starvation and the burning in ovens of some six million humans in the mid-twentieth century of the West?

By the same token, no intelligent visitor's attitudes toward the South Pacific and its peoples should be unabashedly gushing and uncritical. What is best avoided is the air of patronization which newcomers frequently find difficult to conceal. Terminology, for example, is of prime importance. I said it in earlier books, and I say it again, not giving up easily: It is high time—in the South Pacific, in the Caribbean, in South America, in Africa, in Asia —that we stop calling dark-skinned peoples "natives." The American in France calls the nationals of that land Frenchmen. The Swede in Switzerland considers his hosts Swiss. And so it should be in Tahiti, whose people are Tahitians, not "natives." And in all of the other underdeveloped countries, island, mainland, peninsular, or otherwise. Literally, of course, we are all natives of our own regions and countries. But the large-scale application of the word to poorer, non-whites abroad has a disdainful ring of stigma to it. And so does the practice, originated with the British and widely copied, of calling male servants "boys" even when they are grown men, when waiter, steward, bartender (or barman), or houseman are accurate, unpatronizing, and dignified.

Americans abroad, in the South Pacific as everywhere, must be prepared for questions, comments, and criticisms of the racial situation in the United States, and of other aspects of American life and of U.S. foreign policy. They do well to bear in mind the comments of Senator Robert Kennedy to the Council on Student Travel. He suggested that American students (and why not adults, as well?) going abroad "need a real understanding of their own country as well as the rest of the world, so that they can discuss questions intelligently." And he concluded: "Fourth of July speeches are not enough, either. It is just not true that the United States is a perfectly grand place where everyone loves everyone else."

This is not to imply that we need be ashamed as we go abroad. Far from it. There are sound reasons why the United States has become strong, great, and a world leader—and our democratic form of government, with all its imperfections, is not the least of them. It is important to bear in mind, too, that much of the interracial friction which makes current headlines is a result of efforts to insure equal opportunity regardless of color. Americans in the South Pacific do well to remember that sit-ins and other forms of non-violent demonstration originated by Negro Americans and their white supporters, are being emulated by the aborigines of Australia in their campaign for equal rights. They should realize that Fiji—more East Indian than Fijian—is in many respects a segregated society; that all is not sweetness and light vis-à-vis Tahitians and newly arrived French civil servants fresh from service in Algeria, who believe Tahitians will accept the kind of treatment that Algerians fought a revolution to rid themselves of; that the enlightened American administration in Pago Pago must contend with the opposition of certain locals not anxious to see their power eroded; that the Maoris of New Zealand, whose integration into the national life is perhaps that country's finest achievement, *still* remain at the bottom of the social, economic, and cultural scale. I make mention of the foregoing not to be cussedly critical, but only to indicate that all of us still live in an imperfect world; skeletons still are at large in everyone's closet.

Other unasked-for suggestions? Well, yes. Geography is terribly important. New Zealanders deplore the term "Australasia," for it does not imply the existence of their country. (You will not see it appear again in this book.) They are terribly concerned that you not consider them an appendage of Australia, more than a thousand miles distant. And it is well that you know before you go that though they agree on major matters in the lofty range of world affairs, Commonwealth relations, loyalty to the sovereign they share, cooperation in tourism, and the like, Australians and New Zealanders do not always get on terribly well, at a personal level. The New Zealander tends to consider the Aussie a bit brash, far too American-influenced, and not nearly British enough. (But he loves to go to Australia on holiday.) The Australian considers the Enzedder (N-Z-er in American English) provincial, a bit stuffy, somewhat archaic in outlook, and with an attitude toward the Crown and accompanying trappings that is at times excessive. (But he loves to go to New Zealand on holiday.)

The Western Samoans, quite understandably, are proud of their status as a sovereign nation and are not to be confused with their cousins, the colonials resident in American Samoa. The Tongans adored their late Queen, as well they might, and at times appear a bit overimpressed with the homogeneous quality of their populace (no East Indians, few foreigners). And our fellow Americans, the non-white Hawaiians—increasingly strong politically—are not quite as pleased with the economic supremacy of the white power structure as one might imagine.

SHOPPING IN THE SOUTH PACIFIC

Aside from the bonus of a hundred extra dollars' worth of allowable duty-free merchandise from American Samoa (dealt with earlier in this chapter in the Customs section), there are other

lures for the South Pacific shopper, and I detail them, country
by country, in the chapters following. Bargaining is practiced in
certain smaller shops, public markets, and the like, but the larger
stores, in the islands as well as in Australia and New Zealand,
have fixed-price policies. Better establishments will ship parcels
home, although it is wise to remember that only ten-dollar-or-less
gift parcels may enter the United States duty free; more costly
purchases cannot be included in the duty-free allowances of returning U.S. residents unless carried with them. Major shopping
countries, in my view, are Australia, New Caledonia, Tahiti, and,
because of its special duty-free status, American Samoa. The
other islands in this book fall within the middle-interest range,
and at the very bottom of my shopping list is New Zealand. Museums and historical monuments, particularly in Australia, are
excellent sources for postcards bearing reproductions of art
works, handsome illustrated catalogs, prints, and the like. Certain
market stalls and merchants everywhere accept traveler's checks,
usually at rates quite as good as those offered by banks and
hotels.

EMBASSIES AND CONSULATES

Western Samoa, which exchanges diplomatic missions only with
its former occupier, New Zealand, is, I believe, the only non-
Communist, fully sovereign state in the world where the United
States has no embassy or consulate. (Western Samoa does have
excellent relations with the United States, through its neighbor,
American Samoa.) We are also without official representation in
the Kingdom of Tonga, which though self-governing still is tech-
nically under the protection of Great Britain. There are U.S. consulates in Fiji and Tahiti, and in New Caledonia our only official
representation is the delegation to the South Pacific Commission
—a largely technical-assistance organization whose other members
are Australia, New Zealand, France, and Western Samoa. There
are, of course, United States embassies in Canberra, Australia,

and Wellington, New Zealand, and consulates elsewhere in Australia and in New Zealand. (The U. S. Ambassador to Australia, Edward Clark, a longtime personal friend of President Johnson's, is among the relatively few political appointees now heading U.S. missions abroad; not all Australians are, of course, flattered at being among the handful of exceptions to the rule of career diplomats.) It is among the functions of embassies, consulates, and offices of the United States Information Service to assist visiting Americans in professional matters and, upon occasion, unusual difficulties—booking hotel rooms and arranging for sightseeing *not* being among these. It is unlikely that you will need any help in this respect, but if you do, don't hesitate to request it. You will find personnel of varying caliber—often, though, refreshingly high. It is well to remember, when making evaluations in this regard, that a short-time tourist is not to be equated with a long-time resident who must solve problems in the educational, domestic, and health and child-rearing fields, not to mention transacting affairs of state in settings occasionally fraught with sensitive overtones.

CURRENCY

The value of South Pacific currencies, country by country, is indicated in the chapters following. I suggest you take most of your money—almost all of it, for that matter—in traveler's checks, those of American Express being the most universally recognizable. Take a *good many* in ten-dollar denominations, even if they do create rather a bulge; they're most convenient. Carry along, too, about thirty one-dollar bills. These are negotiable for purchases of drinks and cigarettes on most international flights, and also come in handy for last-minute use just before leaving a country when it would be inconvenient to cash a traveler's check. Take your credit cards along; the Diners' Club is particularly strong in the South Pacific, especially in Australia. (Remember, also, that the U.S. dollar is the local currency in American Samoa, as well as Hawaii, should you be stopping there.) There is no need to stockpile Asian currencies in advance of departure. There are no great bargains in these currencies in the United States, as is the case with some European currencies, although you might want a few dollars' worth for use on arrival. You might want to have along, too, Richard Joseph's *World Wide Money Converter and Tipping Guide* (Doubleday, $1.25). It's tiny but compact and easy to use for on-the-spot conversions. There are no black market dealings to be aware of in any of the South Pacific countries. The only confusing situation to be encountered is the current changeover in Australia from pounds, shilling, and pence to new Aussie dollars and cents. But that should present no greater difficulty to the foreigners than to the Aussies. Similar conversions are to follow in New Zealand, Fiji, and other islands.

TIPPING

Well, there is welcome news in this department. Tipping is positively forbidden in Tahiti (don't worry, you'll find other ways to spend your money there), it is practically nonexistent in New Caledonia, Tonga, the Samoas, and New Zealand, and it is done minimally in Australia and Fiji. That doesn't leave much else. And, aside from Hawaii, tips nowhere need be large. *Tips on tipping, country by country, are in the succeeding chapters.* The practice of adding service charges to hotel bills is not prevalent, and there is, of course, absolutely *no* tipping aloft, on airplanes, although porters at air terminals who carry luggage from customs counter to car, bus, or taxi generally expect tips; fifteen cents a bag is a good average. Tipping, wherever it is done, should be based on quality of service; tip for bad or surly service and you encourage more of same for those of us who follow in your footsteps.

Tipping at sea is something else again. It *is* expected. One's most important tippees are the room steward (average one dollar per day for a solitary stateroom occupant, perhaps $1.50 a day for a couple sharing a cabin), and the dining room steward, who should receive about the same. The deck steward, if he's done anything other than assign you your deck chair, should get about from fifteen or twenty cents a day, depending upon his helpfulness. Bar stewards, wine stewards, pages, barbers, hairdressers, porters, and the like are generally tipped as they serve you, much as in a hotel or restaurant, and at about the same rate. On long cruises, there is generally an intermediate point or two at which tips are distributed; pursers know just when. On one-stop voyages, tipping is generally done just before journey's end. Ship's officers, including the purser, are not tipped.

SIGHTSEEING AND GUIDES

You name it—Nukualofa, Tonga, or Sydney, Australia. Anywhere and everywhere in the South Pacific there are guides available, from taxi drivers on Bora Bora who learned a bit of English during World War II from resident Yanks, to the uniformed conductors of bus tours in the New Zealand Alps. Often, of course, sightseeing is included on tours arranged by one's home travel agent prior to departure, in which case there is no problem whatsoever. But should you arrive with no advance arrangements made, worry not. Hotel desks, local travel agents, government tourist departments, all will help you get about. Self-drive or chauffeur-driven cars are everywhere available, including affiliates of Hertz and Avis. The press is worthy of your attention; even in French-speaking Tahiti and New Caledonia there are English-language sections in the papers, and everywhere it is from these sources that one keeps track of what goes on locally as well as abroad, and of what special events might be attractions. I cannot emphasize the dividends which casual walks pay. After the guided tours, strike off on your own as often as you've the time and energy. Peek behind the closed doors of places the bus whizzed by. Relax in the cafes and bars, rest on a park bench, amble through shops if only to browse and converse with the personnel. Don't hesitate to speak up, and do look up those friends of friends of friends; with enough advance notice, chances are they'll be delighted to see you, and getting to know them will be a memorable part of your journey. Don't shy away from Americans but, on the other hand, do remember that there are lots of us at home. Many, while often eminently worth meeting and knowing, and though frequently good stepping stones to local contacts, become rather jaded and cynical after long residence abroad, and the interpretation they may give to visiting firemen may be quite at variance with those of the country's nationals.

PRIVATE CLUBS

A good part of the South Pacific is or was British and that means you're in Private Club Territory. Wherever Britons have colonized—and indeed where Americans have been on the scene —clubs spring up, as a way of life. (The French, in contrast, prefer public cafes.) Many clubs are not entirely devoid of racial or nationality barriers (the British formed them for the express purpose of being able to socialize among themselves). In Australia and New Zealand, there are clubs for every purpose, from golf and tennis to football and bowling. (Rugby or football clubs in Australia's State of New South Wales are among the most affluent in the world; they support themselves with profits from slot machines, which are not allowed in public places. Do go along if invited—and take money.) In the islands, they are frequently with a nautical *raison d'être*. In countries served by Qantas, ask that airline's local representatives if temporary guest memberships may be arranged. And be on the lookout everywhere for service clubs like Rotary and Kiwanis, which delight in welcoming foreign confreres. If you're a golf or country club member, take evidence of your membership with you; it will help pave the way for guest facilities.

MAIL

Except in Tonga, where I question whether the mails arrive more frequently than once a month, if that, mail service is generally good in the South Pacific. (It usually is, where the British and French are, or have been; their mail services at home are far superior to that of the United States.) Still, have your correspondents allow a good week for letters to reach you. If they arrive sooner, no harm has been done, so long as they are marked "Hold for Arrival." If your itinerary has been planned in advance, have letters addressed to you in care of your hotels along the way. American embassies and consulates (where they exist—which is relatively rarely in this part of the world) will hold mail for you, but unlike hotels, which never close, they are not open evenings, Saturday afternoons, Sundays, and holidays (both American and local) so that you can always claim your mail just after arrival. In asking for mail at hotels, big as well as small, make sure that you give your name clearly; for South Pacific English accents are quite dissimilar from those of North America. In some of the smaller places, where mail may be tucked away in crevices or otherwise-occupied drawers, do not hesitate to join in the search for it. Leave a forwarding address if mail you're expecting has not arrived; it will follow *very* slowly unless you leave air-mail postage with the hotel forwarding it.

The regular airmail letter rate from the United States for all destinations in this book, save American Samoa and Hawaii, is twenty-five cents per one-*half* ounce. (For Hawaii and American Samoa it is identical with mainland rates: eight cents per *full* ounce.) International air letters, obtainable at all U.S. post offices, are eleven cents—a fourteen-cent saving for the non-U.S. destinations, but they may not contain enclosures. Similar letter-forms may be purchased by you, for use in writing home, at post offices in most of the South Pacific countries, at comparable prices. If

you are a worry-wart, as I am, affix stamps to your postcards and
letters yourself, rather than leaving the task to the hotel desk
staffs, which I have found are usually reliable, but may, on occasion, slip up.

LANGUAGES

No problem here. Indeed, I know of no world travel area
more consistently English-language-speaking, outside of North
America. English is the official language, or one of the official
languages, of every country in this book with the exception of
Tahiti and New Caledonia. In both of those, French is prime,
but the many Americans in Tahiti and the many Australian and
New Zealand tourists now in New Caledonia (successors to thousands of their countrymen, and of Americans as well, during World
War II), have helped popularize English in those places. Naturally,
all of the island peoples have their own languages, as well. The
language situation in each country is capsulized in succeeding
chapters.

WHERE TO AND HOW MUCH?

Two requisites: It goes without saying: Any trip anywhere re-
quires both time and money, with the former quite as important
as the latter. Naturally, the more of both the better, but it is best
to scotch—at the outset of this section—the belief that a South
Pacific journey is only for the well-heeled. Read along and you'll
see that with as little as a few weeks, and a far from Midas-like
stockingful of collateral, you can have yourself quite a South
Pacific ball.

Your kind of trip—select one of three: I don't like to sound
like an advertisement for a business-management correspondence
course, but How Well Do You Delegate Authority? Your answer
determines the type of travel you select, from one of a trio of

general categories: (1) *Independent* travel, in which *you* do all the work—purchase your transportation tickets, book your hotels, and arrange for your own sightseeing, either in advance or as you move along; (2) *Group* travel on a packaged, escorted tour purchased in advance from a travel agency; and (3) *Individual* travel, *but* by means of a travel agency's *prearranged, custom-tailored-just-for-you itinerary*, with *some* or *all* arrangements—transportation, hotels, sightseeing—made for you prior to your departure.

There is something to be said for each. The traveler without a companion (or mate, as the Australians would put it) might enjoy the company of fellow travelers afforded by group tours. The student on a tight budget, or the veteran traveler who knows the ropes, might enjoy planning his trip as he goes along at his own pace. There is no question but that this method offers one a chance to become well acquainted with the ins and outs of travel, and with the people who staff each country's travel industry. Still, most travelers prefer the third-mentioned procedure, whereby a travel agent makes the basic arrangements—transportation and hotels, for example—and the traveler proceeds unescorted but with the assurance that his major requirements are taken care of, and with the advantage of going precisely where he wants, for a period of time determined by his tastes, interests, and schedule. (If desired, and at a slight cost, he can be met upon arrival at each point by his travel agent's local branch or representative.)

Selecting a travel agent: This is important, *really* important, and can make the difference between smooth sailing and rough seas, on one's trip. It is most desirable that one deal with a travel agent who knows the South Pacific, preferably firsthand, who makes a specialty of South Pacific travel, and who is, at the same time, reputable and efficient. Members of ASTA (American Society of Travel Agents) are invariably good bets.

Itinerary requisites: As you'll see, in the next section of this chapter, it's possible to select air routings which are such bargains that none of the countries covered in this book need be omitted

from your itinerary. Forget the bromide, "If you've seen one
island, you've seen 'em all," for each is distinctive. Try to preface
your South Pacific journey with a stopover in Hawaii, there being
no better living introduction to the area, for reasons I indicate
later on in this chapter. And try to stay *long enough* in Tahiti
to take in Bora Bora and Moorea; in Fiji for an air excursion to
Tonga and an out-island cruise; in the Samoas for visits to *both*
American and Western Samoa; in New Caledonia to get out of
Nouméa into the countryside; in New Zealand—and this, in my
view, is *essential*—to take in the South Island (even at the expense
of the North, if necessary); and last but hardly least, in Australia
to go beyond Sydney-Canberra-Melbourne to the Great Barrier
Reef, Tasmania, Alice Springs, and the Outback, and if you can
swing it, the other capitals, including Perth on the Indian Ocean.

Traveling by air: The economy-minded air traveler does well
to consider South Pacific destinations *in terms of the South Pacific*
as an area. In other words, the bargain tickets for this part of the
world are those which allow stopovers between the starting point
and the most distant destination. Consequently, one's best bet is
a routing with the most allowable stopovers.

Let's start with an example: An air ticket which would take
one from New York (with a wide choice of domestic U.S. stopovers) to San Francisco, Honolulu, Fiji, New Zealand, Australia,
New Caledonia, Tahiti, and then back to the United States via
Acapulco and Mexico City to New York. This is a fine and
direct itinerary, particularly for the traveler who would like to
work the capital of Mexico and its chief resort into a South
Pacific trip. The cost: $1298 New York–New York.

Now then, you're not interested in including Mexico on this
trip; it's close enough to home so that it can be a journey on its
own. But you do want to take in as much of the South Pacific as
possible. Here's the routing for you: New York (with stopovers in
the United States across the country), San Francisco, Honolulu,
Fiji, New Zealand, Australia, New Caledonia, another stop at
Fiji en route home, American Samoa, Western Samoa, a second

welcome stop in Honolulu, then San Francisco and New York. This routing covers every country covered in this book except Tonga, which is cheaply accessible ($89 round trip from Fiji). The rate is the same as the first routing, via Mexico City: $1298 New York–New York. From West Coast cities—San Francisco, Los Angeles, Portland, Seattle, and Vancouver, British Columbia —the fare is, of course, less: $1008. From Chicago, it is $1219, and from Dallas, $1153.

Now then, if you've not been to Asia, or would like to revisit it (see *Asia A to Z,* a companion book in this series) and you've the time and inclination to include still other parts of our planet in your journey, here's a really outstanding transportation bargain: All of the South Pacific countries mentioned directly above may be visited as part of a Round the World air itinerary for but $149 additional, New York–New York. In other words, the total fare would be $1447. And bear in mind that you may go home, on such a ticket, via southern Europe *or*—and here's a twist— Africa (see *Africa A to Z,* a companion book in this series). An African routing could take you from Perth, on Australia's western coast, to the British colony-island of Mauritius into Nairobi, Kenya, through East Africa to that continent's intriguing western countries, and home via Dakar, Senegal. There are, as well, special *group fares,* which require that you and your companions (a minimum of fifteen, sometimes twenty-five) travel together. To qualify for these (rates vary depending on routings, but they are exceptional values) you must have been a member for at least six months, of what the Civil Aeronautics Board terms an "affinity" group—a church, social, union, fraternal, or similar organization with a prime purpose other than travel and a membership of less than twenty thousand. And there are, of course, other routings which your travel agent or airline reservations clerk may work out for you, depending upon your inclinations and your budget.

Foregoing fares are economy-class jet. *First-class fares* are, of course, more expensive. The advantages are wider, more heavily upholstered seats, more leg room, more elaborate meals (served with wines and liqueurs, at no charge), and complimentary cocktails. For example, the Round the South Pacific tickets earlier quoted at $1298, economy class, New York–New York, are $1735 first class. The Round the World fare with the South Pacific included is $2172 first class, New York–New York. (*All* fares are, of course, subject to change by IATA—International Air Transport Association—which sets rates with the approval of the governments of those airlines which are its members.)

Globe-girdling Qantas: A rags-to-riches script writer could not have improved upon the almost melodramatic—and most certainly meteoric—story of the evolution in less than half a century of a "joy ride" service in Australia's Outback to a round-the-world jet airline serving nearly half a hundred cities on routes embracing Australia, Asia, North America, Africa, Europe, New Zealand, and the South Pacific islands.

Qantas is neither an Australian aboriginal word nor the name of any of the country's flora or fauna. It evolved into what has become a household term by means of initials, for it began life as the Queensland and Northern Territory Aerial Service, Ltd. Almost from infancy—in 1920—Aussies, who delight in creating abbreviated versions of even relatively simple designations, christened it Qantas. And so it has been ever since.

The Australian bush is an unlikely setting for the commencement of such an enterprise, but Australia fortunately abounds in the unconventional. It began in 1919 when two young ex-Flying Corps lieutenants (one of whom—Hudson Fysh, later Sir Hudson Fysh, K.B.E.—became Qantas' chairman, to be succeeded upon his retirement in 1966 by Sir Roland Wilson) conceived the idea of an air service while chugging across rural Queensland in a Model-T Ford. The following year, with an initial capitalization in the staggering amount of thirteen thousand dollars, they were in business, with two minuscule biplanes, taking Queensland locals on joy rides, taxi trips, and other missions ranging from the first air-transported Australian maternity case to the initial aerial turkey-shooting expedition.

The first regular service was the 577-mile run linking Charle-ville and Cloncurry, in Queensland, with the first passenger on the service being an eighty-five-year-old pioneer who had first traversed the area half a century earlier by bullock cart. By 1923 Qantas had advanced to the luxury of DH-9C's, which carried two passengers in a covered cockpit that finally allowed them to ride without helmets and goggles. Radio equipment was installed in 1925, and the following year the company built the first com-mercial plane to be produced in Australia, and opened its own flying school. In 1928 it was aboard Qantas that the world-re-nowned Flying Doctor Service (now the Royal Flying Doctor Service) had its beginnings.

A few years later, in 1931, the line teamed up with British-owned Imperial Airways (later BOAC), flying Australian and later overseas portions of its England–Australia route.

World War II saw Qantas in military service, and as a part of its work it found itself operating as far afield as Karachi and Colombo. War's end ushered in a new Qantas era. The Parlia-ment in Canberra passed a bill which allowed the Australian Government to purchase that half of the line owned by BOAC; this was followed, in 1947, by government purchase of all of the line's holdings, so that Qantas became entirely Australian Gov-ernment-owned, and the official Australian-flag overseas airline.

Routes multiplied thereafter. The original England–Australia service became but one of many. Qantas reached out to Japan, Hong Kong, the South Pacific islands, Africa, Southeast Asia, India, Pakistan, and continental European points. In 1954 Qantas flew Queen Elizabeth II and Prince Philip to Australia on a state visit (the first of a number of royal flights). That same year the line made its maiden flights to the United States. In 1956, already a major carrier of international note, Qantas flew thousands of visitors to the Olympic Games in Australia, and carried the traditional Olympic flame from Athens to Melbourne. In 1957 Qantas gained air rights across the continental United States (it was already flying New York–London), thus achieving a complete round-the-world routing via the United States, Europe, Asia, and Australia.

The first of the line's luxurious Boeing 707 jets went into service in 1959, cutting travel time in half, and reducing round-the-world jet air service to 51¾ hours flying time. But there seems to be no end in sight as regards new horizons. In 1964 Qantas opened a new route between Sydney and London, via Hong Kong, and still another—of particular interest to North Americans—which runs from Sydney to London, thence back to Sydney via Bermuda, Nassau, Mexico City, Acapulco, Tahiti, and Fiji. Sydney, Qantas' world headquarters, is the site of its handsome skyscraper office building, Qantas House, and of the spanking new Qantas-operated Wentworth Hotel. From an initial staff of less than a handful, the payroll now numbers in excess of eighty-three hundred; of these more than six hundred are technical aircrew personnel, flying aircraft which cover a network of seventy-two thousand route miles.

Despite its phenomenal size and continued growth, Qantas appears not to forget its ever-so-casual, ever-so-Australian beginnings in the Queensland bush, when its first passenger was an octogenarian. Service continues to have the unique Aussie quality—never stuffily obsequious, invariably gracious, smiling and efficient. Cuisine has an admirably international flavor. (A first-class menu: Consommé Julienne, California Crab, Grilled Breast of Chicken, or Grilled Double Lamb Chops, fresh vegetables, tossed mixed salad, a variety of desserts, assorted cheeses, fresh fruit, coffee, mints.) Tourist-class meals, though necessarily less copious, are delicious. Liquid refreshments? Qantas stewards and stewardesses are as adept at martinis as at more typically Australian drinks. Of course they serve Aussie beers, but in addition they offer a variety of superb Australian wines—one of the big surprises of a South Pacific trip. Always conscious of Australia's cultural contributions, their menus are collectors' items, illustrated with excellent reproductions of such noted painters as Sidney Nolan, Sali Herman, William Dobell, and Albert Namatjira.

And they are not unmindful of other Aussie achievements, including those words their countrymen have added to the English language. They've compiled a complimentary booklet called "Sound the Drum," which I suggest you request from Qantas' North American headquarters, 350 Post Street, San Francisco. And bear this in mind, too: Qantas offices throughout the world double as information centers for travelers with questions of almost any touristic nature. (Women's clothes and packing queries are welcomed by the women's travel consultants in major offices, or by mail to Elizabeth Hunter, Women's Travel Consultant, Qantas House, 70 Hunter Street, Sydney, Australia.) Many of the larger offices (that in New York at 542 Fifth Avenue is a good example) feature comfortable lounges known as Corroboree Rooms, where passers-through may rest their legs, read an Australian newspaper or magazine, look at frequently changed exhibitions of contemporary Australian paintings, meet friends, and catch up on current events of interest—after-dark and otherwise.

Other airlines serving the South Pacific include Air-India, Air New Zealand, Air Polynésie, Airlines of New South Wales, Airlines of South Australia, Alitalia, Ansett-ANA Airways, British Overseas Airways Corporation, Canadian Pacific Airlines, Connellan Airways, East-West Airlines, Fiji Airways, KLM Royal Dutch Airlines, Lufthansa German Airlines, MacRobertson Miller Airlines, Mount Cook Airlines, National Airlines Corporation of New Zealand (NAC), Pan American World Airways, Philippine Air Lines, Polynesian Airlines, Queensland Airlines, Trans-Australia Airlines, Transpac, United Air Lines, UTA French Airlines, and RAI (Reseau Aérien Interinsulaire).

By sea to the South Pacific: Two shipping lines—one American, the other British—make regular sailings to the South Pacific from the North American West Coast, and there are as well a number of other services to choose from.

Matson Lines sails its modern *Mariposa* and *Monterey* (both 365-passenger, fully air conditioned, all first class vessels, built in 1956 expressly for South Seas travel) on frequent forty-two-day cruises. Departure point is Los Angeles, and the route embraces Bora Bora and nearby Tahiti; Rarotonga in the Cook Islands; Auckland, New Zealand; Sydney, Australia; Nouméa, New Caledonia; Suva, Fiji; Tonga; Pago Pago, American Samoa; Honolulu, Hawaii, and San Francisco. All of the handsome staterooms are air-conditioned and with private baths, telephone, and radio, the public rooms are tastefully handsome and spacious, the cuisine justifiably noted, the facilities virtually limitless, and the service first rate, there being as many crew members as passengers. All-inclusive cruise rates range from $1195 to $4500, with a great many staterooms priced midway between the minimum and maximum. One-way passages also are available, so that it is possible to combine both ship and plane on a South Pacific journey. Still another Matson liner, the *Lurline,* plies regularly between the West Coast and Honolulu, on 4½-day luxury cruises, with minimum fares $230 one way, $414 round trip. It, too, could be utilized in connection with air transport.

P & O Orient Lines has wide-ranging global routes (it is the oldest and largest of the world's steamship companies, founded in England in 1837), but the South Pacific is most definitely among its specialties, with a number of its post-World War II fleet of eleven luxury liners (all fully air-conditioned, with at least two swimming pools each) making the Down Under run. P & O's basic South Pacific route extends from the North American West Coast (departures from San Francisco, Los Angeles, and Vancouver) to Hawaii, Fiji, Auckland, New Zealand, and Sydney, Australia. Occasional stops are made also at such spots as Tonga, New Caledonia, Rarotonga, and American Samoa. And on certain sailings passengers may board at Port Everglades (Fort Lauderdale), Florida, and sail into the Pacific via the Panama Canal. Prices for the cruises—about forty days in length—begin at $776 tourist class, $1050 first class. Still longer "Circle the Pacific" cruises—going north into the Orient—begin at $908 tourist, $1326 first class.

There are, as well, a number of *passenger-carrying freighters* plying between North American and South Pacific ports; these include the ships of Columbus Line, Knutsen Line, Pacific Australia Line, Pacific Island Transport Line, and Pacific Shipowners, Ltd.

Travel agents in possession of up-to-date editions of two directories—the *Official Steamship Guide* and the *ABC Shipping Guide*—are able to advise on sailings of these and other lines. Freighter sailings are irregular and dependent more upon cargo schedules than passengers' convenience. The life is informal, facilities comfortable but minimal (depending of course on the ship selected—one does well to investigate most carefully in advance), and ports of call may be altered—again for cargo reasons. Still, freighter *aficionados* are becoming legion. The traveler with a great deal of time and a yen for a quiet, relaxing shipboard holiday might well find them appealing, and, indeed, might want to consider a subscription to a lively periodical which specializes in coverage of this kind of transport: *Freighter Travel News* (Reginald J. Clark, Editor), P. O. Box 526, Caldwell, Idaho.

European luxury liners in South Pacific service include the *Galileo* and the *Marconi* of Italy's Lloyd Triestino Line (Italian Line, New York, U.S. agents), and the *Caledonien, Tahitien,* and *Oceanien* of France's Messageries Maritimes (French Line, New York, U.S. agents).

A CALENDAR OF SELECTED
SPECIAL EVENTS

I don't suggest that you plan a South Pacific journey around the region's special events; the law of averages should assure that you run into more than your share of festivals of one sort or another. Here, though, is a selected sampling.

January: Vakatawase (New Year's Day) Celebrations, Fiji; Surf carnivals, Sydney and other metropolitan beach areas, Australia; Yachting Regatta, International Grand Prix, Auckland,

New Zealand; Start of Samoan-style cricket season, American Samoa and Western Samoa.

February: Royal Hobart Regatta, Barossa Valley Vintage Festival, Moomba Festival begins (Melbourne)—all Australia; Garden Flower Festival, Christchurch, New Zealand; Cherry Blossom Festival, Hawaii.

March: Moomba Festival continues, Australian Industries Fair —both Melbourne; Adelaide Highland Games, all Australia; International Deep Sea Fishing Contest, North Island, New Zealand.

April: Royal Eastern Show, Australia; Merry Monarch Festival, Hilo, Hawaii; Easter Sports Meeting, Levuka, Fiji; Flag Day (April 17), American Samoa.

May: Auckland Festival of Arts, New Zealand.

June: Independence Day (June 2), Western Samoa; National Sheep Dog Trials, Masterton, New Zealand; Ski season opens, Australia and New Zealand.

July: Bastille Day (July 14, but festivities usually precede the holiday and continue thereafter), Tahiti and New Caledonia; Bula Festival, Fiji; Independence Day (July 4) and Hawaii State Fair, Hawaii.

August: International Trades Fair, Wellington, New Zealand; Fire Walking Ceremonies, Fiji; Hula Festival, Hawaii; Public Schools Week Celebrations, New Caledonia.

September: Perth Wildflower Show, Royal Melbourne Show, Sydney Waratah Spring Festival—all Australia; Hibiscus Festival Week, Fiji; Anniversary Day Celebration (September 24), New Caledonia.

October: Great Barrier Reef Islands Festival Week, Brampton-Lindeman, Hayman islands area, Sydney Industries Fair—all Australia; Aloha Week, Hawaii; Agricultural Show, Broadcasting Commission's Annual Singing competition, Tonga; Yearling Thoroughbred Sales, Wellington, New Zealand.

November: Melbourne Cup Horse Race (first Tuesday), Australia; Christchurch Horseracing Carnival Week, Rotorua Rose Festival—both New Zealand.

December: Sydney–Hobart Yacht Race, Australia; Christmas Eve, Christmas Day, and New Year's Eve are observed in many ways throughout the South Pacific.

HAWAIIAN INTERLUDE

Hawaii is not, of course, a part of the South Pacific, but it is so related to it, and so inevitable a stopover point for travelers en route, that it deserves more space than I am able to afford it in this book. It is the fiftieth of the United States, the first overseas state, the second (after Alaska) non-contiguous state— separated from the mainland by a two-thousand-odd-mile span of the Pacific Ocean, and the state whose racial diversity accords it the distinction of being the most polyglot of any American territory. It is the melting pot makeup of Hawaii, not to mention its beauty, that is sure to intrigue the South Pacific-bound visitor, or indeed the traveler on his way home from a South Pacific journey.

The Aloha State is about 16 percent pure and part-Hawaiian (the Hawaiians are, of course, ethnic cousins of the Polynesians of such places as Tahiti, the Samoas, and Tonga, and the New Zealand Maoris), 32 percent of Japanese origin, 32 percent white, 11 percent of Philippine ancestry, and the remainder mostly of Chinese and Korean background. The influences of all these peoples is manifested in the islands and—even though they are now a minority—that of the indigenous Hawaiians remains delightfully pervasive in many facets of daily life, from music and dance to and through feasting and clothing.

When Captain Cook first visited Hawaii (where he lost his life) in 1778 it was a sovereign kingdom and remained so until 1893 when Queen Liliuokalani was deposed and annexation to the United States requested by her successors. President Cleveland blocked the move, convinced that there had been American collusion. The following year, Hawaii became a republic on its own,

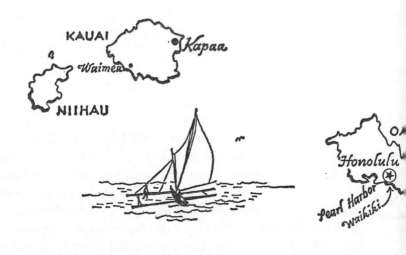

KAUAI

Kapaa

Waimea

NIIHAU

O

Honolulu

Pearl Harbor

Waikiki

Hawaii

0   10   20   40   60   80   10

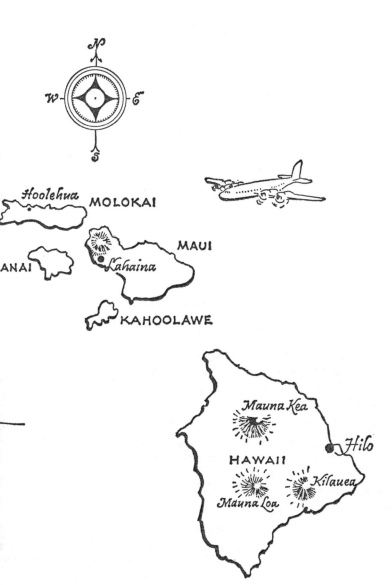

under Sanford B. Dole. In 1898, under President McKinley, the islands were annexed to the United States. They were designated a territory two years later, and, after a long campaign, became a state in 1959 after being voted in by Congress. President Eisenhower issued a statehood proclamation on August 21 of that year, and ordered a new fifty-star flag to replace the forty-nine-star version on July 4, 1960.

Honolulu, the capital and sole metropolis, is on the island of *Oahu*—flower-filled, lighthearted, gay, attractive, and with a good deal to interest any visitor, let alone one bound for the South Seas. The Aloha Tower at the harbor, the handsome University of Hawaii campus, the Honolulu Academy of Art, Iolani Palace (former seat of the Hawaiian monarchy and now the State Legislature), and Chinatown are basic requisites. To these I should most certainly add for those en route Down Under the splendid Pacific collections at the Bernice P. Bishop Museum.

But it is the Waikiki Beach sector, fronting the Pacific with the famed silhouette of Diamond Head crater its trademark, where the visitor will most likely headquarter, swim, surf (surfing was a sport of the old Hawaiian royalty), and dine and dance under the stars. There are a number of splendid hotels, as well as a clutch of good restaurants, bars, and night spots, many of them within hotel premises.

Excursions on Oahu—not the biggest of the islands, but the most populous and still verdant, rugged and beautiful despite its advanced development—might be made to the Pearl Harbor Naval Base, where the attack on December 7, 1941, brought America into World War II; the fish markets and pineapple canneries, distant beaches and rural regions of striking loveliness, and three additions to the scene which should not be missed.

The first, the Polynesian Cultural Center, at Laie, is an imaginatively commendable project of the Mormon Church, which is strong in Hawaii and a number of South Pacific islands. The Mormons have devised a first-rate series of little Polynesian villages, each authentically designed, constructed, furnished, and staffed by residents of the islands they represent: Fiji (not Polynesian, but happily included anyway), Tonga, the Samoas, Tahiti, and, naturally enough, Polynesian Hawaii. Most of the staff are young people from the islands who are also students at the Mormon Church's nearby degree-granting Church College of Hawaii. (It and a vast Mormon Temple are also points of interest, although the temple's interior is open only to Mormons.) They guide visitors about, serve them a typical Polynesian feast in the guest *fale* of the Samoan village, and after dark put on a splendid entertainment consisting of songs and dances of their islands. (Note: If time absolutely precludes a Laie visit, settle instead for the Ulu Mau Village, a reproduced Old Hawaii community, right in Honolulu, and the nightly—7 P.M.—free performances of Pacific Islands dancing, singing, and drumming in Waikiki's International Market Place.)

The second fairly recent attraction of note is the unique East-West Center for Technical and Cultural Interchange, housed in a strikingly ultramodern complex on the University of Hawaii campus. Students are both American and foreign, the latter from many of the South Pacific countries, as well as Asia; there are guided tours and frequent special attractions, ranging from art exhibitions to entertainments in the handsome auditorium. The East-West Center, supported by the U. S. Federal Government, is a bold and exciting step toward uniting American and fellow Pacific peoples, and an important destination for South-Pacific-bound travelers.

No. 3 of the major new attractions is Sea Life Park, which calls itself the world's largest exhibit of marine life—and probably is. On a single visit one can make an underwater descent to a living coral reef, see a fantastic performance by Hawaiian porpoises, a pool of sharks, a twenty-foot replica of an old whaling ship—and a good deal else.

There is inexpensive and frequent air service via Hawaiian Airlines and Aloha Airlines to the other principal islands of Hawaii. (You can take almost all of them in—terribly briefly—on special one-day flying excursions run by Hawaiian Airlines for quickie-tourists, daily out of Honolulu.) *Hawaii,* known colloquially as the Big Island, is the site of Hawaii National Park and the famed Mauna Loa volcano (there is none more active); Akaka Falls, the black volcanic sands of Kalapana Beach, the memorably beautiful Kona coast section and, of course, *Hilo,* the principal city, and the second largest urban center in the state. *Maui's* landmark is the world's largest dormant volcano, Haleakala, with a fantastic, easily viewable crater. There are good hotels, fine beaches, good fishing, and the scenic Lahaina section. *Kauai* is perhaps the most flower-filled of the islands—which is going some. Fine beaches, breathtaking excursion territory galore, and even a sugar mill, if you'd like to visit one. *Molokai* is the least-visited and quietest of the major islands. But there is excellent fishing and hunting, and of course the superb, palm-bordered beaches one finds on all the islands.

Hotels: The Sheraton chain operates a Waikiki group of first-rank hotels, each with its own distinctive personality. The traditional favorite is, of course, the lovely pink pre-World War II Royal Hawaiian, with its justifiably famed gardens, fine dining rooms, coffee shop, and elegant supper club—the Monarch Room —which puts on consistently excellent and eminently enjoyable shows. Bedrooms are refreshingly spacious and high-ceilinged. Others of the Sheraton group include the modern and pleasant Princess Kaiulani ("PK" to the locals), and that elderly landmark, the white-frame Moana, with its dining room overlooking a great banyan tree in the cocktail patio-courtyard which is almost as much an Oahu landmark as nearby Diamond Head. The Surfrider, fourth of the group, is actually an addition—albeit with its own separate entrance, restaurant, and cocktail lounge—to the Moana. The Kahala Hilton, a ten-minute ride from the heart of Waikiki (gratis shuttle service is provided by the management), is one of the most opulently posh of any of the world's Hiltons, with such novelties as playful porpoises in a pool, and his-her bathrooms in gigantic guestrooms. Credit it with distinguished wine-dine-dance facilities and public rooms, and a first-rate staff. Also worthy of attention is the towering new Ilikai, affiliated with the crack Western International Hotels chain, and featuring serving pantries in the bedrooms, a bevy of restaurants including an *intime,* authentically French one which offers some of the finest food and service in the Pacific; convivial watering spots with pleasant entertainment, including an on-high cocktail lounge, with absolutely great views. Other leading hostelries include the Hilton Hawaiian Village, a bustling not-so-small city in itself with every imaginable facility; the quiet Halekulani; an old favorite, the Waikiki Biltmore, and the Waikikian. The leading hotels feature softly lit, interestingly decorated cocktail lounges, restaurants, wine-dine-dance-rooms, and coffee shops. Canlis, a branch of the firm that has restaurants in Seattle and Portland, gets my vote as one of the finest of eating places—superb steaks served by delicately lovely kimono-clad Japanese dolls. The Prince Kuhio, in the Ala Moana Center, excels at Hawaiian dishes, and La Ronde, also at Ala Moana, serves first-rank continental cuisine. Michel's, in the Colony Surf Building, is another distinguished leader in the continental cuisine category. Trader Vic's is, of course, a major drawing card. Other worthwhile restaurants include the charming and most reasonable Willows, with its tropical-pool setting; Fisherman's Wharf, and the Queen's Surf, with its inexpensive, simply delicious buffets. Kalakaua Avenue, the main Waikiki thoroughfare, is dotted with additional spots, many of them—like the Snack Shop and the Kopper Kitchen—good and inexpensive. On the island of Hawaii, there are the Hilo and Naniloa Hotels, both in Hilo; Volcano House in the National Park; Kona Inn and Waika Lodge, among others, at Kona, and the extraordinarily attractive new Mauna Kea Beach Hotel; newest of the Laurance Rockefeller resorts, it has 154 understatedly elegant rooms, an eighteen-hole Robert Trent Jones-designed golf course, fine pool and beach, and still other amenities of the sort which distinguishes Rockefeller resorts in other parts of the world. Maui's standout is the boldly designed Sheraton-Maui, with a magnificent beach, lovely setting, and superb facilities; other Maui hotels include the Hana Maui, the Maji Palms, and the Pioneer Inn. Kauai's leaders include the Kauai Inn, Kauai Surf, and Coco

Palm. Molokai offers the Seaside Inn. Single rates, all European plan, range from minimums of about $10 at the Princess Kaiulani and Moana, to about $16 at the Royal Hawaiian and Ilikai, $22 at the Kahala Hilton, and $33 (modified American plan) at the Mauna Kea Beach. At smaller places (of which there are many) minimums are, of course, lower. The luaus, presumably typical Hawaiian feasts staged for masses of tourists by some of the hotels and restaurants, are expensive (about $10 per person), with food many people find on the dreadful side, and entertainment which can be terribly corny. Watch the paper for the luaus given by churches, often far less touristy, less expensive, and open to the public. *Shopping,* particularly for those bound for the South Pacific, is relatively minimal, although women might want to lay in a supply of *muumuus,* the shapeless Mother Hubbard-type garments which are today's popular refinements of the couture designed by the missionaries. Muumuus come both regular length and ankle length (the shorter version would be more practical for the South Pacific), and there are variations, with fitted waists, called *holomuus.* They are on sale wherever one turns around throughout Waikiki (Iso-shi-ma's, 2209 Kalakaua Ave., has good quality materials at sensible tabs), and at many of the shops (particularly Sears, Roebuck) in the quite splendid, art-filled, and eminently visitable Ala Moana Shopping Center. Men's sports shirts, known as aloha shirts in Hawaii, are of the same bold Polynesian designs as the muumuus, and *de rigeur* with both locals and visitors; indeed, many shops feature His and Hers sets which consist of matching muumuus and aloha shirts for couples who practice as well as preach togetherness; swimwear, for both men and women, is available in similar materials. Clothing aside, I would rank shells and shell objects as the most typically Hawaiian of possible purchases. The shells themselves, and pieces of coral as well, are generally much more expensive than in the South Pacific, but some of the shell jewelry (necklaces, earrings, and bracelets) is most reasonably priced.

Further information: Hawaii Visitors' Bureau, with offices at

2051 Kalakaua Avenue, Waikiki, Honolulu; 400 North Michigan Avenue, Chicago; 212 Stockton Street, San Francisco; 3440 Wilshire Boulevard, Los Angeles, and 609 Fifth Avenue, New York; Qantas Airways, 2051 Kalakaua Avenue, Honolulu.

Australia

Entry requirements: A valid passport and a smallpox vaccination certificate are required of all visitors. American citizens must have a visa, obtainable without charge (and, invariably, within twenty-four hours) from Australian Consulates General in New York and San Francisco, or the Australian Embassy, Washington. Canadian citizens, Commonwealth members along with the Australians, usually need no visas. Special permission is necessary for admission to Australian-administered New Guinea and should be requested when making application for a visa. **Best times for a visit:** Except in the tropical north, where it's always hot, the seasons are the reverse of ours. Generally, summer runs from November through February; autumn, March through May; winter, June through August; and spring, September through October. In planning your visit, bear these points in mind: For a round-Australia tour, don't hesitate to pick any time of year, for even if you visit the far north in Australian summer (the wet season), rains need not be incessant, and at that time of year the south (where most Australians live) has the kind of pleasant climate we experience in our warm-weather months, with eighty degrees the average. The Australian winter (our summer) is without the extremes of cold found in northern United States areas, the average temperature being about fifty-five degrees, with snow only in the mountains, and a fair quantity of showers (interspersed with sunny days, to be sure) in and around Melbourne, Adelaide, and in Tasmania; Sydney, Brisbane, and Perth are not much bothered by winter moisture, nor is the north. Best times for the north (Great Barrier Reef), April to October; for the "Center" (Alice Springs), April to September; for winter

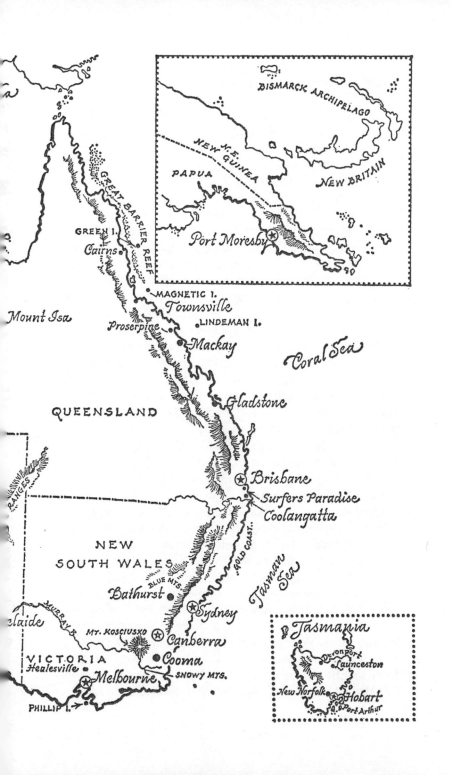

sports in the mountains, July to September; for swimming,
surfing, and sunning at the beaches of the Sydney area, October to April. Sydney and all of the major cities are eminently
visitable the year round. **Currency:** Australia's new decimal
currency system of dollars and cents went into effect in
February 1966, replacing the traditional pounds, shillings,
and pence. However, you're liable to see some of the old
currency in use, as well as the new, so here is a breakdown
for both: $1.12 U.S. equals one Australian dollar which
equals ten of the old Australian shillings. (The old Australian pound, totaling twenty shillings, equaled $2.24 U.S.)
The Australian dollar is worth 12 percent more than the U.S.
one. New Australian paper money comes in one-, two-,
ten-, and twenty-dollar denominations, each a different
color. And the new coins—in animal motifs—come in one-,
two-, five-, ten-, twenty-, and fifty-cent denominations. **Film
availability:** Good stocks of both color and black-and-white
film including Kodak, are available; prices are higher than
in the United States, but note that, in the case of color film,
they include processing. Color processing, done by Kodak
Australia in Sydney and Melbourne, takes from one to two
weeks; black and white as little as twenty-four hours.
Languages: English, of course, although you'll come across
a good deal of Italian in the cities, as well as other continental European languages ranging from French to Hungarian. Australian English, incidentally, is a delight. The
Aussies have enriched the language with many new words,
a number of them adaptations from the tongue of the
aborigines, others locally invented slang which is not a whit
less colorful than that of the United States. There are also
some delightful shortened words: footie (football), Tassie
(Tasmania), lippie (lipstick), cozzie (bathing suit or costume), Paddo (the Sydney inner suburb of Paddington),
telly (television), surfie (surfrider), vegie (vegetable), and
wharfie (longshoreman) are but a few. Somehow or other,
Brisbane has not yet become Brissie. ("Bloody," adopted
from the British, is Australia's No. 1 adjective.) Aussie-
invented additions to the vocabulary include cobber (friend),

billy (tea-brewing bucket, and sometimes tea itself), digger, (soldier), pozzie (position or spot), shelia (girl or young woman), shout (to treat someone—"It's my turn to shout you a beer."), tucker (food), yabber (to chatter), onkus (all wrong), purler (something excellent), give it a burl (try it), fair dinkum (absolutely true), corroboree (aboriginal dance, or social gathering), bonzer (good), and bobby-dazzler (the greatest!). Boomerang—the most noted Australian word to enter the language—is, of course, borrowed, like corroboree, from the aborigines. Not all Australians are proud of the Cockney-derived accent but foreigners, myself most definitely included, enjoy it when they hear it; it is by no means universal and it varies tremendously in degree. (Some Australians make it a point to lose it entirely when they move abroad.) Some say it is less pronounced in city-dwellers than country folk. That may or may not be, but there are, oddly enough, no regional accents, as in most countries. Be that as it may, wherever I travel in Australia, I am used to bellhops querying me thusly regarding my baggage: "Mr. Kyne, are these your kyses?" And everywhere I am easily assured, no matter the difficulty, when I'm told, "She'll be right, mate [often pronounced 'myte']"—the Aussie [pronounced "Ozzie"] catch-all phrase for crises of any and all sorts. **Transportation:** Considering its relatively small population and its location, Australia's accessibility is nothing short of incredible. A dozen international airlines serve its five international airports—Sydney, Melbourne, and Brisbane, on the southeast or east coasts; Perth on the west coast, and Darwin on the north coast. Both Sydney and Melbourne are planning vastly modernized jet-age airports. Qantas, Australia's round-the-world carrier, links its home country with Asia, Africa, Europe, the South Pacific (including, of course, New Zealand), and North America, with a constantly expanding schedule of flights (ten a week at last count) from the United States, via New York and San Francisco, to Sydney. Sydney and Melbourne, on the east coast, and Fremantle (the port of Perth) on the west coast, are the principal seaports. Regularly scheduled luxury lin-

ers of a number of companies—including Matson Lines
and P & O Orient Lines from the United States—link
Australia with the rest of the world, as do passenger-carrying freighters. Domestically, Australia has some eighty thousand miles of air routes. It is served by two principal
lines whose routes embrace the nation-continent: Trans-
Australia Airlines (TAA), frequently pronounced in the
Aussie fashion "tee-aye-aye," a federal government enterprise, and Ansett-ANA, a privately operated company.
Not only do the routes of these two lines virtually parallel
each other (particularly in the heavily traveled south), but
their flights generally leave within minutes of each other;
if one comes up with, say, a dinner flight between Points
A and B, the other will soon follow it, with a flight leaving
at about the same time. The traveler dashing about the
country does well to check his tickets, for it's easy to become confused as to which line's flights one is booked for.
It is possible to have an enjoyable journey on either line,
but—for an air-minded nation like Australia in which there
are as many as forty flights a day between Sydney and
Melbourne—by and large both lines are disappointing.
Ground service can be abrupt, service aloft—by indisputably handsome and handsomely uniformed stewardesses
(there are no stewards for some reason or other)—can be
curt and inefficient upon occasion, and the food served on
board is appalling, no better on one airline than the other.
Indeed, one wishes that Qantas, which is not allowed domestic routes within Australia, were on the scene, or at
least that it were more emulated by the domestic carriers.
Aside from the Big Two, there are regional services by
smaller airlines, including Airlines of New South Wales,
Queensland Airlines, East-West Airlines, Airlines of South
Australia, MacRobertson Miller Airlines, and Connellan
Airways. Jet aircraft are employed only on certain (*not all*)
flights between such widely separated cities as Sydney, Melbourne, and Adelaide in the east, and Perth in the west,
although new jet equipment is gradually being added to
fleets. Otherwise, one generally flies Lockheed Electras and

Viscounts on shorter main routes, and still other planes on lesser routes; these range from Fokker Friendships and DC-3s to tiny Cessnas. Foreign visitors are granted the same luggage allowance as that allowed on their international air tickets. Certain flights offer both first-class and tourist service, with more comfortable seats in the former the only difference between the two. Meals are dismally identical and alcoholic drinks must be paid for in both classes. Food and service notwithstanding, I should emphasize that the domestic airlines' technical and safety standards are most definitely first rate. Also, no matter how small the destination, Australian airlines happily provide bus service from airport to town terminal, and it's always inexpensive—never more than about fifty U.S. cents. There are twenty-seven thousand miles of railways, mostly along the east coast, but also extending across the continent to Perth, and into the "Center," linking Alice Springs with Adelaide. The railways are operated by the federal and state governments, which have not yet gotten together with a standard gauge; as a result there are several, and on a cross-country journey, the passenger changes trains several times because of this archaic feature. Still, you might want to try one of the streamliners, between, say, Sydney and Melbourne. Buses connect the various state capitals and other popular points, as well; many are air conditioned and with reclining seats. It is also possible to get from one part of the country to another via coastal steamers; this type of travel is particularly popular with Australians going to and from Sydney or Melbourne, on the mainland, and the island state of Tasmania. Avis, Hertz, Kay's are the main rent-a-car services and have offices everywhere, including air terminals, so that passengers can rent cars upon alighting from flights; driving is on the *left* side of the road. Urban public transport is modern and cheap; the friendly Aussies will see to it that you don't get lost. Taxis are metered and plentiful except, of course, during rush hours in the big cities, when they're as scarce as at home; solitary male taxi riders always sit up front with the driver; this is considered good Australian "matemanship." **Tipping:** Australians are not, by and large, big tippers, and there is no reason why visitors should be. Ten percent is adequate in restaurants; the equivalent of twenty-five U.S. cents a bag for porters. Taxi drivers *are* generally tipped. **Clothes:** The best rule is to dress as you would at home. Australian clothes are much like those of the United States, and the well-dressed, well-groomed Australians, by and large, are quite as fashion-conscious as Americans, with similar tastes. One does come upon a surprising number of adolescents and young men, shoeless and in shorts, during the warm-weather months in the downtown areas of the larger cities, but by and large, jackets and ties are the rule for men, and dresses for women, in town. At beaches, resort areas, and in the tropical "Center" and north, dress is, of course, more casual. Businessmen in the tropics generally wear walking shorts (the Aussies' are shorter than ours, and far more becoming), knee-length socks (usually white), white short-sleeved shirts, and sometimes neckties. Medium-weight woolens are necessary for the Australian winter, in the south. Don't worry if you've forgotten anything. Clothing is of good quality, is excellently styled, moderately priced, and easily obtainable in fine department stores and shops. **Business hours:** Shops do not close for lunch, but most close at noon on Saturdays; hours are generally nine-thirty to five on weekdays. Banks open from ten to three Monday to Thursday and ten to five on Friday, except in the State of Victoria (in which Melbourne is located), where they open at nine-thirty; they close at three *every* day, including Friday, in Tasmania. **Further information:** Australian National Travel Association offices at 636 Fifth Avenue, New York; 350 Post Street, San Francisco; 22 Old Bond Street, London; 55 Customs Street East, Auckland, New Zealand; 2 Castlereagh Street, Sydney, and, the head office, 18 Collins Street, Melbourne. The foregoing are for information only. But the government tourist bureaus of the various Australian states provide information and perform the booking services of travel agencies, as well. Each has branch offices throughout Australia, but their headquarters are as follows: **Canberra Tourist Bureau,** Civic Centre, Canberra, Australian Capital Territory; New South Wales Government Tourist Bureau, Challis House, Martin Place, Sydney; Northern Territory Tourist Bureau, Herbert Street, Darwin, and Todd Street, Alice Springs; Queensland Government Tourist Bureau, Anzac Square, Brisbane; South Australian Government Tourist Bureau, 18 King William Street, Adelaide; Tasmanian Government Tourist Bureau, Macquarie and Murray Streets, Hobart; Victorian Government Tourist Bureau, 272 Collins Street, Melbourne, and Western Australian Government Tourist Bureau, 772 Hay Street, Perth. In addition, the six states jointly operate the Australian Travel Bureau, Challis House, Martin Place, Sydney. The State of New South Wales maintains a tourism and trade information center at 680 Fifth Avenue, New York, and the Victoria Promotion Committee (mainly for business and economic information) has a U.S. office at 32 East 57th Street, New York. A source of information (non-touristic) is the Australian News and Information Bureau, 630 Fifth Avenue, New York. Principal Qantas offices are at Qantas House, 70 Hunter Street, Sydney (head office); Qantas House, 341 Collins Street, Melbourne; 278 Adelaide Street, Brisbane; 81 St. George's Terrace, Perth, and Darwin Hotel Building, Darwin.

INTRODUCING AUSTRALIA

"Australian history . . . does not read like history, but like the most beautiful lies. And all of a fresh, new sort, no moldy old stale ones. . . ."

—Mark Twain, *Following the Equator*

The One World that many Americans concern themselves with is, by and large, a northern world. The Southern Hemisphere, particularly its southernmost areas, appears to barely exist. We are only just beginning to develop an awareness of countries in the Americas, like Argentina, Chile, and Uruguay. In Africa, were it not for the justifiably publicized immorality of apartheid, I suspect we would draw blanks with the Republic of South Africa. Move along to the world's smallest continent—or largest island, if you will—where there have been a dearth of headline-creating catastrophies, and we are uninformed to the point of cloddishness. I suspect most Americans could point out Australia on a map (it *is* easy to locate), make mention of kangaroos, hum a bar or two of "Waltzing Matilda"—and let it go at that.

The point is: We should *not* let it go at that, for Australia is quite the most exciting country in the Southern Hemisphere, big and bold and beautiful and booming. It is young enough to still be brash, at times boastful, and occasionally unsure of itself. But it is mature enough to express itself with a distinctive, flavorful personality; intelligent enough to be aware of its handicaps and shortcomings; wise enough to ponder the self-criticism of an increasingly sensitive and articulate intellectual community; sophisticated enough to cultivate and value its beauty, with a frequently sardonic, often subtle sense of humor, and happily blessed with enough curiosity to savor, better late than never, perhaps, the customs and cultures of peoples it has heretofore ignored or patronized.

A detached New World: Australia, when you think about it— and we up north simply *don't* think about it—is amazing. It has a good deal in common with the United States, to be sure. We are both, after all, New World countries, despite Australia's geography. But it is, in many ways, even newer than the United States. It did not achieve complete sovereignty until the twentieth century, and its states, which had been colonies, did not become self-governing until the middle of the nineteenth century.

Yet, despite a terrain which is largely uninhabitable, a population which, considering the area involved, is relatively sparse, and a location half a world away from the continents whose culture it shares, Australia is "with it." The North American or Western European in one of its great cities today finds himself immersed in the complexities of modern life which are familiar to him and which appear incredible when one considers the corner of the world in which Australia is situated. This former British outpost—ignored by the monarchs of its original continental European discoverers and ultimately utilized by London as a penal colony only after the American colonies were lost— is today one of our planet's brightest corners.

The contrast between it and neighboring New Zealand could not be stronger. Nor could the personalities of Australians and New Zealanders, between whom there is sometimes very little love lost. Much smaller New Zealand had its European beginnings as a model British colony, populated by carefully selected, eminently respectable cross sections of mother country communities. It more than fulfilled its promise into the beginnings of this century, but recent decades have seen it sink into mediocrity— largely self-satisfied, generally without the sparks of vitality which engender self-criticism and progress. Australia, on the other hand, could not have had a less promising genesis, as indeed how could it with its initial function that of one vast jail?

Tough, ambitious, visionary: Its early settlers, convicts though a lot of them were (many were nothing more than what would be minor civil offenders today), were made of strong stuff, however. They were tough (withstanding early privation), resilient (they stayed on as freedmen after working off terms of bondage), ambitious (they pushed across the eastern seaboard to new western frontiers), visionary (they came to realize the tremendous potential of their new nation-continent), talented (there were among them brilliant planners, engineers, and architects, as today's visitors easily perceive in the older sections of the country, where their tastefully inventive handiwork is in startling contrast to nondescript constructions of the early New Zealanders).

The incredible vastness of their land imbued them with the chronic loneliness which has always been a hallmark of their greater artists's work, right up to such modern greats as painter Sydney Nolan and writer Patrick White. This loneliness, born out of isolation, has been responsible for their willingness to rely not only on their own labors but on the functions of modern government. The cult of "mateship"—the strong reliance on one's comrades, the compulsion toward cameraderie and mutual aid—is nowhere more developed or a part of a culture than in Australia. At the same time, the Australian has had far fewer objections to government participation in economic life than, say, the American. Governments run his railroads, telephone services, and telegraph companies. And he has pioneered in government welfare services, all the while expressing his individuality through strong, successful private enterprise.

The Aussie personality: Today's Australian, if one would but give him a bit of thought, is an oddball in the very best sense, almost instinctively adapting only the most sensible facets of his heritage. He speaks the English of his forebears but he has adapted the language into one of his own—graphic, racy, indigenous, reflective of his environment and his refreshingly informal outlook on life.[1]

---

[1] Australian-ese, developing into a language all its own—currently termed "Strine" (a contraction of "Australian") by tongue-in-cheek students of the subject—has not been surpassed, in writing at least, since C. J. Dennis wrote *The Sentimental Bloke*. Let me tempt you with a few verses of "At the Play":

> Doreen an' me, we bin to see a show—
> The swell two-dollar touch. Bong tong, ye know.
> A chair apiece wiv velvit on the seat;
> A slap-up treat.
> The drarmer's writ be Shakespeare, years ago,
> About a barmy goat called Romeo.

> "Lady, be yonder moon I swear." sez 'e.
> An' then 'e climbs up on the balkiney;
> An' there they smooge a treat, wiv pretty words
> Like two love-birds.
> I nudge Doreen. She whispers, "Ain't it grand!"
> 'Er eyes is shining; an' I squeeze 'er 'and.

> This Romeo 'e's lurkin' wiv a crew—
> A dead tough crowd o' crooks—called Montague.
> 'Is cliner's push—wot's nicknamed Capulet—
> They 'as 'em set.
> Fair narks they are, just like them back-street clicks,
> Ixcep' they fights wiv skewers 'stid o' bricks.

Polynesian beauty:
A young Western
Samoan.

Coconut-gathering: climbing
high in Western Samoa.

R.L.S.: Stevenson's portrait and
writing chair, at Vaalima, where
he lived, in Western Samoa.

ındry day in a Western Samoan village.

Lava-lava-clad American Samoans play Yankee-style baseball.

The Stars and Stripes fly from the Post Office in Pago Pago, American Samoa, replete with its own Zip Code number.

Visitors ascend Mount Alava, American Samoa, in this cable car, for a superb view.

...pical of Fijian coastal villages is this ...e, where the Gary Cooper movie *...urn to Paradise* was filmed.

A Fijian dances the *meke* in
traditional costume.

...ng mariners: Fijians, like this trio,
...no time in taking to the sea.

The white-frame Royal Palace *(right* and Royal Chapel, Nukualofa, Tong

Tonga's famous flying foxes make their home in this venerable tree.

Loading copra, Tonga.

The harbor, Papeete, Tahiti.

He shares a Head of State—the monarch of the United Kingdom is also the monarch of Australia—with his British cousins. But he's his own boss, respectful toward the Royal Family but without the self-conscious obeisance toward it of his New Zealand neighbors. He retains much of the British pattern in his way of life—a passion for a home and garden of his own, a near-madness for sports (including Aussie-type football or tennis, golf, swimming, surfing, cricket, and lawn-bowling), a proclivity for private clubs of all sorts and sizes, a thirst for beer and for tea as well, a fondness for governmental, judicial, and military organization and ritual, and the view—inherited in the Americas, as well—

[Subsequent verses continue to detail the plot, and the poem ends with the stanza below.]

> Then Juli-et wakes up an' sees 'im there,
> Turns on the water-works an' tears 'er 'air,
> "Dear Love," she sez, "I cannot live alone!"
> An' wif a moan,
> She grabs 'is pockit knife, an' ends 'er cares . . .
> "Peanuts or lollies!" sez a boy upstairs.

The aforementioned "Strine" language has been committed to paper in a remarkable little book entitled *Let's Talk Strine,* published by Ure Smith, Sydney; in late 1965 it was in its eighth printing after publication earlier that year; it costs seventy-five Australian (oops, Strine) cents, and I suggest you pick up a copy upon arrival. The author, using the pseudonym Afferbeck Lauder (Strine for alphabetical order), is described as Professor of Strine Studies at the University of Sinny, and his work is based on articles originally run as a Sydney *Morning Herald* series. Professor Lauder came to conclude that the book would be helpful to "stewnce, vistas and new Strines" after a newspaper reported an autographing party in a Sydney shop at which English writer Monica Dickens was inscribing copies of a new book for purchasers. One woman, offering a copy to the author, intoned, "Emma Chisit," and Miss Dickens, believing that the name of the lady, wrote "To Emma Chisit" on the flyleaf, to personalize the inscription. The customer then repeated "Emma Chisit," and only then did poor Miss Dickens realize that she was simply asking the book's price, not indicating her name. Helpful Strine terminology might include *aorta* (Aorta build another arber bridge), *cheque etcher* (Where cheque etcher hat?), *Dismal Guernsey* (the new *Dolls and Sense*), *Egg Nishner* (air conditioner), *Gloria Soame* (glorious home), *Scummin Glerser* (coming closer), *Rise Up Lades* ("sharpened steel wafers, now usually stineless, used for shiving"), and—should you be traveling by *trine—Rye Wye,* which is easily translatable.

of Anglo-Saxon superiority, with which are coupled the racial and ethnic prejudices so many of us are finding it so difficult to break away from. At the same time, the Australian—good-looking, well scrubbed, healthy—is superbly flexible. The country is by no means without the anti-intellectualism still too prevalent in America, but the Australian is developing an open-minded dynamism that comes of his fending for himself in an alien part of the world.

Migrants and neighbors: Since World War II, he has opened his eyes to the non-British world. He has brought to his shores some two million European immigrants, about a million of them the Continentals so eschewed by his New Zealand neighbors. Most of the rest are Britons, or "Pommies," as the Aussies call them because their pink cheeks at one time reminded the tanned Down Underers of pomegranates. The continental Europeans have given Australia what New Zealand so needs—a blending of cultures and habits and foods and sights and smells and attitudes. He has turned toward the Americans whom he befriended—and who befriended him—during the World War II conflict, and adapted their New World ways—not all of them, to be sure, the most desirable kinds of imports.

And he has begun to consider his Asian and South Pacific neighbors, and to accept, at long last, the reality of his proximity to an immense non-European world with which he must come to terms. Fierce patriot though he is, there is instilled in him a sense of impatience, a feeling that he may not be moving along as quickly or as intelligently as he might be. And there is no question but that the doubters in his ranks have much reason to be critical. Still, all things considered, Australia's transformation from *terra incognita australis* (unknown southern land) is one of our planet's greatest success stories.

A backward glance: A very old land geologically (it is without the jagged peaks of newer continents) Australia has probably been inhabited for something like twelve thousand years by tribal groupings of aborigines believed to have come from the Asian continent via Indonesia. Overwhelmingly isolated, and devoid of

the contacts with other cultures without which no people pro-
gresses, the aborigines found themselves without motivation to
live, other than, for the most part, as nomads, exceeded in their
quite literal primitiveness by few other peoples.

It was not until the second century of the Christian era that
the rest of the world had any idea of Australia's existence. At
that time, the Greek genius, Ptolemy, convinced that there was a
land mass below the Asian continent, indicated a *terra incognita*
far to the south of what was then known of the Asian coast.
More than a millennium later, Europeans—Spanish, Portuguese,
and Dutch—chanced upon the mystery land. Torres sailed
through the strait, now bearing his name, which separates Australia from New Guinea, in 1606. A Dutch vessel later sailed
through the nearby Gulf of Carpentaria that same year, and less
than two decades later, part of that northern coastal region was
charted by other Dutch navigators.

Later decades saw other ships following the continent's western coast and, gradually, going east along its southern extremities.
Abel Tasman came upon what is now the island-state of Tasmania
in 1642, and a later Dutchman, Wilem de Vlamingh, discovered
the Swan River, on which the Western Australian capital of
Perth is built, in 1696. By this time the area had come to be
known as New Holland. But its fertile, temperate-zone southeast
coast had still not been chanced upon and none of its explorers
had been enthusiastic about development, not even the first English visitor, William Dampier, who landed in the northwest in
1688.

The consequences of Cook: It was not until nearly three-
quarters of a century later, in 1770, that a European visit was
to be of true consequence to Australia's future. The British Navy's
Captain James Cook—ubiquitous is too commonplace a word
for him—sighted land near Cape Everard in the favored southeastern corner of the country, as part of a momentous journey
on which he had undertaken an astronomical mission in Tahiti
and then circumnavigated New Zealand. The date was April 20,

1770. Nine days later, after charting the coastline as he proceeded north, Cook landed at Botany Bay, so named by him because of the profusion of unusual botanic specimens encountered there. But that was not the end of his Australian explorations. He continued north along the coast for some thirteen hundred miles, stopping only when his ship, the well-named *Endeavour,* struck a coral reef at Trinity Bay. Two months later, after repairs, he again resumed his northern course, and after sailing through Torres Strait, landed on an island just off Cape York which he named Possession Island, and on which he flew the British flag, formally taking possession of the eastern extremities of the Australian continent for his sovereign.

It was a beginning. But a slow one. Cook was enthusiastic in his reports to London, but there was little response. Timing, though, is everything. Britain had just awakened to the significance of its loss of the American colonies. It needed a distant spot to send convicts, the penology of the time embracing the theory that the transportation of lawbreakers to underdeveloped areas abroad not only solved the problem of incarceration but simultaneously aided in the colonies' settlement and, indirectly, made possible a fresh start in a new environment for those convicts desirous of such new beginnings. It should be pointed out, too, that the eighteenth century was largely a have and have-not era, with the bulk of the people in the latter category, with tremendous poverty, and no modern social services to cope with it. As a result, debtors were commonplace and petty thievery rampant. The exorbitant prison term was the exception rather than the rule—this obtained, indeed, through much of Dickens' time—and harsh sentences were meted out for the most minute infractions.

And so, on May 13, 1787, just a day before the Americans' Constitutional Convention began deliberations in Philadelphia, fifteen hundred persons—some eight hundred of them convicts—set sail from England in a fleet of eleven ships under the command of Captain Arthur Phillip, the first governor of what was to be the Colony of New South Wales. The flotilla landed at the

Cook-discovered Botany Bay over eight long months later, on January 18, 1788, transferring a week later to Port Jackson, which was to become Sydney, Australia's largest city.

Smallest continent, biggest island: The land they had begun to populate embraces roughly the area of the forty-eight conterminous United States or of Europe with Russia excluded, embracing some twenty-five hundred miles from east to west, some two thousand from north to south, with about half of the approximately three million square miles of area in the tropics. With the Indian Ocean on its west coast and the Pacific flanking its eastern shores, Australia, at once the smallest continent and largest island, stands quite by itself. The southern tip of Africa is nearly five thousand miles distant, India's lower flank is about three thousand miles away, the West Coast of the United States is nearly sixty-five hundred miles from Sydney, and London more than ten thousand. The coastline exceeds twelve thousand miles, a part of which— some 1250 miles—is bordered by the Great Barrier Reef, extending from the northeast corner south to near Brisbane. The highest mountain, Kosciusko, is 7316 feet, and a giant, as peaks go, in this geologically ancient land.

But Australia's great age and isolation have been responsible for a remarkable quantity of flora and fauna found nowhere else on the planet. The latter include marsupials (animals whose young are born and nurtured in their mothers' pouches) like the kangaroo and its smaller relative, the wallaby; the docile, cuddly koala (meaning "dry" in the aboriginal languages), which subsists entirely on the leaves of certain species of eucalyptus (or "gum") trees found only in Australia, the oil of the leaves taking the place of water; the dingo, or native dog of the aborigines; the incredible platypus, a small, amphibious creature with a fur coat, a ducklike bill, webbed feet, and all of the talents of a ham actor; the gawky, ostrich-like emu; the exquisitely beautiful lyrebird, the kookaburra bird, or laughing jackass, and quantities of quite splendid parrots and cockatoos.

Modern Australia extends beyond the continent, and includes tiny Norfolk Island, mostly inhabited by descendants of the

Bounty mutineers who were brought from Pitcairn Island in 1856; the Territory of Papua and New Guinea, comprising the Australian (eastern) portion of the island of New Guinea (the remainder is Indonesia's West Irian) and with a population exceeding two million, mostly Melanesian; the twenty-seven Indian Ocean islands of the Cocos (Keeling) group with a total populace under seven hundred, about thirteen hundred miles from Australia's west coast; Christmas Island, whose phosphates are mined by the employees of a joint Australian-New Zealand commission; Nauru Island, over eighteen hundred miles northeast of Australia, a UN trust territory jointly administered with New Zealand and Great Britain; and 2,263,000 square miles of the Antarctic, where Australia maintains four research stations. But I digress.

Westward, ho: The 1788 settlement had a rough time making ends meet in its initial period. There were no fierce aborigines to fight off, in the manner of American settlers vs. American Indians. (Almost everywhere they were encountered, Australian aborigines were unhostile; still, they became completely extinct in Tasmania, and many thousands on the mainland perished with the coming of the white man.) But farming was not easy, for want of good soil, and foodstuffs had to be imported, until Governor Phillip scouted around for better land. His men explored inland as far west as the barrier of the Blue Mountains. And there was additional coastal exploration, too, the most significant being that of Captain Matthew Flinders who, during 1802–3, circumnavigated the entire continent, and by so doing ended the two-century era of Australia's discovery. Flinders is honored in almost every Australian city by streets bearing his name and by a mountain range. In October 1965, the remains of one of his ships, the *Porpoise,* including cannon and anchor, were found off the coast of Queensland, near Rockhampton, by an underwater photographer.

Not that there was not more to be encountered. The enormous interior beyond the coastlines was still virgin territory, until a series of expeditions resulted in its being discovered. The Blue Mountains were finally traversed in 1813, and a settlement ensued in and about the town of Bathurst. In 1827, the Darling

River and other vital inland waterways were discovered. A few years later, southeastern South Australia was traversed. And in the interim, there had been settlements in Hobart, Tasmania (1803), on Queensland's Brisbane River (1824), on Western Australia's Swan River (1829), in Victoria's Melbourne (1835), and South Australia's Adelaide (1836).

Then came treks to the arid west and the tropical north. Edward Eyre reached Albany, Western Australia. Ludwig Leichardt went all the way north to Darwin. The three Gregory brothers explored the Indian Ocean coastal area north of Perth. John McDougall Stuart went north from Adelaide to Alice Springs. And all the while, Australia grew. Colonial governors were empowered to make free grants of land to any residents willing to employ convicts and take over their maintenance from the government. As a result, early Australia's landowners were emancipated convicts, free settlers, former army officers, ex-merchant sailors. They took to the established towns but they had itchy feet, many of them, and settled west of the Blue Mountains, and on the great sheep stations which developed after Spanish Merino sheep were imported and began to thrive on the dry plains. By 1831 the wool industry had been well established, with some two and a half million pounds exported.

Gold and progress: And migration was swelling the populace. Free settlers were entering in such quantities that the need for imported convicts was lessening. There were more than four hundred thousand people living in Australia in 1850, and a decade earlier, "transportation" (as it was called), or the importing of prisoners from Britain, had been stopped in most eastern colonies. (It ended in Tasmania in 1853, but it did not *begin* in labor-short Western Australia until 1850, coming to a halt as lately as 1868.)

And then came a new shot in the arm, not dissimilar to those experienced by the United States, Canada, and New Zealand: a gold rush. Gold discovery, at Bathurst in 1850, was the impetus for a phenomenal population increase. The 405,000 of 1850 grew to well over a million in 1860, and half a million more within the decade ensuing. Many of the prospectors—ambitious, bright, bold—stayed on as farmers and townsmen, adding to the solid development of the country. They were followed by still more newcomers in the second Gold Rush of 1892, in Western Australia.

And all the while the country progressed, with new roads and railroads, new towns, new industries, and a public education system which helped create a people anxious to govern themselves.

The original New South Wales colony, with Sydney its nucleus, was split up into other colonies (Tasmania, Queensland, Victoria). And the others—South Australia and Western Australia —developed on their own. New South Wales was the first to gain limited legislative powers of its own, in 1823; this was strengthened two decades later, and by 1850 the eastern colonies had authority to determine their own forms of government. By 1855 New South Wales had full responsible government, with the other colonies following.

The colonies federate: Beginning in the 1860s, the colonies' premiers began meeting together periodically to discuss problems of mutual interest. The result, in 1891, was the first federal convention, under the sponsorship of New South Wales' Premier Henry Parkes. By 1898 an acceptable federal constitution had been drawn up, and two years later, on September 17, 1900, Queen Victoria proclaimed the creation of the Commonwealth of Australia, whose actual birth date was January 1, 1901.

The Commonwealth was a remarkable achievement, for it was brought into being by a group of already self-governing states which voluntarily relinquished some of their powers for the mutual good—and did so under no external pressures, such as was the case of the American colonies, whose only hope for independence lay in their united efforts against Britain. Australia had never known war or even rebellion. Its leaders at the time of federation were Australian-born democrats with vision and purpose to appreciate the value of their subdivided continent banding together as one.

The country has not had time to look backward since, and unlike the United States, and more recently Canada, has never entertained second thoughts about federation. The Duke of Cornwall and York (later King George V) opened the first Parliament at Melbourne on May 19, 1901, and in 1911—following provisions of the Constitution—a portion of the State of New South Wales was designated as the Australian Capital Territory. Construction of the new capital city, Canberra, began. Not until 1927, though, did the Duke of York (later King George VI) open the first Canberra Parliament.

Two world wars—and thereafter: World War I had a profound effect on Australia's development. Nearly a half million of its population of some five million were in the armed services, and of the 332,000 who went overseas, almost 70 percent were casualties—the highest proportion for all Commonwealth forces. World War II saw Australia contribute almost a million men, one out of every four of its males, with more than half of these overseas, and about half of that number were casualties. The war cost the country, then with a population of under eight million, some five billion dollars. Fortunately, it had by then become strong enough to effect a revival. It had become one of the world's major wool markets, but had also created heavy industry as a major factor in its economy. And it had not neglected the expansion of its education system (private and parochial schools complement its state schools) nor the social services, which include old-age pensions, unemployment compensation, maternity allowances, child endowments, workmen's compensation, and voluntary health and medical benefits.

At the same time Australians nurtured their democracy, with innovations like the pioneering secret ballot first introduced in the Victoria Legislature in 1856, nationwide by 1870, and now universally known as the Australian Ballot. Voting is compulsory in all the states, and women have had the vote since 1902—almost two decades before they were granted suffrage in the United States.

Evatt, Menzies, and Holt: Politically Australia is a generally three-party country, the Big Three being Liberal, Labor, and

Country. The Communist Party is legal and not without some influence, though small and without any representation in state or federal Parliaments. There is, as well, the small Democratic Labor Party, offshoot of Labor. The Labor Party, oldest extant, has become a vast if diffuse organization, generally progressive, but with diverse factions which tend to impair its effectiveness. The Country party is what its name implies: a generally conservative, rural minority group.

The Liberals came into being during World War II to supplant the older United Australia Party, and are, by and large, middle-of-the-road moderate in their general point of view. They are currently in power, as a result of a coalition with the Country party, and their leader is the Prime Minister, Harold Holt, who succeeded Sir Robert Menzies in January, 1966. Holt, born in Sydney in 1908, and a Melbourne University law graduate, is an economics-labor expert, and as sports-minded as most Aussies (skin-diving, spear-fishing, horse racing). He was the youngest member of the 1940 Menzies Cabinet, and also has served as Minister of Labor and National Service, Minister of Immigration, Acting Air Minister, Deputy Leader of the Liberal party, and House of Representatives leader. He had been Treasurer since 1958. His attractive wife, Zara, is a noted dress designer with salons in Sydney and Melbourne.

Sir Robert Menzies, Mr. Holt's predecessor, retired at the age of seventy-one, and was the senior government chief, from the standpoint of service, in the British Commonwealth. He first governed (without his knighthood title of "Sir") from 1939 to 1941. He resumed office from Labor's J. B. Chifley in 1949, and his detractors claimed that his chief asset was the ability to survive in office, many convinced that much of Australia's progress during the Menzies period had been despite the Prime Minister's leadership rather than because of it. (Analogies were made here to the United States during the Eisenhower administration, although Menzies was an undeniably superb politican who, unlike Eisenhower, relished politics.)

There were Australians who hoped that the accession of Prime

Minister Holt would see the end (and not only as regards personalities) of the Menzies Era—the era of a passing Australia. Sir Robert's comments on the 1965 Commonwealth Prime Ministers' Conference indicated that he looked back with nostalgia at the day when the Commonwealth was the small "white" coterie of Great Britain, Australia, New Zealand, Canada, and white-governed South Africa (now no longer a member), rather than the dominantly dark-complexioned group it is today. "This is not the old Commonwealth," he told a Canberra press conference upon his return home. And he appeared pessimistic about its continuance when, asked if he could see a future for it, he replied, "I wish I knew."

A factor in the remarkable Menzies longevity—and the continuance of his party in power—was his chief opponent, Arthur Calwell, leader of the Labor opposition, who does not appear any more palatable to many Australians—even younger ones who would like a change—as a potential Prime Minister. Calwell took over the Labor Party leadership in 1960 from the late Dr. Herbert V. Evatt, the dynamic progressive who became one of Australia's most controversial figures and one of its best-known and most respected leaders in international affairs. Calwell represents Labor's conservative wing, that faction of the party which had opposed Evatt's policies, the most significant being an Evatt criticism of a Royal Commission investigation of Soviet spying in Australia. Considerably earlier, it was Evatt who fathered modern Australian foreign policy. Until he was appointed Deputy Prime Minister and Foreign Minister by Labor Prime Minister John Curtin in 1941, Australian foreign policy largely reflected British views. It was Evatt who, though pro-British, insisted that Australia must recognize the facts of geography, and that London was half a world away. He plunged Australia into the international sphere, and as its delegate to the San Francisco conference at which the United Nations was created, became a forceful spokesman for the smaller nations, and an important contributor to UN charter provisions covering the Four Freedoms, the rights of colonial and dependent peoples, and international progress and welfare. He was honored by his colleagues in the General Assembly when they elected him its President for the 1948–49 term.

Contemporary ebullience: The modern Evatt approach has survived him. The million continental European immigrants have added new life, luster, and style to Australia's cities (and Australians are dominantly urban). Foreign investment (much of it American) has increased tremendously and helped bolster the economy. The standard of living, always high, has climbed higher, and with it has followed increasing sophistication in matters aesthetic and cultural. The jet aircraft and the television set have brought widely scattered Australians closer together, more interested in each other's home territories. And Australians, more than ever before, are traveling abroad.

Social stratification—never as rigid as Britain's nor as provincial as New Zealand's—has been relaxed. Australians have begun to take more pride in their own accomplishments. They flock to art galleries to see the paintings of William Dobell, Russell Drysdale, Sidney Nolan, Arthur Boyd, Tom Roberts, Sir Hans Heysen, and Soli Herman. They line up for tickets to performances of the Australian Ballet (whose co-artistic director is Aussie-born Robert Helpmann). They are moved—as have been many foreigners, myself most definitely included—by such superb contemporary dramas as Ray Lawler's *Summer of the Seventeenth Doll,* Alan Seymour's *The One Day of the Year,* and Douglas Stewart's *Ned Kelly.* They delight in the international acclaim which has come to their Patrick White for his epic novels, including *The Tree of Man* and *Voss,* and they have made a phenomenal best seller of Donald Horne's recent *The Lucky Country—Australia in the Sixties*—a fascinatingly candid critical analysis. They enjoy the folksy humor and nostalgia of Steele Rudd's *On Our Selection* stories, and the derring-do of the legend of Ned Kelly, an Australian Outback hero who was at once Robin Hood and Billy the Kid. They revel in the engaging vernacular poetry of C. J. Dennis's earlier-quoted *The Sentimental Bloke.* And they enjoy poking fun at their foibles, and criticizing themselves in such magazines as *The Bulletin* (which has been on the scene since 1880 and has played a major role in the development of an Australian literature), *The Nation, Quadrant,* and the outrageously irreverent *Oz* (i.e., "Australian"). There are, as well, mass-circulation magazines like *Australian Women's Weekly,* an Australian edition of *Vogue,* the handsome travel magazine published by the Australian National Travel Association, *Walkabout,* and hundreds more. The number of newspapers—more than 650—is astonishing; of these fifty are dailies. Leading papers include the Sydney *Morning Herald,* the Melbourne *Age,* and the recently established, nationally circulated *Australian.*

Aussie arts and artists: The Aussies excel at music. The Sydney Symphony is of international note, and but one of a number of such orchestras. The number of Australian singers and instrumentalists of international renown are out of all proportion to the country's size: Dame Nellie Melba, Percy Grainger, Eileen Joyce, John Brownlee, and Joan Sutherland and her husband Richard Bonynge (a 1966–67 conductor at New York's Metropolitan Opera), to name some of the more prominent.

In the theater one finds productions of plays like those mentioned earlier, of many others by Australians (including novelists Patrick White and Morris West), of hilariously satirical revues (the recent *Is Australia Really Necessary?* and *A Cuppa Tea, a Bex, and a Good Lie-down* were of Broadway or West End caliber), and of musicals and plays from New York and London by the resourceful impresarios, J. C. Williamson, Ltd. (The *Hello, Dolly!* Australian company—except for its imported American leading lady—was first rate.) Happily, although it persists in such reactionary practices as banning the import of "undesirable" books and films, the government has not hesitated to help subsidize the arts, through the Australian Elizabethan Trust (named for Queen Elizabeth II and not dealing exclusively with Elizabethan drama, as a foreigner might think); the Arts Council, and the Australian Broadcasting Commission are all active in the performing arts. The Little Theatre movement is everywhere, and there are numbers of legitimate theaters in the major cities.

Sydney's long-time-abuilding Opera House promises to be among the world's greatest. Melbourne is building a new Cultural Center and Adelaide is the site of a national Festival of the Arts, held every other year. Australian movies are mostly documentaries produced by the National Film Board, but cinema is a national pastime, with most of the offerings American and British; some continental European. There are both government and commercial TV networks, with the latter showing more third-rate American fare than might seem necessary. And the disc jockey has become as much a national institution as is the case in the United States, with Beatle-type music equaled in popularity only by the type of dancing it induces everywhere on the planet, and the inevitable bizarre clothing fads which also follow it.

Involvements, East and West: And so Australia goes its mostly merry way. It is much more a part of the world today than its earlier citizens could ever have dreamed. It maintains some threescore diplomatic, consular, and trade missions abroad. It remains good friends with Britain through its association with the Commonwealth of Nations. By means of its monarchial system of government, Elizabeth II is Queen of Australia as well as of Britain and the other Commonwealth monarchies like New Zealand, Canada, Jamaica, Trinidad and Tobago, and Malta. The Queen's son and heir, Prince Charles, became the first member of the Royal Family to study in a Commonwealth country when he enrolled for a term in the Anglican Church's rough and rugged Geelong Grammar School near Melbourne. Still another Royal Family tie—not overly successful—was the post-World War II Governor-Generalship of the Queen's uncle, the colorless Duke of Gloucester. The Queen's representative is the Governor-General, who may or may not be a Briton. (The current incumbent is Lord Casey an Australian.) Britons are often appointed governors of the various states. Many Australians would prefer that these posts be held by Australians, as they have been under Labor governments. (In Canada, Governors-General have been Canadians for some time, as have Lieutenant Governors of the Canadian provinces, whose functions correspond with the

Australian state governors.) Australia is allied with the United States and New Zealand in the ANZUS Treaty of mutual defense. It is a member of the Southeast Asia Treaty Organization —which may or may not endear it to certain Asian states. But it promotes ties with its Asian neighbors through full membership in the UN's Economic Commission for Asia and the Far East and in the Colombo Plan, a commendable organization of Asian and European nations engaged mostly in technical cooperation. Australia has contributed some twenty-seven million dollars to the Plan and trained several thousand Asian students in its universities through the Plan. In addition more than fifteen thousand Asians study privately in Australian universities. Australia is, of course, a charter UN member, contributing some twenty million dollars annually, in recent years, to its aid schemes, in addition to its administration, as a UN trusteeship, of New Guinea and adjoining Papua, for which it expended a total of more than fifty million dollars in cash grants in 1964.

Australia not only supports the United States in its Vietnam policy but has contributed soldiers to the forces there and, according to the Canberra government, the Aussie casualty rate has been twice that of the Americans' (as of October 1965 about sixteen hundred Australians served in Vietnam, according to the Australian government, which stated that the casualty rate was one out of twenty contrasted with one out of forty in the case of U.S. troops).

Asia and Australia: Not all Australians, as indeed not all Americans, support their government's involvement in Vietnam. U. S. Vice President Humphrey was greeted by a substantial chorus of demonstrators opposing the Vietnam war, on his visit to Canberra in 1966, and there were protest teach-ins in 1965 not unlike those of the United States. At an 8½-hour one, in Canberra, Morris West—whose popular novels include *The Ambassador,* which has a Vietnamese theme—suggested that his fellow countrymen consider Vietnam not only as an outgrowth of relationships with the United States, the West, and the entire Commonwealth, but as a matter involving "all our future relations with eight hundred million people in China, with one hundred million people in Indonesia, with all the other nations of Asia, with the emerging nations of Africa as well." He questioned the wisdom of a Vietnam policy "tied to the policies of another nation" (the United States). Alluding to the "White Australia" immigration policy, he questioned the claim that "we are sending troops to Asia to defend brother Asians against Communism [whom] we do not think well enough of . . . to admit as residents of our country," and he opined that "the greatest problem that we have in Australia is that we have not yet framed for ourselves any philosophical and moral concepts about the true nature of our relationship with the rest of the world."

The black Australians: Mr. West's statement reflects the growing concern of Australians with their newly discovered neighbors and their older allies. But the relationship of Australia to Asia is possibly no more pressing a current problem than is the relationship of the white Australian majority with the relatively tiny aboriginal population. Only recently has an appreciable concern been shown for the aborigines—dark-skinned, smooth-haired descendants of the original Australians, only a relative few of whom remain nomadic hunters who wander with their dogs in search of the wild game and edible roots on which they subsist. Although numbers have served with the Army as expert trackers, as horsemen, as sheep station hands, and as handicraft artisans (their bark paintings now enjoy a vogue), few have been able to distinguish themselves. Among the handful of exceptions are painter Albert Namatjira and singer Harold Blair. About a fifth of them live in the sparsely populated Northern Territory, where they are under federal jurisdiction (but where substantial numbers live, albeit voluntarily, in reserves run by private church groups). Those aborigines resident in the various states (Queensland has the largest number) are under state authority and are not protected by the federal government. They continue to meet the kind of discrimination the Negro American is battling with the aid of his federal government and many of the American state and municipal governments, and their status is at least as pitiful as that of the American Indian. Lately, though, the aborigines—particularly those living in and near cities—have begun to actively oppose discrimination, with the aid of sympathetic whites, inspired by the widely publicized success of sit-ins and other forms of non-violent resistance as practiced by civil rights adherents in the United States. Despite enlightened policies of the federal government, and attempts at betterment by state governments, the status of the aborigine—there are no more than about a hundred thousand in this immense, rich, and resourceful land with a populace of 11,500,000—remains the shame of Australia.

Looking forward: Equally worth serious consideration is a liberalization of the earlier-mentioned restrictive immigration policy, under which Australia's doors are, by and large, open for permanent settlement only to whites. (All races, it must be emphasized, are welcomed as tourists, students, and otherwise as temporary residents.) The schemes whereby Europeans are given "assisted passage" to Australia, as migrants, is most commendable and has benefited the country tremendously. But Australia, now booming and with a severe labor shortage, remains heavily underpopulated, even considering great arid portions which are not habitable. It has reached the point where authorities are urging people (some two-fifths are Roman Catholic, the rest mainly Protestant, with Anglicans dominant in this group) to increase the birth rate, it having been deduced that too many wives prefer working rather than rearing large families. Alternatively, Australia might also consider swelling its ranks, at least partially, with some of the residents of the nearby, desperately overcrowded Asian lands. The result would be a country even more excitingly cosmopolitan than it has become since World War II. But it is unlikely that that could happen—at least with success—before Australia comes to terms with its own non-whites.

Still, there are grounds for optimism. A 1965 Gallup poll indicated that 73 percent of the population (as against 44 percent in 1958) would not object to a small annual trickle of skilled Asian migrants. Today's Australian has open eyes as well as a zest for the good life. As a result of his incredibly heavy involvement in two global wars—only the bloody Allied victory in the Battle of the Coral Sea kept the Japanese out of the country in World War II—he knows the importance of being at peace with Asia, and one hopes he can expand his already solid democratic concepts to the point where he will take in, as fellow Australians, close-by neighbors as well as distant friends.

YOUR VISIT TO AUSTRALIA

I need not delude myself. By no means every foreign visitor to Australia is in a position to traverse the entire country, taking in the requisite bits and pieces which combine to delineate the tremendous sweep and vitality of the land. But I can hope, and I can plead. Ideally, in my view, an Australian visit would embrace a taste of every state and of the Northern Territory; naturally, Papua-New Guinea and Norfolk Island would be frosting on the cake.

In order of significance, though, I would suggest the following as requisites: Sydney, because it has become one of the world's great cities; Canberra, because it is a planned city which is the federal capital; an island or two, at least, of the tropical wonderland which is the Great Barrier Reef; Melbourne, because it is the No. 2 city and offers a good deal of interesting contrast to Sydney; Tasmania, principally because it evokes so graphically the country's convict period and because it is architecturally superb; Alice Springs, because it is Frontier Australia; Perth, because it is Australia's sole west coast metropolis, half a continent removed from any city its size; and then the other major visitor areas: Adelaide and the vineyard country, southern Queensland, with Brisbane and the nearby Gold Coast, and Darwin, gateway to the vast aboriginal reserves of Arnhem Land and of crocodile-hunting country.

I have, earlier in this chapter, detailed the transportation picture in Australia, and at this point let me add that guided tours of limitless variety are everywhere available. There is no major visitor center without excursions of half-day, day-long, overnight, and even longer durations. Additionally, one may book regional tours with varying itineraries. One, for example, covers in twelve days four capital cities: Sydney, Canberra, Melbourne, and Adelaide, as well as Alice Springs and Ayers Rock, with transport via plane and car, and all-inclusive costs approximate $535 for one person, $340 for each of two persons. Another tour, this one transcontinental, takes you, in fifteen days, from Sydney to Perth, via Canberra, Melbourne, Tasmania, and Adelaide, using planes, cars, trains, and buses, and costing about $460, single, less per person for groups of two or more. And still another starts in Sydney and, via plane and car, takes you on a nine-day journey to Brisbane and thence to and through Papua-New Guinea, for about $430, single; $385 each of two persons, double. At the other extreme are half-day bus tours of the cities, which average about $1.50 per person.

Thanks to mostly comfortable modes of transport, a friendly and helpful populace, and no language barrier, it is not at all difficult to plan one's own Australian explorations, and travel independently and inexpensively, or to have travel agents prepare individual itineraries, tailor-made, according to budgets and tastes. Point is: It's a big country, so stay as long as you can, setting yourself a deadline for departing from Sydney, one of our planet's toughest-to-leave cities.

Sydney: Few cities are aesthetically able to please from every angle. London is at its most elegant from the surface. Rio is most brilliant from on high. To enjoy Tokyo one must open the doors of an outwardly drab façade. New York can offer squalor on one block, excitement on the very next. Sydney, though, is an urban gem. To fly over its harbor, bisected by the great bridge which is as much an Australian symbol as the kangaroo, is to savor one of the happiest blendings of man and nature—inner waters dotted with the billowing white sails of graceful craft, irregular shorelines of placid green interspersed with the red roofs of neat houses and the crystal walls of slim skyscrapers, all set against the clearest of blue skies, and flanked, north and south, with the fiercely steep cliffs that enclose white sand beaches pounded by heavy surf.

The approach by sea, past the great clifflike headlands which protect the fingerlike projections of the harbor which create its coves, is quite as lovely. There is no feeling of anticlimax, once one sets out to explore, on foot, for Sydney is a grab bag of surprises: a city which is at once Australia's biggest and oldest, and which is the essence of Australia at its best.

Sydney came about as an afterthought. It was Botany Bay, a few miles to the south (Kingsford Smith International Airport now flanks its north shore) which was the original destination of the fleet of eleven ships which arrived to settle Australia as a penal colony in January 1788. Naval Captain Arthur Phillip, who became the first governor, was not at all happy with what he found—a low, swampy region. He went north to what was then Port Jackson, described it, hardly with English understatement, as "the finest harbor in the world," and without delay moved his brood to it, at the same time retitling it Sydney Cove after the same British Cabinet member, Viscount Sydney, for whom another then-new community on the other side of the world— Sydney, Nova Scotia—was named at about the same time.

Sydney's beginnings were anything but happy. There was much sickness and little food, but Governor Phillip persevered, and by the time he retired in 1792 it was on the road to survival, even overcoming a grim period of anarchy, military misrule, and great confusion, which ended with the so-called Rum Rebellion in 1808. Lachlan Macquarie, a newly appointed governor, brought back law and order. And he did a good deal more: By means of a visionary town-planning and public-works program he transformed a ramshackle outpost into a handsome town.

A cultivated man of excellent taste, he put to work one Francis Greenaway, a brilliant architect who had been convicted of forgery in his native England and was serving his sentence in New South Wales. The Macquarie-Greenaway collaboration resulted in Sydney's emergence as a Regency city, of which there still remain handsome remnants. Before the nineteenth century had reached its midpoint, a Municipal Council had been formed, and later, with the cessation of convict transportation and the granting of representative government by London, Sydney assumed increased stature as the seat of the first Parliament in Australia.

With the gold rush in the 1850s, it prospered even more, as the port of entry for newcomers. Paddington and Darlinghurst, residential sections graced by charming houses faced with rococo iron lacework balconies (the iron was ballast in ships), went up at this time. And the city's boundaries continued to expand. In something like 175 years, Sydney has become the fourth-largest city in the Commonwealth (preceded only by London, Calcutta, and Bombay).

Today, Sydney is the core of Australian industry, its cultural center, and its good-time town par excellence. But neither the tinsel of after-dark rendezvous nor the stacks of outlying factories have spoiled it. It has managed to retain its natural beauty, preserving its shorelines and its parkland and a substantial quantity of its old landmarks. At the same time, it fairly bristles with the energy of contemporary Australia, pleasurably absorbing the mores of its new European migrants, adapting a good deal from America, all the while retaining much of its British heritage, not to mention that which is solidly and peculiarly Australian. Sydneysiders are not unlike New Yorkers in that they come from everywhere. They are as *au courant* with the state of the world as counterparts in other great global centers—well-informed, well-dressed, smartly groomed, sufficiently impatient with the tried and tested to sample the new, the imported, the exotic, the unusual, and jealous of their city's reputation as the place fellow Australians look upon with mixed feelings of admiration and envy.

Nothing of contemporary Sydney more typifies its forward look than the Opera House, begun in 1959 and scheduled for 1969 completion. The site is Benelong Point, at the tip of Sydney Cove, where the colony had its beginnings. The architect is a Dane, Jøern Utzon, chosen as the result of an international competition, and the design sufficiently avant-garde to have created what is probably the most discussed architectural controversy of modern times. The building is a soaring bevy of tile-surfaced sail-like components, astride a massive base, with the effect that of a free-standing sculpture blending in with the waterfront setting, and eye-filling from the harbor, the city, and the air. Within will be a main auditorium seating twenty-eight hundred, a smaller auditorium for eleven hundred, a chamber music hall seating three hundred, a four-hundred-seat experimental theater, a large split-level restaurant, twenty rehearsal rooms and fifty dressing rooms, as well as refreshment bars and lounges. The Opera House has had anything but an easygoing history. There have been delays in the completion date and costs have mounted to where the finished product is estimated at more than fifty-five million dollars—a third more than New York's relatively unexciting and conventional new Metropolitan Opera House. And opinions about the building are not all complimentary. Australia's own Joan Sutherland termed it "that great effigy," and the Sydney *Sun,* "The Mad Scene from Benelong." But it has had its supporters, among them the late great architect Eero Saarinen, the theater's Sir Tyrone Guthrie, and Australian art critic Robin Boyd, who has opined that "Sydney will live to be proud of it." Sydneysiders, more power to them, are financing it by means of a lottery which brings in six and a half million dollars a year, and though impatient, are enjoying watching it take shape.

Opera House-watching is, of course, but one phase of Sydney sightseeing. The visitor does well to get his bearings by means of introductory bus tours of the city and the surrounding area, boat tours of the harbor, and thereafter proceed at will, on his own, by foot, by inexpensive public transport (including the South Pacific's only subway), by cab or by hire car.

Downtown, or central Sydney, is a mainly rectangular area extending south from the harbor. Its core is statue-filled Hyde Park. At its northern apex Queen's Square leads into elderly and elegant Macquarie Street, aptly named for the early governor-builder. Here is to be seen the gracefully colonnaded white-frame colonial structure which has been the seat of the New South Wales Parliament since 1829, but was built as a hospital almost two decades earlier. (Step inside and ask a guard to be shown about.) The finely proportioned stone-walled Old Mint, dating from the same era and a work of the earlier mentioned convict-architect Francis Greenaway, is just down the street, and now houses state government offices. Also on the same street is the handsome Public Library of New South Wales, whose Mitchell section—with first-rate collections of paintings, manuscripts, and books relating to early Australia and the South Pacific—is eminently suited to browsing. Here too are two other Greenaway-designed buildings: the Law Courts, which had been the barracks of prison laborers who helped build the city during Governor Macquarie's day, and St. James Church, reminiscent of Sir Christopher Wren's London churches, with its green copper spire and graceful Regency design.

Macquarie Street leads into Martin Place, which might be called the center of the center of Sydney. Here one finds the General Post Office (some say its plans got confused with those for Bombay, so redolent is it of Victorian-Indian public buildings) and the Cenotaph Monument to World War I dead, before which the annual Anzac Day ceremonies commemorating Australia's great losses at the Battle of Gallipoli and in World War II take place. It is also the site of the Changing of the Guard ceremonies every Thursday noon. (Newcomers cannot fully appreciate the significance of Anzac Day without reading Alan Seymour's searing play, *The One Day of the Year,* a part of the Penguin paperback, *Three Australian Plays.*) And here, too, are information offices, at Challis House, for Sydney, New South Wales, and the other Australian states as well.

The leading business streets, running parallel with Macquarie, cut through Martin Place, and include Elizabeth, Castlereagh, Pitt, and George, the latter humming with the activity of fine department stores, specialty shops, cinemas, banks, coffee shops, snack bars, tearooms, and restaurants. On George Street, too, are the elaborately colonnaded Italian Renaissance Town Hall (which houses, besides the Council Chambers and city offices, an immense concert hall with one of the world's biggest organs) and the Gothic structure which is St. Andrew's Cathedral (Anglican)— the oldest such in the country (1888) and containing within a painting of the Queen's 1954 visit, a sixteenth-century Great Bible, and the Air Force Memorial and Book of Remembrance. Also off George Street is the wholesale produce market; it's open on Friday only, when it is worth at least a brief visit.

Museums? Most certainly to be included on the itinerary of any visitor who would know Australian fine arts is the Art Gallery of New South Wales, in the great parklike Domain (soap-box orators on Sunday afternoons); half of the painting in the collections are of Australian origin, and there is a good section on aboriginal art, as well, with Oriental and other foreign galleries, too. The Australian Museum, opposite Hyde Park, contains an excellent ethnological section, which brings alive the early pre-European days of the country. And first rate, too, is the glimpse of modern technological Australia afforded by the exhibits of the Museum of Applied Arts and Sciences.

Almost a museum, in that it is a peephole to the past, is a superbly preserved section of the city which dates back to Governor Phillip's era: The Rocks. Far too few visitors bother having a look at this bit of Georgian and early Victorian Sydney at the approach to the Bridge. Its core, green-lawned Argyle Place, is lined with fine houses of the early city and dominated by the splendidly proportioned old Garrison Church. Quite as charming is the earlier-mentioned inner suburb of Paddington (Paddo to Sydneysiders), which is being restored to its early Victorian grandeur by the new proprietors of many of its old houses, each with whimsically elaborate wrought-iron grillwork façades. Two other mementos of old Sydney are within the splendid Botanic Gardens which adjoin the domain and fringe the harbor: the Conservatorium of Music, designed by Greenaway in 1818 as the stables of Government House, and Government House itself (not open to the public), with its romantic crenelated towers; it is the work (1837) of the same architect who designed Buckingham Palace. (Vaucluse House, near the harbor's southern entrance, is frequently included on city tours. It is an elderly residence, far more distinguished by its gardens and setting than its interior.)

Sydney's zoo is a special treat mainly because getting there is half the fun. It's across the harbor from the main part of town, and gained by ferries from the Circular Quay at the harbor. At the destination one finds almost every conceivable variety of Australian fauna. The koalas, however, are behind bars and not pettable. One finds them in more natural surroundings at Koala Park (along with kangaroos, emus, and other wildlife) in the northern suburb of Pennant Hills.

The ferry to the zoo is but one way of seeing the harbor. There are a variety of sightseeing tours by boat, all delightful, and there are two excellent elevated observation points. Best known is that atop the southeast pylon of the Harbour Bridge, from which (on a clear day, naturally) one may see as far as a hundred miles with the aid of the binoculars and telescopes which are available. (Sydneysiders, it is well to mention at this point, are inordinately proud of their Harbour Bridge, and I suggest you be enthusiastic about it when asked, even though you may secretly harbor admiration for the Golden Gate or the Verrazano. Connecting the city with its northern suburbs, it was erected in 1932, has a single-arch span of 1650 feet, with the crown some 440 feet above sea level. There's an eight-lane roadway for cars, two lines of railroad tracks, and a ten-foot-wide sidewalk as well. The total length, including approaches, is two and a half miles, and—I doubt if you'll be quizzed on this point, but be prepared—the high-water clearance for passing ships is 172½ feet.)

Bridge lesson completed, let's pass to the newer of the observation points, which I think affords an even more breathtaking view, thanks to increased height (almost a hundred feet) and better perspective. I refer to the tower of the twenty-six-story AMP Building (at Circular Quay), Australia's highest skyscraper at this writing, but due to be succeeded by even taller towers, Sydney sprouting new buildings with incredible rapidity.

But we've still more of Sydney to consider. King's Cross, a few minutes by cab and a bit longer by public transport from the city center, is a blend of Greenwich Village, Soho, and some extremely pleasant residential sectors, which is at its liveliest at night, thanks to virtually limitless quantities of restaurants, coffee houses, bars, night clubs, late-hour shops and art galleries, excellent hotels and streets pleasantly noisy with a babble of languages. "The Cross" is a Sydney requisite for visitors to the city from throughout Australia, as well as for the locals and, it goes without saying, the foreign tourists.

There remain the beaches. And it is difficult to do them justice. No urban area in the world can surpass them. There are thirty-four all told, nestled among coves protected by steep cliffs, along a forty-mile stretch, on either side of the city. Bondi, the nearest to the city center (about five miles), is understandably about the most popular, with crowds of over fifty thousand not uncommon on weekends of the long summer. (Its rock-bound sculptured mermaids are at least as lovely as Copenhagen's.) Other popular beaches include Manly, Coogee, and Bronte. Palm and Whale beaches to the north are quieter and of exceptional beauty. The beach lifeguards are uniquely Australian. All of them are volunteers—members of local beach lifeguards' clubs which are associated with the Surf Life Saving Association. Each beach's guards wear distinctive bathing suits and caps. Besides saving lives (more than one hundred thousand since the turn of the century) they're very big on carnivals, mass displays, and competitions, held during summer weekends. Newcomers do well to swim only where there are lifeguards and then between the two red flags, for the undertows can be heavy and sharks are by no means unknown.

Other sports? Aside from the favorite spectator one—racing at huge Randwick, Warwick Farm, and other courses—there's golf (some three-score courses, a number of which welcome foreign tourists), tennis (at many open-to-the-public courts), and fishing, for shark, marlin, mullet, and many other species.

Sydney shares primacy with Melbourne in the realm of shopping, so that I should allow time for that activity in my schedule, which should not be so crowded that exhaustion will set in before night-fall—for Sydney offers more diversion in this respect (see Creature Comforts) than any other Australian city—indeed, any city in the South Pacific, be it the watching of the Australian Ballet or the consumption of Australian beer.

New South Wales excursions from Sydney: There are far larger Australian states, but New South Wales, with a thousand miles of coastline and an area twice that of California, is considerably more than a dot on the map. Named in the eighteenth century for Glamorganshire, the maritime county of *old* south Wales which it was believed to resemble, New South Wales is a land embracing Australia's highest mountains, vast sheep stations, rolling valleys, a considerable sprinkling of urban settlement, and, of course, the already alluded to splendors of one of the most magnificent of shorelines. I should not leave the area without at least taking in *Palm, Whale,* and the intermediate beaches to the north of Sydney, either by means of public bus, guided tour, or private car. Just south of town is *Sublime Point,* where the vistas are quite what the immodest name implies. Also to the south, at Kurnell, on the headland dominating Botany Bay, is *Captain Cook's Landing Place Reserve,* a 260-acre memorial to the historic landing of 1770, with monuments to Cook, botanist Sir Joseph Banks, and other figures. Earlier-mentioned *Koala Park* at West Pennant Hills, twenty miles from town, is a recommended excursion, and an alternative might be *Kuring-gai Chase,* an immense wildlife and bird sanctuary (with more than its share of koalas and some aboriginal rock paintings as well). It is at the southern border of the *Hawkesbury River,* another popular spot. Located thirty miles north of Sydney, the river area can be covered on day-long combination bus-boat tours. Even more of an attraction is the *Blue Mountains* region. Some sixty miles from Sydney, these were the peaks that settlers found impenetrable during the colony's early years. Though hardly alpine—they rise no higher than four thousand feet—they embrace quite spectacular sandstone cliffs, fantastic rock formations, sparkling waterfalls, dramatically precipitous gullies, and hills embroidered with the fragrant leaves of a great variety of eucalyptus, or gum, trees. This is a land for hikes and picnics and rubbernecking, most easily come by on day-long excursions from Sydney, to *Katoomba,* with lunch at an elevated revolving restaurant. Some fifty miles beyond Katoomba, and also accessible on tours, are the *Jenolan Caves,* whose caverns and tunnels are presumed to be something like half a million years old. There are stalagmites and stalactites in profusion, and of varying hues, with a six-thousand-acre wildlife reserve and good accommodation to boot. At one point or other, during one's Australian stay, *a visit to a sheep station* should be a requisite. All-inclusive one-day air tours are conducted to stations in the vicinity of *Bathurst,* a pleasant city and one of Australia's most historic (with a recently opened historic museum in a fine old house) and *Dubbo.* Visitors see sheep being herded by incredibly skilled dogs, watch shearing operations, visit stockyards, meet hospitable neighborhood folk often stopping for a beer at a local pub, and pan for gold in long-since-deserted streams, with meals taken in the farmer's homestead. I add a word of caution, however: *Make sure the homestead to be visited is all it's cracked up to be.* The day's excursion is a long one and spending much of it in fly-infested, shacklike surroundings can be most unpleasant, particularly at the rates charged.

Canberra and the Snowy Mountains: Australia's national capital is a new, planned city, in many respects not unlike Brazil's Brasília, and the Indian State of Punjab's Chandigarh. It has, heaven knows, had a difficult time aborning—two World Wars intervened after its conception, and it is still far from completed, although it is developing with such speed that residents find new additions each time they return from an absence of even moderate duration. Still, one does well not to expect either the excitingly radical departures from the conventional, which make Brasília so exciting, or the distinctive stamp of the virtually inimitable Frenchman Le Corbusier, which makes Chandigarh such a startling new addition to the ancient façade of India.

Canberra owes its original design to Chicago architect Walter Burley Griffin, who was selected as its planner as the result of a worldwide competition held in 1911, after the newly federated Commonwealth of Australia had decided to move its seat of government from Melbourne, in the State of Victoria, to a plot of "neutral" federal territory, not unlike the American District of Columbia. The land selected was a 910-square-mile chunk of the State of New South Wales, conveniently located between the chief Australian centers of population, Sydney and Melbourne, with the Pacific about seventy miles to the east and the Snowy Mountains—Australia's Alps—about the same distance south.

The city got its name (presumably a corruption of an aboriginal place name, and pronounced *"Can*-b'ra") in 1913 when it was officially christened by Lady Denman, wife of the then Governor-General. But it was not until 1927 that Parliament moved from the elegant Melbourne building (which now is the seat of the State of Victoria legislature) to what was planned as a "provisional" Parliament House in Canberra. Nearly five decades have passed and the "provisional" Parliament remains in use. It is a capacious white cement building, sufficiently dignified, to be sure, but by no means distinctive or overly pleasing in its design. It is, though, the first building to which you should beeline, for it is the core of the Australian government. The entrance foyer, King's Hall, doubles as a gallery of paintings of distinguished Australians and sovereigns, and from it one gains the two chambers. The Senate, or upper house, is decorated in red, as are London's House of Lords and upper houses in all Commonwealth legislatures, including those of all Australian states.

The federal Senate numbers sixty members, ten from each of the six states, all elected for six-year terms by proportional representation. It is in this chamber—again following traditional British practices—that Parliament is officially opened each year by the Sovereign's representative, the Governor-General. The lower chamber, the House of Representatives, has 124 members, each state's strength being based on its population. (Breakdown, to give you an idea of where political power lies: New South

Wales, 46; Victoria, 33; Queensland, 18; South Australia, 11; Western Australia, 9; Tasmania, 5, and—having votes only on matters concerning their territories—Australian Capital Territory, 1; Northern Territory, 1.)

Quite as worthy of a visit as Parliament House is the Australian War Memorial, a massive building constructed around a great reflecting pool in its inner courtyard, whose cloisterlike galleries are walled with plaques on which are inscribed the names of the more than one hundred thousand Australians who lost their lives in the wars in which Australia has participated. The Hall of Memory, beneath the building's great dome, is a massively proportioned chamber with mosaics decorating its ceiling and walls, and handsome stained-glass windows honoring each of the armed services. Of particular note are the galleries containing splendidly designed dioramas of major battles in which Australians have fought, collections of war mementos, and some excellent paintings, including superb work by William Dobell and Stella Bowen.

Other Canberra destinations might include the modern, functional, and aesthetically unexceptional campus of the Australian National University, the rather unusual igloo-shaped Academy of Science, the High Court, the foreign embassies (America's is a traditional, red-brick Colonial building), the attractive Civic Square, with its sculpture-flanked, fountain-filled reflecting pool around which are grouped shops, stores, and other business establishments; Lake Burley Griffin, the manmade body of water which separates the governmental and non-governmental sectors of the city and which is best viewed from observation points atop Mount Pleasant or Black Mountain. Outside of town is the Royal Military College and Government House, the substantial if not particularly handsome official residence of the Governor-General (not open to the public).

Canberra's youth and the precision with which it, like all planned cities, has been created, combine to prevent its having the warmly inviting façade of most Australian cities. But its people (there are something like eighty thousand of them) are a cross section of Australia. Get acquainted with them and the outwardly austere, antiseptic quality of the city gives way to Aussie "mateship" at its best.

A Canberra visit, except for the visitor with a special mission, need not be longer than a couple of days. (It can, if one is *really* pressed, be as little as one day; en route between Sydney and Melbourne one can arrive on an early morning flight, sightsee the day long, and take off in the evening, again by air, for whichever of the two major cities is one's destination.)

Ideally, though, one will stay long enough for a trip into the nearby *Snowy Mountains* of New South Wales. *Kosciusko State Park,* which covers one and a third million acres of the area and is named for Australia's highest peak (7316 feet), is at once an alpine wonderland—skiing from June to October, fishing from September to April, eminently photogenic panoramas the year round, and the site of the remarkable Snowy Mountains Scheme, a nine-hundred-million-dollar program, begun in 1949, under which the Snowy River is being diverted, through a series of tunnels and dams, to irrigate a vast interior area. The town of *Cooma* is the unofficial capital of the region, and base for engineers and workers from thirty nations (their flags line its main street) who are undertaking the job. There are good hotels in Cooma and smaller places such as *Adaminaby, Jindabyne, Khancoban, Perisher Valley,* and at *Mt. Kosciusko.* Fishing is at its best on *Lake Ecumbene,* where one may also go sailing, sightseeing by launch, feed kangaroos and emus at wildlife sanctuaries, and inspect the ingeniously wrought dams and tunnels of the area. One can take in the *basic* basics in as little as a full day, but at least twice that time is the ideal minimum.

Melbourne (pronounced *Mel*-burn, or if you really want to sound Aussie, *Mel*-bun, but please, *not* Mel-*born*) and Sydney—you might as well know from the start, if you don't already—are about as rivalrous as two cities within the same country can be. Sydney, the larger of the two in population, is expected to be overtaken by Melbourne within a decade (it is already way over the two million mark), but quantity of residents notwithstanding, the two are vastly dissimilar. Geography has a good deal to do with it, Sydney being lucky enough to have one of the most beautiful of settings. But personality enters in, too. Melbourne likes to think of itself as being more British in tone than its competitor. And even though it is taking in more New Australians—immigrants from Europe, half of them from the Continent—than Sydney, it somehow or other manages to retain a certain staidness and reserve, the much-appreciated contributions of its newcomers notwithstanding.

The visitor, then, must take Melbourne on its own terms, blocking out, if that is at all possible, contrasts with Sydney. For Melbourne has a great deal to recommend it. Despite its flattish terrain and a location on immense Port Phillip Bay, without the Pacific to flank it, it has made the most of the Yarra River, which flows through it. Its central sector is laid out gridiron-style, making it supremely easy for a newcomer to get about on its extrawide principal thoroughfares. It offers excellent accommodation, fine eating places, the best art museum in the country, first-rate theater and musical events, a rather grand and substantial mode of public architecture which is Victoriana at its best, some of the loveliest of urban parks and gardens, and a stylish elegance easily discernible in its people, which happily manifests itself in the great stores and the shops which line its elaborately decorated arcades.

Melburnians are not nearly as likely to strike up a conversation with you in a pub, as would be the case in almost any other Australian city. But they are not, conversely, nearly as difficult to know as Sydneysiders might lead you to believe. The important thing is to approach their city with an open mind and not a *word*—unless you're asked—about the capital of New South Wales. (Even a remark about the Sydney Opera House will bring a retort: Melbourne is building, in stages, an elaborate cultural center, costing some fifteen million dollars; the first part, an Art Gallery, is scheduled for 1967 completion.)

Chances are you'll be staying in the aforementioned gridiron-shaped city center, in the vicinity of the two principal thoroughfares—Bourke Street (remember it because it has the gracious

State Parliament overlooking its upper end) and Collins Street (*it* is dominated by the elegant State Treasury Building, in a similar position). Flinders Street, just beyond Collins, is flanked by the Railroad Station beyond which flows the Yarra River, and these three streets are cut through by half a dozen additional streets of import—Spring, Exhibition, Russell, Swanston, Elizabeth, Queen, and William. Many, but not all, of the city's parks and gardens, the lovely St. Kilda Road, and the handsome residential areas, are on the other side of the Yarra, which is traversed by four bridges.

A half-day sightseeing tour is ideal for orientation, after which it's easy to stroll about on one's own. I would head first for the Fitzroy Gardens, where the big surprise—after going through a magnificent plant-filled conservatory—is the charming house in which Captain James Cook was born almost two and a half centuries ago, in England's Yorkshire. It was brought to Melbourne, stone by stone, in 1934 as a part of the city's centennial celebrations. You'll want to go through its low-ceilinged rooms and stop for a chat with the caretaker, who is one of Melbourne's most knowledgeable experts on matters relating not only to Australian history, but that of the entire South Pacific area.

Worthy of attention, also, are the National Gallery (paintings and sculpture, many of them Australian), National Museum (Australiana exhibits), and State Library, all housed in the same complex of buildings; the beautiful Parliament House, far more impressive than the "provisional" Federal Parliament in Canberra (as indeed are most of the State Parliament Houses); the good-looking campus of Melbourne University (and, if you've time, the still-abuilding Monash University, with the Douglas Annand murals in its Wilson Hall); ever-so-impressive Government House (not open to the public) and its grounds; the Shrine of Remembrance, a memorial to the dead of the two World Wars; and, aside from the many areas of Victorian houses with wrought-iron fronts, two open-to-the-public houses of note, both a century old: exceptionally beautiful Como, and Caroline House.

Aside from the aforementioned Fitzroy Gardens, with the Cook House and Conservatory, I should certainly list a stroll through the Royal Botanic Gardens (only three such parks in the British Commonwealth have been granted the title "Royal"); the delightful Treasury Gardens, just a step from the heart of town and a favorite alfresco lunch spot for nine-to-fivers; the King's Domain, within which is located the ultramodern Sidney Myer Music Bowl, and the fifty-five-acre Zoological Gardens, or at least those portions with Australian animals.

Melbourne, aside from being a manufacturing center and great port, is Australia's financial headquarters, so that you might want to take in its Stock Exchange; visitors may watch trading from the public gallery. Melbourne was, as you'll recall, the site of the 1956 Olympics; and the stadiums and swimming pool erected for the games may be seen, along with the immense Melbourne Cricket Ground. Summer visitors will want to be aware of the chain of beaches which ring the east shore of Port Phillip Bay, including St. Kilda (with an amusement park, cinemas, and all manner of facilities from cabaret to Turkish baths), Brighton, and Black Rock. There is racing at noted Flemington (scene of the annual Melbourne Cup in November—Australia's fashionable answer to Britain's fashionable Ascot), night trotting races at the Royal Showgrounds, golf at a number of links which admit foreign visitors, tennis at Kooyong (where Davis Cup matches are played), and, in March, Melbourne's Moomba Festival, when the city is at its least inhibited, imbibing in a mélange of festive and cultural events.

Excursions into Victoria from Melbourne: Victoria is Australia's smallest mainland state and is proof positive that big things can come in small packages. Two day-long outings from Melbourne should be considered requisites. The first, a trip to *Phillip Island,* fifty-five miles southeast of town, is so special that friends back home are liable not to believe your description of it. What happens is this: Each evening like clockwork, at seven o'clock, at but one smallish strip of beach on this island's coast, dozens upon dozens of tiny fairy penguins waddle ashore from the briny deep, where they've spent the day feeding on fish. The State of Victoria has protected the area, and as darkness falls, attendants train giant spotlights on the beach. Visitors, all behind guide ropes, kneel down and watch the parade. The penguins, quite as hammy as those you've seen in zoos, seem to enjoy their audience tremendously, and stare right back at the visitors. They rarely make the trek individually, however, most preferring to wait at the shoreline until eight or ten have been bounced in by the surf. From the beach, they proceed into bordering sand dunes (enclosed by fences, but you may look through) where their young await them in the burrows which are their homes. They then feed their offspring by means of regurgitating down their throats what they've eaten during the day, at sea. Sleep for the family follows, until four in the morning. Visitors may return at that hour, if they wish, to watch the adult penguins return to the sea for another day's nutrition. On the same island is a rocky peninsula where, if you're lucky, you'll see seals sunning themselves during the day. And on the road which leads to the island from the mainland (there's a bridge) look sharp for shy koalas up in the gum trees.

The second requisite is the forty-nine-mile drive from Melbourne, through the very green and very scenic *Dandenong Mountains,* to the *Sir Colin Mackenzie Wildlife Sanctuary* at *Healesville.* There is probably no better public place in Australia in which to see koalas (keepers will let you pick them up if there's not too big a crowd), emus, lyrebirds, kangaroos, wallabies, and—the big treat—platypusses, two of which cavort rather wildly and with much abandon in an immense glass-walled tank known, sensibly enough, as a platypussery.

Other Victorian destinations for those with more time to savor the state might include the *southern Australian Alps* (winter sports, fall hunting, summer trekking at Mount Donna Buang and Lake Mountain, and other spots more distant from Melbourne, particularly Mount Buffalo National Park) and a leisurely cruise of five days' duration along the *Murray River,* Australia's longest, via paddle steamboat, through an attractive region of orchards and vineyards which in earlier days utilized the paddle-wheeler as its chief means of transport.

Tasmania: Separated from the mainland by Bass Strait, Tasmania, Australia's smallest state and its only island-state, appears to remain the most tradition-bound region of the country. Despite some success by its government to lure European emigrants, it retains the provincial Anglo-Saxon flavor—eminently respectable but a bit bland—of the neighboring island-country of New Zealand, both of which, coincidentally, were discovered by the Dutchman for whom Tasmania is named.

There are other similarities with New Zealand. Both are endowed with spectacular natural beauty (New Zealand, it must be admitted, has the edge, its overpowering South Island Alps being higher and more jagged than any Tasmanian peaks), both are without large cities, and if one wants to carry it a bit farther, both have capitals plopped beneath quite splendid mountains, the one behind Tasmania's Hobart bearing the same name (Wellington) as New Zealand's seat of government.

Tasmania is 150 miles from the closest mainland point, and with an area roughly extending 180 miles north to south and east to west, Tasmania is now expanding its permanent population of about 365,000, with great quantities of summer Australian tourists, and an increasing number of foreigners who include it in their itineraries. Early visitors, though, gave it short shrift. Abel Tasman came across its west coast as long ago as 1642, but it wasn't until a century and a half later, when explorers sailed through Bass Strait, that anyone had quite realized it was an island. Long known as Van Diemen's Land, it became a British territory in 1802, and served mainly as a penal colony until the mid-nineteenth century when Britain ceased sending over felons. In 1855, islanders replaced Mr. Van Diemen's name with Mr. Tasman's, and the following year received responsible government from the Crown.

Things have been moving along with a degree of rapidity ever since. But, happily for the visitor, not with overwhelming alacrity, at least until relatively recently. In consequence, Tasmania—almost from stem to stern—is rich in the monuments of its past, possibly more consistently so than any other state. I wouldn't say it was necessary to tour it in its entirety, but I would advise at least a minimal length visit to it on any Australian itinerary. Access is most direct by air from Melbourne, although one may fly from other points, and there is ship service (slower, of course, but comfortable) as well. Guided tours go everywhere, roads are good for those who would get about on their own, and distances, of course, are not great.

Hobart, the capital, is the largest urban center and is, as well, Australia's second oldest city. With a population of about 120,000, it is able to offer first-class amenities, touches of modernity (the new campus of the University of Tasmania, the modern Civic Fountain complex), a smashing view of town and port from atop 4166-foot Mount Wellington, a delightfully photogenic harbor, and some rather charming bits of the past. These would include the exhibits of the Narryna Folk Museum; Australia's oldest theater, the Royal (1837); St. George's, one of the fine churches designed by convict architect James Blackburn (1838); Anglesea Barracks (1814) and Battery Point, which is dotted with structures of century-plus vintage. Old Hobart, like much of Tasmania, took a long time in getting word of new modes and styles during colonial days, and for this we may be grateful: Its dominant architectural style is classic Georgian, even though a lot of what was constructed went up in the Victorian era. As a result, one finds the severe, clean-lined Georgian all about.

I would suggest, in this regard, that a requisite excursion be the short trip to the tiny village of *Richmond,* but fifteen miles distant. Never restored, progress has happily passed it by and it remains as it was a century and a quarter ago. Richmond is an almost perfect Georgian preserve. Its graceful bridge, spanning the narrow Coal River, dates to 1823 and is the oldest still in use in the country. St. John's is the oldest Roman Catholic Church in Australia (although the Anglican St. Luke's is a year older— 1834). To be seen, too, are the jail (with walls three feet thick), and a number of staidly grand houses still used as residences. *New Norfolk,* a bit more distant from Hobart than Richmond, is the

site of Australia's oldest licensed hotel, the Bush Inn, and of other
similar vintage remnants.

And fifty miles southeast, on the *Tasman Peninsula,* which
affords the motorist as splendid a sampling as he can find of
Tasmania *au naturelle,* are the magnificent ruins of *Port Arthur,*
which lie twelve miles coastward from the narrow bit of land
known as Eaglehawk Neck. Port Arthur housed some thirty thousand convicts between 1830 and 1877, when it was closed, and
the visitor will hear tales about it from the locals, some of whom
have published their theses in locally obtainable brochures and
booklets. The point that they try to make is that the prison was
not nearly as brutal as earlier histories implied, and convict transportation from England is, in varying degrees, defended as a
therapeutic system which resulted in placing felons in far more
wholesome, less evilly tempting, and less socially disreputable en-
vironments than those of the British Isles. Well, there are alterna-
tives to colonization other than penal settlements. But there is
no doubt but that many ex-Port Arthur habitués (and many
other former convicts) did find success in young Australia and
that their descendants, along with the descendants of other colonists, have built themselves quite a country. And theories of
humanity, or lack of it, notwithstanding, the ruins are a sight to
behold, even though they are all that remain of a near-disastrous
fire which occurred after the prison was closed. Most striking is
the beautifully designed Gothic-style prison church, possibly lovelier now, with its roofless, windowless façade, than in its prime,
and the work of the same James Blackburn, architect of the
earlier-mentioned St. George's in Hobart. There are, as well, the
so-called "Model Prison," a euphemistically named solitary con-
finement quarters, the main prison block, the turreted powder
magazine, the homes of prison officials. All are quiet now, on
pleasing green lawns, within view of the little Isle of the Dead
where thousands, both deceased convicts and civil personnel, are
buried.

From Hobart, one can make still other excursions. There can
be trips to the exceptionally rugged *West Coast,* parts of which

have still not been explored, so wild is the terrain. Or there may be excursions along the *East Coast,* for milder terrain and fine beaches. What I would suggest, though, particularly if time is at a premium, is the *123-mile drive inland, from the capital to Launceston,* the No. 2 city, along the historic route of the Old North Road. It took the early builder-governor, Macquarie, five and a half days to make the journey in 1811, but now it can be done in a leisurely day, and so much remains from the Macquarie era that one must be judicious about stops for photos, let alone inspections. All along the route are Georgian-design structures—places like St. Mark's Church, near Bridgewater; Dysart House, in the village by that name; the mill at Oatlands; the classic bridge at Ross; the Grange, a National Trust house at Campbelltown and, just a few miles before reaching Launceston, the tastefully restored Franklin House, a convict-built mansion dating to 1838, which was inhabited until 1960, when it was taken over for restoration by the National Trust. (Good teas in the adjoining lunchroom, and greeting-card reproductions of old Van Dieman's Land scenes on sale at the desk.) Entally, an old house of un-distinguished design also near Launceston, is highly touted by the state tourist department, but has been restored by it with non-descript Victorian pieces, and cannot compare with Franklin House, if one must make a choice.

Launceston itself is as Victorian as so much else of Tasmania is Georgian. And delightfully so, with its gingerbread buildings gaily painted in primary hues, good collections of early Tasmania (including the island's aborigines, now extinct) in its Queen Victoria Museum, and a honey of a park—Princes Square, with wrought-iron fences enclosing its gardens over which play the waters of a Paris-imported fountain, the spires of churches form-ing the background. *Devonport,* where ferries from Melbourne land, is sixty-five scenic miles to the north. The visitor may return to the mainland by that means, or by air, from Launceston.

Adelaide and South Australia: Each Australian state, possibly not by plan but at least by execution, has a major city which is at once its capital and metropolis. South Australia's is Adelaide, a community of some six hundred thousand, with a conservative ambiance not unlike that of Melbourne, a pleasant setting between the Mount Lofty Mountains and Gulf St. Vincent, and its most distinctive quality, an ingenious layout wherein its almost rectangular gridiron-design center is framed by lush parklands separating it from residential areas. The city plan, indisputably the finest of any of the country's state capitals, was the handiwork of its first Surveyor-General, Colonel William Light. He had to put up a fight for his scheme, and contemporary Adelaide thanks him for it. The parklands that enclose the city's core embrace some seventeen hundred acres, within which one finds a race track, golf courses, bowling green and croquet courses, bridle tracks, botanical gardens, and children's playgrounds, all interspersed with lovingly tended, beautifully landscaped areas of flowers and greenery.

The city center is enclosed by four thoroughfares—South, East, West, and North Terraces. Bordering the last-named are the most imposing of Adelaide's public buildings, and it is on these that the visitor does well to concentrate. The colonnaded Parliament House of South Australia, with its elaborate classic façade of local marble and the elegant chambers of its Legislative Council and House of Assembly, is one of the country's handsomest structures. The nearby National Gallery of South Australia is a tastefully arranged treasure trove of Australian art and sculpture, and contains a substantial collection of foreign art as well. The zoo, in a country abounding in zoos, is among the most enjoyable, with its koalas, the most sought-after specimens of foreign visitors, easily viewable.

King William Street, which bisects the central rectangle at midpoint, is the principal commercial thoroughfare, and with Rundle and Hindley streets, is pleasant for strolls, to see the department stores and specialty shops during the day, and for cinema-going and theater after dark. There are a substantial number of old and elderly buildings. Government House is a modified Regency edifice dating to 1839. Parts of the University of Adelaide date back to later Victorian times. Ayers House goes back to 1846, is open to the public, and serves as the National Trust of South

Australia's headquarters. Other vintage places of import include the Friends Meeting House (1840), Christ Church, and its rectory (1849), the Town Hall (1859), Treasury (1860), Old Legislative Council (now the State Land Tax Office) dating back to 1854, and the fine Gothic St. Peter's Cathedral (Anglican, 1869). (A good walking tour leaflet is available from the aforementioned National Trust.)

Adelaide has more than its share of recreational facilities within the shadows of its downtown area, but *beaches* are a bit more distant. Within twenty miles of town are a score of them, including Lars, Semaphore, Grange, Genley, and Glenelg. Locals are proud (overly so, I think) of the views obtainable from the Mount Lofty summit, eleven miles from town. But other excursions might be considered. One would be by air to *Kangaroo Island,* where the lures are superb deep-sea fishing, and the Flinders Chase Reserve, positively abounding with native fauna, easily observable in natural surroundings. Still another—highly recommended for the visitor who, like me, becomes enamored of Australia's excellent wines—would be to the *Barossa Valley,* some forty miles north, and still about as Teutonic in atmosphere (including language) as it was when German settlers founded it more than a century and a quarter ago. Wineries open their doors to visitors, and there's a splashily colorful vintage festival during March and April of every year, when the grapes are harvested. Barossa can be done in as little as a full day, but for the in-a-hurry passer-through, consider the Penfold Winery—one of the country's finest, just outside of town, which may be inspected within an hour or so.

Aficionados of river cruises, with five days at their disposal, can cruise the pleasant *Murray River* in a paddle-wheeler from the town of Murray Bridge to Morgan. And, for the mountain buff, there is the sufficiently rugged terrain of *Flinders Ranges,* with *Walpena Pound* and its chalet the favored headquarters region. South Australia is always, of course, visitable, but I should make a point of getting to it, if my travels took me within the neighborhood during March, on even-numbered years. It is then that Adelaide stages its Festival of Arts, which has become one of the best-quality such events on any continent.

Perth and Western Australia: Australia's west is its miracle country. The State of Western Australia, almost a million square miles in area, occupies a third of the nation-continent, is fringed on the south, north, and west by the Indian Ocean, and borders the immense Northern Territory and South Australia on the east. Though much older than one might imagine (it was first settled at Albany in 1826 and became a British colony three years later), it has, because of its great geographical separation from the east and the aridity of much of its tremendous area, taken considerably longer to develop. But recent decades have seen it making up for lost time. Now, with a population of some eight hundred thousand, it is, after Victoria, the fastest-growing state of Australia. Its capital and sole urban center of consequence, *Perth,* is one of the most joyous of Australian cities. Blessed with an incomparable climate (the sun, locals insist, rarely takes a holiday from dawn to dusk) and an inspired setting astride the swan-shaped Swan River estuary, a few miles from the sea, Perth is one of those rare places where the pace is moderate but the atmosphere still fairly brisk. Its nearly half a million residents—many of them transplanted easterners, many newcomers from Europe—know how to enjoy themselves, placing heavy emphasis on the out-of-doors, but by no means neglecting other urban pleasures.

Perth's international airport and its modern port of Fremantle (with excellent facilities at its passenger ship terminal) bring it the newcomers without which a city cannot become cosmopolitan. But its own people make the major contributions. They have retained a good bit of the old and blended it harmoniously with the zestful additions of our century, and I suggest you sample both. First, though, contact the Western Australian Tourist Bureau and arrange to be invited for a meal or an evening into the home of a private family, by means of the "Perth is People" scheme, an Australian counterpart of Denmark's pioneering "Meet the Danes" plan. Next, scoot up to King's Park, an incredibly lovely thousand-acre garden ablaze with species of the wildflowers for which

Western Australia is so justifiably noted. And from the city's restaurant terrace, or simply a bench, take in the skyline and the river below. Then, amble about downtown—past the smart shops of Hay and Wellington streets, of the charmingly Tudor London Court Arcade, and of St. George's Terrace.

Stroll along the riverfront Esplanade. Inspect the onetime jail which is now the nucleus of the Western Australian Museum and Art Gallery. Contrast the old Perth with the new. In the former category note the convict-built Town Hall (1867), the turreted Victorian Gothic palace which has been Government House for more than a century; strikingly designed, the similarly aged brick barracks, for long military quarters, are now government offices, and in dire danger of destruction. See the Western Australiana collections in an 1835 windmill on the edge of town. Admire the classic façade of the old Esplanade Hotel. And then take a look at modern Perth—skyscrapers like the T and G Building (with a rooftop observation tower), the splendid campus of the University of Western Australia (just outside of town), and the spanking new Parliament House of Western Australia, just above the aforementioned barracks.

Beaches? The yellow-sand shores of the Indian Ocean are among Australia's finest; some, like Scarborough, Trigg Island, and North Cottesloe, are for surfing; others, like Cottesloe, Port, and Leighton, are calmer, and for non-surfers. More of those famous wildflowers? *Yanchep National Park,* thirty-two miles north of town, abounds in them, and has koalas and kangaroos as well.

An excursion might well be made to unique *Rottnest Island,* a kind of Alcatraz turned resort; many of its original limestone buildings now provide accommodation for pleasure-bent visitors; there's swimming, golf, tennis, and good boat service from nearby Perth and Fremantle.

Other Western Australia destinations involve more travel. Some eighty miles north of Perth is something of a surprise—a Spanish Benedictine monastery at *New Norcia,* of traditional Iberian design and with venerable art and ecclesiastical treasures in its library and chapel. Historic *Albany* and the surrounding area of the southwest are also of interest, and *Broome,* way, way to the north, is a pearling center with a heavily aboriginal populace.

The Northern Territory—Alice Springs and Darwin: Australia's newest frontier, even less developed than Western Australia, is the enormous half-million-square-mile Northern Territory, an area more than twice the size of France, taking up nearly a fifth of the continent, the great bulk of it tropical, and with a population of but about fifty thousand, more than a third of whom are aborigines. Federally administered only since 1911, when it was taken over from South Australia, the territory made relatively little progress until after World War II. Since that time it has had a Legislative Council of its own, with power to enact local ordinances, and it has a representative in the Parliament at Canberra.

The territory makes its living mainly through cattle-raising, mining (mostly copper), a bit of agriculture, some pearling, and, in recent years, tourism. Oil experts are currently optimistic about finding liquid gold near Alice Springs. Federal expenditures now, averaging about fifty million dollars yearly, are tiding the region over into the mid-twentieth century. But a crash development program of truly major proportions is still awaited. Planes, many of them small craft, fly everywhere, but there are relatively few roads or railroads. Amenities of near-first rank are to be found only in the two principal towns, Darwin, the seat of government, and Alice Springs. The territory is not a part of the world for everyone, as its population attests. But the visitor with a yen for the lush tropics, great desert-like spaces out of which rise barren rocky peaks, the life and lore of the aborigine, and an informal, hearty atmosphere, will not be disappointed.

Alice Springs, the touristic heart of the Territory, was settled more than a century ago, but not until 1929 was it connected by rail with Adelaide, a thousand miles to the south. Growth, consequently, was feebly slow until very recently. Now, though, The Alice (or just plain Alice), as the Aussies sentimentally call it, is a surprisingly modern town of some five thousand population. Set amidst the barren Macdonnell Ranges, it is a flat, neat place, low-slung, with broad streets, a few comfortable hotels, and a number of local landmarks. These would include the springs from which the town is named (for the daughter of the builder of its original telegraph line); Anzac Hill, with a war memorial monument, and a fine panoramic view; the headquarters of the estimable Royal Flying Doctor Service (open to visitors but with a management apparently so busy that it cavalierly welcomes them with a pile of brochures and a contribution box designed to take the place of a guided tour); a School of the Air, by means of which rural youngsters get their lessons via radio; the handsome Flynn Memorial Church, dedicated to the Flying Doctor Service's founder; a populace of white, aborigine, and mixed-blood stock-men, in from the outlying cattle stations, in outfits not dissimilar to those of the U.S. cowhand; tourists from urban Australia and abroad; and business and government personnel, most of whom profess affection for their new, or relatively new, hometown. From Todd Street, Alice's main drag, one is in the countryside within minutes. Excursions take one to such nearby points as *Standley Chasm* and *Palm Valley.*

Ayers Rock, though, is more distant—some two hundred miles from town. There are package tours, taken by many Aussies, which keep one there overnight or for several days, but the accommodation is so primitive and the flies so bothersome (take some sort of head net if you can), that I suggest a day-long flying excursion. The rock is indeed worth seeing. Some five and a half miles in circumference, with a height of 1143 feet, it is the world's largest single rock, and its massiveness is accented by the flat desert country surrounding it. Fascinating too are the various colorations it takes, according to the time of day—whitish yellow in the midday sun, purple when in shadow, and at sunset it is a brilliant ball of red fire. Aborigines have affixed paintings on the walls of its crevices (they considered it a sacred place but none are about now). And the hardy may climb to the top. Twenty miles distant are the Olgas, some thirty dome-shaped monoliths embracing a fifteen-square-mile area. The longer tours take one to them; day-trippers must be content to view them from Ayers Rock.

A taste of authentic cattle station life can be had at *Ross River,* a "homestead" ranch house a few hours' drive from Alice, which takes paying guests in simple but attractive adjacent cabins, and feeds them in the homestead dining room with plain, if wholesome, food. Activity includes swimming in a cleverly improvised (and capacious) pool, riding, and learning how to toss a boomerang from one of the aboriginal hands. Even city slickers like me learn after a few tries, and I—like all "students"—have the boomerang I learned on to prove it!

Many of the aborigines in the Alice region live on reserves run by Lutheran and other church groups, and I suggest you get to at least one during your visit. Additionally, you might consider a day's flying with Connellan Airways, whose small craft take tourists along, when there is room, on the milk-run flights to outlying *cattle stations* and *aboriginal reserves.* The same airline also offers a variety of packaged tours. Alice and the surrounding area—the Center, as it is known, or the Outback—is an unforgettable part of our planet—harsh, dry, almost eerily red and yellow in coloration, and with minimal facilities. Still, there is a certain attraction to the great sweep of the region—thousands upon thousands of square miles still more populated by kangaroos and lizards and emus than by people—or even cattle, for that matter.

Darwin, at the "Top End" of Australia, is at once an international air terminus for jets arriving from Asia and Europe, and a small, just-developing, humidly tropical port, with a smallish populace and a minimum of amenities for the visitor. The setting is pleasant—the town straddles a promontory on the sea. There are wide streets, enlivened by vivid tropical plants and flowers, and there's a fine botanical garden, and good facilities for swimming, snorkeling, water skiing, and fishing. Beyond the town is crocodile-hunting territory (safaris may be arranged in Darwin and equipment rented there). And one may, as well, make excursions of as little as a day to such phenomena as giant anthills, uranium mines, picture-book jungles, and, in vast *Arnhem Land,* government and church aboriginal reserves. This is a region with aborigines who are still nomadic hunters, a part of the world which has known few outsiders. As recently as June 1965, Melbourne University anthropologist Donald F. Thomson reported coming across a Stone Age tribe, the Bindibu, who had never before seen whites, subsisted largely on lizards, seeds, and small birds, fashioned their own tools from stone and wood, and used their teeth and feet as tools. They were, Professor Thomson reported, "friendly, fearless, poised and happy."

Queensland—Great Barrier Reef, Brisbane, Gold Coast: I suspect it would not be quite fair to term Queensland the most inelegant of the Australian states. Still, one cannot help but note how it contrasts with its neighbors to the south and west. Despite its eastern locale it is not without a frontier kind of atmosphere, a quality which one would be less surprised to encounter in newer regions. It has, of course, been handicapped in its development by the great portion of its area which is overhumid, tropical, or barrenly arid. But it is not without blessings and some quite special attractions.

Occupying a quarter of Australia and extending south some sixteen hundred miles from just below New Guinea to the New South Wales border, it has known white settlement since 1828, when *Brisbane* (pronounced *Bris*-b'n) had its beginnings. Though it is the country's No. 3 city, Brisbane is, in at least one visitor's view, the state capital with the least to tempt the visitor for any but the briefest stay. The Town Hall, the city's landmark, is properly elaborate and imposing, with its 240-foot tower. The ornate French Renaissance State Parliament House and the gardens which border it are attractive. Shops and department stores are in the Queen, Adelaide and George streets area. There is an old lighthouse-like observatory, convict-built in 1829, and the State Government Stores building is of similar vintage. Australian paintings may be seen at the Moreton and Johnstone galleries, as well as the National Art Gallery which offers foreign works, too. And there are two interesting museums, the Queensland

Historical Society, in Newstead House, the town's oldest; and the Queensland Museum, with some interesting exhibits on the state, particularly its tropical sectors. The University of Queensland is modern and functional, and eight miles from town I should consider a requisite, at least for koala fanciers, the Lone Pine Sanctuary which is absolutely loaded with the animals.

The Gold Coast, an hour's drive south from Brisbane (and connected with Sydney and Melbourne by what is almost an air shuttle service) is a twenty-mile strip of tinselly Pacific Coast resorts which I would have no hesitation in describing as the most tawdry, tasteless, and vulgar piece of real estate in all Australia. The Gold Coast is a prime object lesson in how not to develop an area. All that is worst of contemporary United States culture has been freely transplanted by its entrepreneurs, to the extent that Miami Beach and Coney Island are positively restrained in contrast. New Zealanders, anxious for a place where they may live dangerously and where bars don't close at six each evening, adore the place, as do many Aussies who flock up from the south in winter, when Sydney and Melbourne are unswimmable, the climate being undeniably superb, as are the beaches and surf. Foreign visitors, except perhaps for the most tired of businessmen, do well not to waste their time, but for those who insist, the basics are as follows: *Coolangatta* is the site of the airport which brings holidaymakers by the planeload. Going northward from there, one passes resort community after resort community, none being very distinguishable from its neighbors. *Surfers Paradise,* with its ever-so-modest appellation, is the focal point of activity, a maze of hotels, motels, guest houses, shops, bars, restaurants, and nightspots. Within the area is the *Currumbin Bird Sanctuary,* where twice each day customers sit around a great outdoor oval, plates of feed in hand, to await the arrival of thousands of brilliantly plumed parrots and other winged creatures. The birds zoom in on schedule and perch themselves all over their benefactors—head, arms, lap—while enjoying a meal. It's gimmicky, but quite a show. There are also a porpoise pool and daily water-ski shows in the general neighborhood.

ook's Bay, on the island of Moorea, near Tahiti.

Polynesia beckons: a young
Bora-Bora, near Tahiti.

Floral headgear is traditional
with Tahitian men.

France's *tricoleur* flies above a New Caledonia school, as a multiracial class emerges.

France in the South Seas:
The Cathedral, Nouméa, New Caledonia.

6

A secluded beach on the
Isle of Pines, New Caledonia.

Mitre Peak protrudes above a
cloud, Milford Sound, New Zealand.

Fly to a glacier: the author,
and the plane on which he was
flown to New Zealand's Franz
Josef Glacier; note special skis,
for landing, beneath its wheels.

Advance headquarters of the
American Navy's Operation Deepfreeze, Christchurch, New Zealand.

A pair of towheaded New Zealanders in the harbor's sands, Queenstown, New Zealand.

A Maori-carved gateway frames traditionally costumed guide Rotorua, New Zealand

Maoris on New Zealand's North Islar make practical use of the thermal waters; here a lad bathes in a natural hot-water pool.

Sydney's great port: the famo Harbour Bridge, to the left, ar a landmark-in-the-making—t Opera House, righ

The Great Barrier Reef is quite something else again; indeed, a visit to it can be almost reason enough for an Australian journey, for it is—to understate—a wonder of the worlds both of tourism and nature. It extends some 1250 miles from the tip of the continent's Pacific coast, near the town of Cairns, to Gladstone, a point just a bit more than three hundred miles north of Brisbane; the reef is a great mass of coral, probably thirty million years old. It protrudes from the ocean's floor to create a protective barrier for the series of exquisitely tropical isles which lie between it and the shoreline of the mainland. Its crystal clear azure waters shelter some three hundred species of coral—coral of many shapes and formations, coral whose hues appear too brilliant to be natural —purple, pink, scarlet, yellow, varying shades of green. And, adding to the brilliance in the undersea grottos formed by the coral, are incredibly lovely varieties of marine life, untold quantities of tropical fish which make tank collections of friends back home seem pallid and artificial. At low tide, the wide beaches of the region are a treasure trove for fossicking, or shell collecting. Nowhere in the Pacific is there more wonderful snorkeling and scuba diving. For the more sedentary, the undersea world may be inspected from glass-bottomed boats. It should go without saying that swimming and sunbathing are nowhere more idyllic.

The reef is as wide as five miles, at certain points, and in the south extends as much as a hundred miles out to sea. By no means all of its islands are developed, let alone inhabited. But a number are, so that the visitor has a wide choice. The principal islands are reached via various coastal towns, some by air and launch, some—those closest to the mainland—by launch only. A good way of seeing several is a Barrier Reef cruise on modern craft taking as many as twenty-five passengers. From Mackay, the Roylen launches depart for five-day excursions, and the *Esmerelda,* on three-day trips. There are, as well, five-day cruises on the *Eveley,* out of Townsville.

The visitable islands? Let's start at the top—up north—and go southward toward Brisbane. If your itinerary gives you enough time, I would suggest flying to *Cairns,* from the south, or even from Alice Springs or Darwin, via the economically important but hardly scenic little town of *Mount Isa,* with its great copper mines (and a much-needed good new hotel). Cairns, with a population under three thousand, is the farthest north mainland town of consequence, with good accommodation, a welcoming, informal-living populace, and proximity not only to the northernmost inhabited island in the reef, but also the quite special *Atherton Tablelands,* a plateau of fern-filled valleys, splendid crater lakes, sparkling waterfalls, and deep, tranquil ravines, eminently viewable on tours as brief as a day. Also within the neighborhood of Cairns are fine beaches, immense cattle stations, and sugar plantations of the kind made so memorable in the play *Summer of the Seventeenth Doll.* But major area billing goes to *Green Island,* a pleasant launch ride from town. Green Island is unique because of its Underwater Observatory—one simply walks down a flight of steps into an undersea cabin and watches sea life from great windows on all four walls; and its Marineland Museum, an alfresco, *au naturelle* collection of the fascinating fauna of the area. There is a pleasant hotel, great fossicking, swimming, sunning, and skin-diving.

Going southward, the next mainland town for departures for the reef is *Townsville,* a commercial center whose chief aesthetic distinction is a graciously sweeping bayfront location, but without any of the charm of Cairns, which it much exceeds in population. From this point one may go by launch to *Magnetic Island,* considerably developed, or the much quieter *Orpheus* and *Dunk Islands.* Continuing south on the coast, one comes to *Proserpine* and nearby *Shute Harbor.* These are departure points (by helicopter or launch) for *Hayman Island,* probably the most developed and most visited of the lot. Also accessible from Proserpine and Shute Harbor are smaller *South Molle Island* and more tranquil *Long Island. Mackay* (pronounced Ma-*kiy,* in typical Aussie fashion) is the takeoff town for well-developed *Lindeman Island,* and also-popular *Brampton Island;* both have comfortable, modern facilities. *Gladstone,* closest point to Brisbane for reef departures, is the means of access to *Heron* and *Quoin Islands,* neither of which have more than minimal amenities.

Norfolk Island: Discovered by Captain Cook in 1774, a penal colony for transported convicts until 1855, and since 1854 the home of European-Tahitian *Bounty* mutineers' descendants (brought from Pitcairn), tiny Norfolk Island is a delightful get-away-from-it-all Australian destination, some 930 miles northeast of Sydney. There still are less than a thousand inhabitants, but Qantas flies regularly. One finds the life quiet and ever so relaxed, the local accent a quaint blend of elderly—if not Old—English and Polynesian (*Wut a way you*—how are you), and the family names typically Bountian—including, of course, Christian. Norfolk pines—this is where they're from—abound in the rolling countryside, there's good swimming at Emily Bay, excellent fishing, simple accommodation, and silent ruins which evoke penal colony days.

New Guinea (or, more properly, the jointly administered Australian territories of Papua and New Guinea, which share the main New Guinea island with the Indonesian territory of West Irian) has still not been developed for tourism. Although both of the principal domestic Australian airlines (TAA and Ansett-ANA) make flights from the mainland, hotels are without frills, and most visitors are on non-touristic missions. Still, this is an area of unparalleled interest, with a populace of some two million Melanesians, many still yet to make the breakthrough from Stone to Atomic Age eras, through the good offices of the thirty-five thousand Australians on the scene. The terrain is nothing short of splendid—a verdant central chain of jagged peaks, lushly fringed coastlines, dense lowland jungle. *Port Moresby,* the capital —at once twentieth-century European and traditional Melanesian —is the principal center, and from it one can take brief excursions to nearby coastal villages on stilts, and teak plantations, or longer trips to *Lae,* facing the Huon Gulf; *Goroka,* the coffee capital of the interior which is the site of massive Melanesian "sing-sings" in May of even-numbered years (and of less elaborate such events tailor-made for visitors at any time); *Mount Hagen,* where the sing-sings take place in the intervening years, and exquisitely tropical *Madang*. Internal air services link scores of isolated communities, many of which can be worked into the itineraries of the more adventurous. And handicrafts, as museumgoers know, are among the most ingenious of the South Pacific.

WHAT TO BUY

Australia is a shopper's surprise package. With its exceptionally high standard of living, it has, in recent years, been able to match traditional quality of workmanship with smartness of design, in both manufactured and handcrafted products. Department stores in every city and the smaller towns, but most particularly the state capitals, are among the best-merchandised in the world, offering quite as wide a range, department by department, as one is accustomed to in New York or London, special sales (both advertised and otherwise), with staffs invariably efficient and gracious, and such amenities as escalators, restaurants, tearooms and barber shops, and even, on occasion, art galleries. There are, as well, smaller specialty shops in the big cities which are quite as *à la mode* as those of major European and North American cities, and there are, too, shops which specialize in the frequently interesting crafts of the aborigines. The same high standard of living which has made all of this possible is also responsible for the price scale: there are few bargains. Tabs are just about what one would expect to pay at home, if sometimes a bit less. The better shops and big department stores are adept at shipping purchases overseas. And Sydney's Kingsford Smith Airport has a duty-free shop selling such commodities as liquor, cigarettes, French perfumes, Japanese cameras and tape-recorders, Swiss watches, and the like, to passengers departing for overseas.

Sydney and Melbourne, the Big Two cities, are the best shopping centers, with the most diversity and a good deal of high style and elegance in their offerings, but one can find good stores elsewhere too.

Most interesting buys? Well, Australian wool is, of course, of
international note, and the Aussies do fine things with it. Men's
sweaters, women's knitwear, blankets, traveling rugs, and sheepskin coats and rugs are eminently purchasable in this category.
Kangaroo skins are offbeat buys, as throw rugs and coats, moc-
casins, and as the covering for the little koalas which nary a
tourist departs without. (The koalas' own fur cannot be used in
these as it is forbidden to kill them.) Australian opals are fashioned
into rings, brooches, and bracelets, and so are other native stones.
There is a considerable range of handcrafted ceramics, many of
which are attractive, and leather goods are first rate, with wallets,
briefcases, and women's handbags in cowhide, calfskin, crocodile
skin, and kangaroo hide. Australian-written, -illustrated, -photo-
graphed, and -printed books make excellent mementos, and most
are not available in the United States. Paintings are available in
every major city's profusion of art galleries, and many are the
work of gifted Australian artists. Aboriginal crafts—the highly
popular bark paintings, model canoes, wood carvings, spears,
woven grass products, and boomerangs—are unlike those of any
other South Pacific culture. Note, though, that many souvenir
shops sell boomerangs which are factory made, or otherwise mass
produced by Europeans. And lastly, there are the offerings of the
museums—from Perth to Brisbane—almost all of which sell at
their information desks attractively produced catalogs and albums
of their collections, postcards of the paintings from their collections, reproductions of paintings, and, as at Sydney's Australian
Museum, hand-blocked adaptations of aboriginal bark paintings.
I suggest starting one's browsing in the big department stores.
They have souvenir counters and book sections as well as regular
departments, with most of the other types of aforementioned
merchandise. Then branch off to specialty shops. In *Sydney,*
major department stores include the first-rate David Jones (which
has branches in towns of all sizes throughout the country and which
is known to Aussies simply as "DJ's"), and also-excellent Farmers.
Authentic aboriginal work, at fair prices, is to be had at the
Church Missionary Society's shop, at 135 Bathurst Street. Koalas,

kangaroo and sheepskin rugs, and other fur products are a specialty of the long-established Koala Bear Shop, 43 Park Street. Clay's, 103 Macleay Street, King's Cross and Grahame's, Martin Place, are among the leading bookshops. Alan J. Davis, Martin Place, and Percy Marks, 49 Castlereagh Street, are good for opals. Ceramics, leatherware, and the like are specialties at Benelong, 128 Bourke Street. Note also the myriad of small—and frequently excellent—shops for paintings, clothes, accessories, jewelry, and books in the compact King's Cross area; many of these are open evenings. Browse through the downtown arcades like Victoria, Imperial, and Her Majesty's—they're full of intriguing little shops, as is short, alley-like Rowe Street. *Melbourne*'s leading department store—one of the world's largest, and with branches in other towns —is the Myer Emporium. (The Aussies still use the word "emporium" but not as much as the Indians.) Myer's is a prime Melbourne sightseeing attraction, and so is Georges, Ltd., perhaps the country's most elegant shop for men's and women's clothing and accessories. The Anglophile proclivities of the well-to-do Melburnians are reflected in this store's stocks, more of which appear to be imported from Britain than locally made. Other Melbourne sources: Primrose Pottery Shop, 367 Little Collins Street, for ceramics, handwoven place mats, other craft products; Arts and Crafts Society of Victoria, Albany Court, Collins Street, aboriginal artifacts, other crafts; Feitel Furs, 290 Little Collins Street— kangaroo skin coats and rugs, koalas, and the like; and the shops of Melbourne's justifiably noted arcades—delightful Victorian carryovers such as the Royal and the Block. *Adelaide* numbers a Myer Emporium among its department stores, and the shop of the South Australia Department of Aboriginal Affairs, 132–40 Grenfell Street, is one of the country's best sources for aboriginal products; its staff, in direct contact with the department's aboriginal experts and the artisans themselves, is exceptionally knowledgeable. Other centers: **Hobart:** Myer Emporium; **Perth:** David Jones, and the shops of the charming Tudor-style St. George Arcade plus David Ffoulkes' Gift Shop—full of offbeat wares, on Broadway, in the Nedlands district; **Brisbane:** McWhirter's (a part of the Myer chain), Queensland Department of Native Affairs retail shop, William Street—aboriginal crafts; **Canberra:** David Jones, Georges (a branch of the Melbourne specialty shop); **Alice Springs:** Tmara-Mara Galleries—prints, watercolors, paintings of local artists including Rex Battarbee, teacher of aboriginal Albert Namatjira, his sons, and other aboriginal painters; **Great Barrier Reef:** David Jones has branches in such towns as Cairns and Townsville; all along the coast as well as on the reef's islands, lovely shells and coral are on sale in hotels and souvenir shops.

CREATURE COMFORTS

Hotels—There are exceptions to the rule, as in every country, but, by and large, one lives in considerable comfort, eats extremely well, and is rarely at a loss for after-dark diversion in Australia. Fine, modern-design hotels have sprung up everywhere in the last half decade, and highly regarded older places have refurbished. The result is accommodation in all the capitals and major visitor areas, with air conditioning, all rooms with bath and, frequently, with radio and television, room service, licensed restaurants and cocktail lounges, and amenities including gift shops, barber shops and beauty parlors, branches of airlines and travel agencies, and same-day laundry and pressing. Even in the less luxurious places, service is generally cheerful and cleanliness commonplace. What follow are a selection of better hotels (and occasionally, where outstanding, motor hotels), in principal centers of tourist interest. Rates, of course, vary, but at the leading hotels such as those below, they range from $8 to $12 single, with $10 being a good average; $12 to $18 double, with $14–$15 being a good average. Australian hotels do *not* add a service charge to bills, nor are hotel rooms taxed. All of the major cities, and most smaller places too, have perfectly adequate less luxurious hotels and motels with correspondingly lower tariffs.

Most Australian hotels—particularly the larger ones—contain, in addition to restaurants, a staggering variety of bars and cocktail lounges, more than are found in hotels elsewhere, thanks to the peculiarities of Aussie drinking customs and laws. All of these are open to men, of course, but, generally, only cocktail lounges —in contrast to largely stand-up bars—welcome women.

Sydney: Visitors stay either in the central downtown area or in King's Cross, and it's a toss-up as to which is the more convenient; downtown hotels are within walking distance of department stores, leading shops, office buildings, and the like, and a step from theaters. King's Cross, on the other hand, is Sydney at its liveliest after dark, and but a seven- or eight-minute taxi ride from downtown. Australia's newest major hotel is the $11.2-million, 20-story, 452-room Wentworth. Built and operated by Qantas Airways, it bears the name of the old Wentworth, which closed when its replacement opened, but which had been a hostelry, in one location or another, for more than a century. Other downtown hotels include the new, elegant, opulently decorated 252-room Menzies, with topnotch service, and every imaginable facility; the 305-room Australia—spacious, gracious, with all services, and attractive traditional decor; and the very good, 100-room Carlton-Rex. In King's Cross, the undisputed leader is the lavish Chevron (formerly the Chevron Hilton)—228 rooms (I suggest you insist on one with a harbor view—it's splendid), and a number of interesting restaurants and bars. Directly across the street is the smaller Sheraton (no relation to the U.S.-operated Sheratons, but, withal, The Hotel Where The Beatles Stayed). And not far away is the attractive Town House. **Canberra:** The federal capital's leaders are the elegantly modern Canberra-Rex, 158 rooms, all facilities; the older Canberra, with 125 rooms, and the comfortable Ainslie-Rex. **Melbourne:** In what must be an attempt to dispel the popular Victorian-era image of conservative Melbourne, its newest hotel, the Southern Cross, is vividly ultramodern. There are 435 eminently comfortable rooms, a commendable variety of wine-dine-dance places, any number of auxiliary services, including a mammoth shopping plaza, and the attentive service that is to be expected of hotels which are members of the excellent U.S.-origin Inter-Continental chain. More typical of the city and its architecture are the lovely, elderly, and first-rank Windsor, with 254 up-to-the-minute rooms and a heavy sprinkling of MPs, what with Parliament House just across the street; the Menzies—marvelously Victorian, with 133 guest rooms and great, high-ceilinged public rooms; the agreeable 147-room Savoy Plaza, and the smallish (79 rooms) but ever-so-posh Ress-Oriental. Better motels include the Royal Park, Palm Lake and John Batman, all with good licensed dining rooms, and about two miles from the city center. **Tasmania:** Hobart is happily blessed with the Wrest Point Riviera (and that *is* the correct spelling of the first word, strange as it seems to Americans who are inclined to omit the "r"), handsomely straddling a peninsula jutting into the Derwent River, just minutes from midtown, with 108 rooms, all facilities, including a swimming pool, and delightful service. In town are the newer 42-unit Travelodge, unlicensed but with a swimming pool, and the central Hadley's Hotel. In Launceston, there are the Tasmania and the Cornwall, both smallish but both modernized and with good facilities. **Adelaide's** newest is the Australia, perhaps the most continental European-flavored of major Australian hotels, spanking new and ultramodern, with a panoramic city view from many rooms and its rooftop restaurant. More traditionally Australian—its façade is one of the handsomest in a city of handsome buildings—is the 81-room South Australian, with a convenient central location, and an ambiance of dignity and charm. The modern Travelodge Motel has 78 units, a swimming pool and a licensed dining room. **Perth's** newest is the Travelodge, about a mile from the center of the town, with a pool, licensed rooftop restaurant, and 54 functional rooms. More central, though, and more traditional, are the 53-room Palace and the 49-room Adelphi, both elderly but atmospheric and agreeable, particularly the Palace. The Mount Private Hotel (unlicensed) occupies a recently modernized old house and is most comfortable and attractive, with a fine river view. **Alice Springs:** The Stuart Arms, built on the site of an earlier, similarly named hostelry which perished in flames a few years ago, is proof positive that everything's up to date in The Alice—comfortable, central, and the focal point of local life with a pleasant dining room, a huge, ever-busy lounge-bar, and outdoor patio for dancing, and a beer garden. Also good are the Mount Gillen Hotel/Motel—half a mile from town, with 17 units and a swimming pool, plus a licensed dining room; and the Oasis Motel, about the same distance from town as the Mount Gillen, also with a pool, and a first-rate licensed restaurant. **Darwin:** The 44-room Darwin Hotel leads, along with the Fannie Bay Hotel, two miles from town, both licensed, with restaurants and air-conditioned rooms, and both are under the same management as Alice Springs' Stuart Arms. **Brisbane's** No. 1 is modern, 257-room Lennon's, central and with all amenities. Other leaders include the small but good Criterion and the 40-unit Travelodge, at Kangaroo Point, with swimming pool, and the new multi-facility 11-story, 70-unit Tower Mill Motel. **Gold Coast:** The 169-room Chevron Paradise has a pool, central location, all facilities, and a decor and ambiance more than faintly derivative of Miami Beach at its most flamboyant. Lennon's, at Broadbeach, is more restrained, with 100 rooms, all amenities including a pool, but a location a bit away from the center of things if, indeed, it is the center of things one desires in this tawdry area. Coolangatta, which has the Gold Coast's airport, offers the 41-unit Beachcomber Motor Lodge, with swimming pool. **Great Barrier Reef:** In Cairns, the favorite is the 17-room, centrally located Great Northern, with truly luxurious rooms, fine food, and pleasing service. Across the water, at Green Island, the hotel is the 33-room Coral Cay (half with private baths); Dunk Island—the 22-room Great Barrier Reef (half of the rooms with baths); Orpheus Island—Orpheus Island Lodge, six of ten rooms with baths; Magnetic Island—Magnetic Hotel, with new cocktail lounge and guest rooms; Arcadia Hotel, individual, self-contained cottages, unlicensed; Hayman Island—Royal Hayman Hotel, 118 rooms all with bath, swimming pool, nightly dancing and entertainment, barber and beauty shops. South Molle—South Molle Island Tourist Resort, more than half the 57 rooms have private bath, swimming pool; Long Island—Happy Bay Resort, 14 of 27 rooms with bath; Lindeman Island

—Lindeman Island Hotel, 32 rooms all with bath, swimming pool, dancing; Brampton Island—Brampton Island Hotel, 63 rooms all with bath. Quoin Island—Quoin Island Tourist Resort, nine self-contained cabins, dining room, swimming pool, unlicensed. Coastal towns, from which access is had to reef islands (aside from Cairns, above) include Townsville (Hotel Allen, modern, attractive, 16 rooms all with bath, full facilities); Proserpine (Motel Astro, 10 self-contained units); Mackay (Kooyong Motor Hotel—12 units with bath, licensed dining room; Caravilla-Reef Motel—30 units with bath, unlicensed restaurant); and Gladstone (Port Curtis Motel, 16 units, all with bath). At **Mount Isa,** a stopover point for travelers en route to the reef from Alice Springs and Darwin, there is the new, first-rate Barkly, 31 rooms, all with bath, excellent restaurant, delightful service. **Norfolk Island:** Kingfisher Airtel, Anson Bay—a onetime cable station recently transformed into a series of cottages, each with bath; dining room, bar, pool, and shuttle bus service to beach and shops. **New Guinea:** Port Moresby—Hotel Papua, 16 of whose rooms have baths, and Hotel Boroka, with fewer such accommodations. The 35-room Gateway was set for late 1966 completion. Goroka—Hotel Goroka, about half of whose 17 rooms have private baths; Madang —Hotel Madang, 28 rooms with bath, swimming pool.

RESTAURANTS, NIGHTLIFE

In no sphere is the tremendous contribution of the continental European migrant to Australia more evident than that of the Inner Man. Since World War II the new Australians—Italian, Hungarian, German, Greek, Dutch, others—have virtually transformed the country's restaurant scene, introducing their own cuisines with great success, and making life far more pleasant for visitors as well as locals. One now finds foreign-cuisine restaurants —particularly Italian—in even smaller towns like Alice Springs, while the capitals boast a delightfully wide range. Naturally the native-born Aussies deserve a lot of credit too. More widely traveled than ever before, they scout around the world for new ideas and successfully import them with their own adaptations.

At the same time, the traditionally favored means of relaxation —the consumption of a beer or two or three—remains the most popular, the pub in Australia being quite as significant a social center as in Britain. Pub closing hours are controlled by state governments, and the Federal Government in the territories. Closing time is 10 P.M. in New South Wales, Victoria, Tasmania, Queensland, Western Australia, the Australian Capital Territory, and the Northern Territory. It is 6 P.M. (catch the bars between five and closing for the famous "six-o'clock swill" when homebound workers guzzle what they can before the curfew) in South Australia, which, hopefully, will 'ere long, extend to ten. Almost everywhere, drinks are available in nightclubs until the wee hours, and through late dinner, in licensed restaurants. Licensed hotels (only "private" hotels and many motels are not licensed) may serve their registered guests liquor at any time. Bars everywhere are closed Sundays, although exceptions are made for hotel guests. What follows is a selected list of interesting places in the major cities; no attempt is made to be exhaustive. Most of the state government travel departments publish gratis leaflets on dining in the major cities of their states, and in all capitals hotels distribute guides, published weekly, in all guest rooms; these contain a variety of current dining and entertainment suggestions. The Diners' Club has done a fantastically exhaustive recruiting job in Australia—restaurants and hotels everywhere are affiliated with it, so that members will find their cards most convenient in this country.

Sydney: The top hotels have excellent restaurants and night-spots. At the Chevron there is the Silver Spade nightclub (for nightly shows and dinner-dancing), excellent and inexpensive smorgasbord in the Oasis, the elegant Golden Grill dining room, a main floor cocktail lounge, and additional bars below, as well. The Menzies offers the handsome Emperor Room nightclub, the Red Lion Pub, the Main Lounge and Diamond Bar for cocktails, a moderately priced—and very good—coffee shop, and the Keller, a free-for-all German *bierstube* which is a lot of fun. The Australia's gracious high-ceilinged Jade Room is but one of a number of its wine-dine spots. The Carlton-Rex has its Carlton Restaurant and Elizabethan Lounge. For excellent steaks and other hearty beef dishes and wines by the goblet or bottle, there are the Bistro-Dorset Horn Chop House, downstairs, on Angel Place (downtown) and the Angus Steak Cave, a similarly excellent *bistro*-type steak-and-wine spot, on Abercrombie Lane, off 254 George Street, downtown. Chelsea, 119 Macleay Street, King's Cross, is Sydney dining at its most festive, with Edwardian decor, music, dancing. Countess Teleki's small-as-a-sixpence but excellent Salad Bowl, Springfield Avenue, King's Cross, serves superb Middle European cuisine. The Ozone is well worth the drive out to Watson's Bay; Frenchman Michel Ray offers first-rank French food, and from his Marine Parade location—with an outdoor terrace—one has a splendid view of the harbor and the distant city skyline. More expensive, also French, and with dancing and a fine setting, next to the Flying Boat Base, is Caprice, Sunderlay Avenue, Rose Bay. The Trianon, 29 Challis Avenue, King's Cross, is French, in a charming converted terrace house. Romano's, 34 Castlereagh Street, is a onetime Italian restaurant turned discothèque. The Sukiyaki Room, 32 Martin Place, is a pleasant bit of Japan. The Hungry Horse, Surrey Hills, is a modest but amusing dinner spot. Coachman, 763 Bourke Street, Redfern, is traditional, with excellent meals. The Four Canoes, Village Centre, Springfield Avenue, King's Cross, offers a panoramic view of The Cross from its upstairs tables, and good, medium-priced meals. Cahill's is a chain of eleven restaurants, each with its own subtitle and decor, all good bets. Ye Olde Crusty Taverne, 255 George Street, occupies rather ancient cellars; substantial food, good wine. Sorana's, 73 Macleay Street, King's Cross, has continental specialties. Maharani, William Street, King's Cross, is the genuine Indian item. The Music Hall, 156 Military Road, Neutral Bay, offers amusing spoofs of old-time mellerdrammers on its stage, during dinner. Chequers, Goulburn and Pitt Streets, is a big-and-brassy-type nightclub, best visited after dinner for the late, or late, late shows. Pruniers, 308 South New Head Road, Double Bay, has good steaks, continental specialties, entertainment, and dancing. The Weinkeller, 37 Pitt Street (near Circular Quay) specializes in smorgasbord, and you may have Indonesian food at Slamat Makan, 362 Victoria Street. The Gas Lash is among the livelier discothèques, and the atmospheric Marble Bar of the Adams Hotel is pleasant for a drink. Sydney is Australia's biggest theater center and I suggest you check the papers for current attractions—domestic and imported dramas and musicals, the Australian Ballet, even lunchtime performances at the "Q" Theatre in the AMP skyscraper. Watch, too, for performances of the fine Sydney Symphony (the talented American, Dean Dixon, is its music director) at the Town Hall Auditorium, and other musical events at that location, at the Conservatorium of Music and elsewhere. Principal cinemas are downtown and there are some in King's Cross, too. Last performances generally begin at about 8:00 P.M., but they usually open with at least a half hour's worth of ads flashed on the screen, so you don't miss much if you arrive a bit late; most feature films are British, American, or continental European with subtitles. **Melbourne:** The Southern Cross Hotel offers lunch and dinner-dancing in its posh Mayfair Room, hearty steaks in the excellent Club Grill, drinks in the lobby Willawa Cocktail Lounge and the downstairs Pub. The Ress-Oriental Hotel's Rib Room is a favorite for steaks. The Windsor Hotel's traditional-design dining room is for quiet, *table d'hôte* dinners. The Menzies boasts its elaborately Victorian Chandelier Room for dinner, dancing, and entertainment, *à la carte* meals in its restaurant, and the pleasant Club Bar. The Savoy Plaza's Rainbow Room has Indonesian and continental specialties, dancing and entertainment. Florentino, Bourke Street, across from the Southern Cross, is absolutely great for Italian food, either in the upstairs restaurant or the less expensive ground-floor Bistro. Antonio's, Toorak Road, is another good Italian place. The Top of the Town is a striking new restaurant atop the new MLC skyscraper, fine for lunch or dinner, with a great view and impeccable service. Mario's, Exhibition Street, is a traditional favorite for dinner, dancing, and entertainment. Fanny's, 243 Lonsdale Street, is another old-timer, elegant and excellent. Other good bets include the Walnut Tree, the Hermitage Bistro, and the Flagstaff Hotel Restaurant (smorgasbord). Melbourne is a lively theater city; watch the press for programs at more than half a dozen locations, for musical attractions in the Town Hall auditorium, and for movie suggestions. **Canberra:** The ever-so-modern Canberra-Rex Hotel has an excellent dining room overlooking its swimming pool, patio dancing and entertainment in its Club Lounge, and a pleasant cocktail lounge and coffee shop. Good restaurants include the Taverna, Civic Centre; Charcoal, London Circuit; Noah's, Rudd Street (Italian), and—particularly for lunch—steaks at the Carousel, atop Red Hill, for a fine view. **Hobart:** The Wrest Point Riviera's dining room is excellent, particularly for local sea food; cocktail lounge, too. The Travelodge's Fountain Room has good food, and a lovely view from its rooftop setting, although it's unlicensed. The Golden Dragon is Chinese, with dancing and entertainment Saturdays. Consult the press for theater, music, and other special events. **Adelaide:** I don't believe there's a posher dine-dance-floor show setting in all Australia than the Colonel Light Room, atop the Hotel Australia; and the continental food is first rank; the downstairs Matthew Flinders Room has excellent meals too, as well as several good cocktail lounges. The old-fashioned ambiance of the South Australian Hotel makes both its dining room and cocktail lounge inviting. There's good beef at La Cantina Bistro, 106 Hindley Street; a fine view from Ernest Torren's Lake Restaurant, Memorial Drive; continental food at the Red Wine Grill, 160 Glen Osmond Road; entertainment and dancing at the Paprika Club, 145-A Hindley Street. Adelaide, next door to the country's major vineyards, is the perfect wine-sampling city. Check the paper for plays in any of several theaters, and musical events as well. **Perth:** The Palace Hotel dining room is delightfully Old World, the Adelphi Hotel has an amusingly decorated Bistro, for good steaks, in its basement, and the Travelodge has the rooftop Chester-Ford Restaurant (licensed). Luis' Restaurant, 2 Sherwood Court, serves good continental food, Heidelberg is

German continental, and the Tum-Tum Inn, in the nearby port of Fremantle—which is fairly lively after dark—is a pleasant steak house. Though unlicensed, the King's Park Garden Restaurant offers a sweeping view of town, and is perfect for lunch. The Bistro of the Red Castle Motel has quality steaks and wines, but an out-of-town location near the airport. Perth offers plays and musical events in half a dozen theaters and is the seat of the Western Australia Ballet. **Brisbane:** Lennon's Hotel, in its Rainbow Room, features nightly dinner-dancing and entertainment; there's a coffee shop and cocktail lounge as well. The National Hotel's Sovereign Room also offers dinner-dancing and cabaret. Leading restaurants include Rowe's, Rowe's Arcade, with continental cuisine; Chez Pessa, 87 Wickham Terrace, Italian food; The Colony Club, 232 Edward Street, French continental, and the Camelia, 119 Queen Street (continental). The foregoing are licensed but many of the additional places are not; some offer what they call liquor messenger service; order a bottle of what you'd like, and it will be delivered to your table from a nearby shop.

AUSTRALIAN FOOD SPECIALTIES

Aside from the continental European foods now so prevalent, there is the traditional Australian regimen. Beef is the mainstay, although lamb is not unpopular. Not every Australian, despite what you may have heard, has steak and eggs for breakfast—but many still do. One must clearly *specify* (and hope for the best) when ordering rare or medium-rare steaks, for most Aussies, unlike their British cousins, prefer beef well done. In only a handful of the very top restaurants is it ever possible to obtain rare or even medium-rare roast beef; if you don't like it well done, order something else! Sea food, particularly lobster tails and Sydney Rock oysters, is excellent, and you'll want to try carpetbag steak, which is steak stuffed with oysters. Water is everywhere potable (but you must always request it in restaurants), and a variety of soft drinks are available. Milk is, of course, pasteurized, and milk drinks (sodas, shakes, and the like) excellent, ice creams and sundaes are delicious, and the candy is good, too. My favorite candy bar—I developed a passion for them—is a dark, chocolate-covered something called Cherry Ripe.

The first thing Australians ask visitors is their opinion of the country's beer, and it's very easy to answer in the affirmative; it is excellent and it is, again unlike England, served cold; barmaids often dispense it into glasses by means of long rubber hoses with spouts at their ends, which extend from under the bar. Leading brands include Tooth's, Toohey's, Foster's, and Swan. A good deal of coffee is consumed (Italian-type espresso lounges are everywhere), but tea is quite possibly even more popular, and good. Australian cigarettes (many of them filtered) are good-quality and reasonably priced; popular brands include Rothman's, Craven A, and Philip Morris. Biggest surprise of all to most visitors is the wine. The better Australian wines (rarely, if ever, imported into the United States) are truly first rate, particularly the reds. Always a good bet for ordering at lunch or dinner are the bottlings of such vintners as Penfold, Lindeman, Hardy, McWilliams, and Leo Buring, who produce whites like hock, reisling, and chablis, burgundy and claret in the red category, rosés, and sherry, port and champagne, as well. Prices are most reasonable. Also Australian-produced are gin, rum, brandy, liqueurs, and even whiskey, although imported brands are everywhere available. Mixed drinks at good hotel bars cost almost what they do in the United States; beer and locally made liquor are less expensive. Meal prices are only a bit under what they would be in comparable United States places.

Fiji

Entry requirements: American citizens need no visa, just a valid passport and vaccination certificate, and proof of onward transportation (air or steamship ticket). **Best times for a visit:** The ideal season for visitors are the months of May through November, when Fiji is at its coolest and driest. The balance of the year is rainier, particularly on that side of Viti Levu (the main island) where Suva, the capital, is situated. Viti Levu's windward side—site of Nadi and Lautoka—from which excellent cruises to outer islands depart, is invariably drier than the leeward (Suva) side. Hurricanes are apt to occur during the wet months, most often between December and March. But the "wet" period has its share of dry and sunny spells and need not deter the visitor. Suva's year-round temperature average is in the low eighties, and the humidity percentage averages in the seventies. Nights tend to be quite pleasant. **Currency:** The Fijian pound, which equals $2.54 in United States currency. It's divided into twenty shillings, with twelve pence to each shilling. A shilling, in other words, is worth a bit more than twelve U.S. cents. Note—Fiji will probably follow Australia and convert to the decimal system. **Film availability:** Both color and black-and-white film (usually Kodak) are available, as is black-and-white processing. **Languages:** English is the official language, is studied in the schools, and is quite widely spoken. Fiji's Fijians, predominantly Melanesian, speak Fijian as their principal language. And the majority of those citizens of East Indian origin regard Hindustani as their mother tongue. **Transportation:** Nadi International Airport, with a 10,400-foot jet runway and a modern air-conditioned terminal with free-

Fiji Islands

port shops, cocktail lounge, and snack bar, is one of the busiest in the South Pacific, and is served by half a dozen airlines. Qantas jets, connecting the U. S. West Coast with Australia, call here daily. Nadi is about 150 miles by road from Suva, but is linked with it also by Fiji Airways' frequent Heron service, with a number of flights every day. Fiji is an excellent departure point for neighboring islands, including American Samoa, Western Samoa, and Tonga. The port of Suva is visited by passenger-carrying ships of such lines as Matson, P & O Orient, and Union Steamship of New Zealand, as well as freighters, many of which carry small complements of passengers. Small ships link the islands of the Fiji group, carrying passengers and copra—particularly copra. And there are some excellent cruises, designed for tourists, which visit the islands, departing from Lautoka (the seaport near Nadi) and Suva. Taxis are plentiful both in Suva and Nadi, and rates are moderate. Visitors should note that the leading Nadi hotels provide *free* taxi service for their guests arriving and departing for the International Airport. Rent-a-car services are available, and chauffeur-driven cars may be engaged through hotels or travel agencies for sightseeing. **Tipping:** Tips are not refused but are not expected and not offered by the locals. And if you choose to tip, tip minimally. I might add that service is nowhere more pleasant or gracious. **Clothes:** Men wear ties with shirts to dinner in the better hotels. But otherwise, dress is informal, although women do *not* wear shorts downtown in the larger towns, nor after dark. **Business hours:** Larger stores are open from 8 A.M. to 1 P.M. and 2 P.M. to 4:30 P.M., Monday through Friday, and from 8 A.M. to 1 P.M. Saturday. Smaller shops close Wednesday afternoons, but usually are open evenings. Bars are open from 10 A.M. to 10 P.M. every day but Sunday. **Further information:** Fiji Visitors Bureau, Suva, Fiji (headquarters for mail inquiries); Fiji Visitors Bureau, Nadi International Airport, Fiji; Qantas Airways, Nadi and Suva, Fiji.

INTRODUCING FIJI

It is not often that a country is more known by a foreign designation for it, rather than its own. But it happens. In Europe, the Finns long since resigned themselves to their land being known abroad as Finland—a Swedish word—rather than Suomi, which is what they call their country in their own language. In the South Pacific, take the case of Fiji. Its own people call it Viti but neighboring Tongans long ago began pronouncing it Fiichi, and En-

glish-speaking visitors soon changed that to Fiji. The Fijians—
although the principal island of their group still is called *Viti* Levu
—have gone along; indeed just about everyone has but the French,
to whom these islands remain *les Îles Viti*. Now Viti, at least to
me, more connotes a hair preparation or perhaps a pep pill rather
than the palm trees, blue lagoons, and thatch villages which come
to mind when Fiji rolls off one's lips. Therein may lie the rub.
Fiji *is* quite as alluring as its name implies. But there's a good deal
more to it, and I suspect its significance is rarely appreciated by
most of us who live half a world away.

Size and population alone make Fiji a standout, as South Pacific areas go, for its half million people inhabit a hundred of a
group of more than five hundred islands which straddle the 180th
degree meridian—with the International Date Line bending to
the east of the cluster, to make time uniform throughout.

Methodists and Hindus, too: But go on from there: Name another land where the number of Methodists about equals the
number of Hindus. How many countries *asked* to be annexed—
and during the imperialistic era of the nineteenth century—by
three major powers, and were turned down by all three? (One, of
course, finally agreed.) What other underdeveloped land can one
name that owed a relatively piddling debt to an American and
was dunned for it by the rich United States? Where else was a
notoriously cannibalistic populace turned into as hospitable a
Christian people as one can find—in less than half a century?

And where else in the Pacific has the indigenous population
had to take second place, numerically, to an originally small
group which has been on the scene but eight decades?

Fiji is, in a word, fantastic. And I don't know of any Pacific
island group which has had fewer dull moments in its formative
period. It's likely that the first Europeans to come upon it were
Spaniards, but Abel Tasman, for whom Tasmania was eventually
named, is considered its European discoverer. He happened into
the area in 1643, had a terrible time navigating the northern
reefs, and passed the word so well that the Fijians were left un-
disturbed by visitors for well over a century.

Early visitors: In 1774, the English Captain James Cook (who else?) did some surveying, and a few years later the *Bounty*'s Captain Bligh rather gingerly traversed the shores of the main isles in the *Bounty*'s launch—with a Fijian war canoe in hot pursuit. There were occasional other visitors in ensuing years, but it was not until 1840 that America's Commodore Charles Wilkes (the same naval officer who surveyed the Samoas so well) made the first clear charts that the outer world really had a comprehensive idea of just where the Fiji Islands were.

There had, of course, been earlier white contacts, none of them representative of the European at his best. Traders came down for *bêche-de-mer* and sandalwood, escaped convicts made their way from Australia and settled in, and there were assorted other beachcombers who introduced European firearms into already explosive local situations. Missionaries came, of course, but the first, surprisingly, were Tahitians of the London Missionary Society, in 1830.

King Cakobau—and crises: Five years later, two British Methodists, William Cargill and David Cross, followed. And one cannot but admire their guts and courage. For the Fijians—intelligent, proud, warlike, and cannibalistic—were anything but tractable. They had, by the time the whites arrived, divided themselves into a number of mutually antagonistic chiefdoms, and after gruesome battle followed gruesome battle throughout the first half of the nineteenth century, there emerged a pair of dominant confederacies, or kingdoms. One, under a Tongan chief named Maafu, was supreme on Vanua Levu, the second-largest island of the group. The other was the great Fijian whose name is variously spelled Cakobau and Thakombau (and pronounced as the second spelling reads). He had come to gain control of the main island, Viti Levu, and was indeed the first chief to envision a united Fiji, to conceptualize the Fijians as members of a single nation rather than subjects only of the various tribal groups of the islands.

But Viti Levu, big as it is, was not all of the envisioned United Fiji. Cakobau needed support and it came to him from still another monarch, Tonga's King George Tupou I, who himself had earlier embraced Christianity for himself and his kingdom. The Tongan monarch made clear that if Cakobau became a Christian he would ally himself with him. Cakobau made a difficult decision—and went along. His realm at the time was glutted with rich and selfish white traders and sub-chiefs not at all disposed to dispense with cannibalism.

An American "debt": Cakobau had still other troubles. Some years earlier, Fijians had burned and looted the house of a conniving, disreputable, and intensely disliked United States agent resident in Fiji. The American had appealed to Washington for action and eventually he got it. In 1855 he persuaded the captain of a U.S. naval vessel visiting Fiji to investigate his claims. The captain arbitrarily assessed damages of $43,531 against Cakobau and told him that if he didn't sign a note promising to pay within two years that he would be hauled off to America. The amount of the debt—far in excess of the damages to the American's house—might well have been four million dollars, so completely beyond payment as Cakobau's coffers were concerned. By 1858 it was still unpaid, and another American ship came to collect—this time with interest. Desperate, Cakobau could but sign a second promissory note, and it was largely as a result of his helplessness that he appealed to Britain to take over Fiji. (Earlier, resident whites had similarly appealed to the United States but in vain.)

But Britain was busy fighting the Maoris in New Zealand and declined. That was in 1860, and Cakobau still was threatened by attack from rival chief Maafu—which might result in the dissolution of the kingdom he had fought to weld together. He turned next to the United States, asking them to take over. But the Civil War was on, and there was not even the courtesy of a reply.

Poor Cakobau. He had, at the same time, continuing domestic troubles, for his kingdom was not nearly as united as had been envisioned. By 1871 he had gotten his feuding chiefs to agree to a constitution. An election for the first parliament followed, but the government turned out to be one with European traders the powers behind the throne. Even more desperate, Cakobau asked

Germany for protection in 1872. But Bismarck, at that particular time, wanted no Pacific colonies. He, too, declined. Negotiations resumed with Britain and a spark of interest was kindled.

Pax Britannia: Finally, in 1874, the Crown sent Sir Hercules Robinson, governor of Her Majesty's Colony of New South Wales (now the Australian state by that name) to conclude an agreement with Cakobau, Maafu (still a major power), and other chiefs. It was known as the Deed of Cession, and it was signed October 10, 1874. As a token of his appreciation, Cakobau sent Queen Victoria his war club, accompanied by this memorable and moving message: "Before finally ceding his country to Her Majesty the Queen of Great Britain and Ireland, the king desires . . . to give Her Majesty the only thing he possesses that may interest her. The king gives Her Majesty his old and favorite war club, the former, and until lately, the only known law of Fiji. In abandoning club law and adopting the forms and principles of civilized society, he has laid aside his old weapon. . . . Many of his people, whole tribes, died and passed away under the old law; but hundreds of thousands will survive to enjoy the newer and better state of things. The king adds only a few words. With this emblem of the past, he sends his love to Her Majesty, saying he fully confides in her and her children who succeeding her shall become Kings of Fiji, to exercise a watchful control over the welfare of his children and people, who having survived the barbaric law and age, are now submitting themselves under Her Majesty's rule to civilization."

Maturing colony: The war club was presented by King George V to the Fiji Government in 1931—after a search had been made for it in Britain. For years it was thought to have reposed in the British Museum in London. It was found, though, in Windsor Castle, which it had probably never left after having been given to Victoria. At any rate it now—most appropriately—serves as the ceremonial Mace of Fiji's Legislative Council, a memento of the much-set-upon man who, though hardly without faults, transformed a cannibalistic collection of tribes into a peaceable and united people. Cakobau visited Australia with his two sons after he abdicated. They returned home with the measles—heretofore unknown in Fiji—and the epidemic which followed was the worst Fiji has ever known, with countless thousands of fatalities. The old man survived, though, and when he died in 1883—after strongly supporting the new British Government—he was given the salute by a British warship, and all of Fiji mourned him.

Cakobau's successor was the first British Governor of the Crown Colony of Fiji, Sir Arthur Gordon, a Scottish peer to whom the clan system was no novelty. From the first he appreciated the appropriateness of the Fijians' form of tribal government, and throughout the years of British rule the aim has been to preserve Fijian customs, to have Fijians govern themselves in local matters, and to protect them—and most particularly their land—from non-Fijian exploitation. Indeed, only a limited amount of so-called Crown Land could pass into the hands of whites, Fijians were prohibited from selling any of their lands to settlers, and a good bit of land previously transferred to unscrupulous Europeans was given back to its original Fijian owners.

Puritanical missionaries: Sir Arthur met with opposition, not only from the land-holding Europeans, many of them Germans whose protests resulted in protracted London-Berlin negotiations which culminated in a settlement in 1889, but from missionaries as well. They had, before annexation, come to enjoy tremendous power and prestige in their communities. Their communicants were being charged what amounted to compulsory church taxes, collected with the aid of Fijian magistrates. They refused to recognize traditional Fijian (non-Christian) marriage ceremonies— which the new British government *did* decide to accept. They resented the Gordon administration's reversal of their prohibition against dancing. And they fought his efforts to relax their bans on such harmless and charming practices as the wearing of flowers in the hair.

The East Indians arrive: Meanwhile, Fiji's economy was developing. Cotton was followed by sugar as chief revenue producer —which was all well and good except that there was a labor shortage. The Fijians, dominantly a Melanesian or Negroid people, were not dissimilar from Polynesians (like the Samoans) in that they lived communally in their villages, sharing their crops, and finding the cash economy of the Westerner of little appeal. The result was that there were not enough people to work the cotton fields, and later the sugar and copra plantations. Earlier white settlers had virtually kidnaped labor from other South Pacific islands in a barbaric practice known as blackbirding. It fortunately became illegal, and consequently eyes turned to India —and the beginning of a new era in Fijian history.

Between 1879 and 1916 some sixty thousand Indians were brought to Fiji as indentured laborers. Only about a third of those who came chose to go back to India after their terms of indenture. The rest remained, as small farmers, sugar mill workers, and later as business and professional people and civil servants. They did not, however, stay a minority for long, for they believed in large families.

What has happened, in consequence, is that there now are more Indians in Fiji than there are Fijians. And the two groups have retained their own identities. Although English is the official language of the colony and the *lingua franca,* Fijians continue to speak Fijian among themselves, and the Indians speak mostly Hindustani. They did away with the caste system of their homeland, but they have their own villages and settlements, and their own places of worship (the majority—about 70 percent—are Hindus but there is a substantial Moslem community and a populace of bearded, turbaned Sikhs as well). The lovely sari is still worn by most Indian women, and the traditional Indian cuisine, built around the famed curries, are the mainstays of their diet. (The situation in some respects is not unlike that of Trinidad, although there neither the Negroes nor the Indians are indigenous to the island.)

Land and sugar: Fiji's Indians staff the sugar cane industry almost entirely, and they have contributed immeasurably to the business, commercial, and professional life of the colony. The only truly critical period in Fijian-Indian relations came during World War II when Indian sugar workers and growers struck

for higher wages, and—as a measure of their dissatisfaction—
virtually ignored the need for their cooperation in the prosecution
of World War II. (Hardly any Indians enlisted in the military
forces, in contrast to substantial numbers of Fijians and Europeans.) But wages—better now, of course—were only one of the
Indians' grievances. The other still is a major problem, and that
has to do with the land—that same land which the British gen-
erously offered to protect for the Fijians when they took over Fiji
years before Indians were on the scene. Certain Indian migrants
were able to buy parcels of Crown-owned land, but in recent
years they have been able, by and large, to do nothing but rent.
As citizens of the colony, they quite naturally resent what they
consider discrimination.

The Fijian-Indian-British triangle: The problem, not surprisingly, extends beyond economics into politics, for it is the Fijian
minority, fearful of the Indian majority, that tends to prefer British rule to independence. Fijians realize that under the British
their rights are protected, and many don't want to risk the Indian
domination which might come with sovereignty.

Fijians continue to largely govern themselves, as they have
since Britain took over. Put briefly, it works out like this: The
Colony is divided into administrative units called *tikina,* each
under a Fijian *buli* who presides over the *tikina's* council at
monthly meetings. *Tikina* are grouped together as provinces, or
yasana, each under a *Roko Tui* who governs with a provincial
council. The whole system works under the Secretary for Fijian
Affairs, who is advised biannually by deliberations of the colony-
wide Council of Chiefs—invariably held amidst considerable and
exceptionally elaborate festivity.

Colony-wide, the British-appointed Governor is, of course, the
chief executive, although legislation is enacted by the Legislative
Council, which, through the years, has continually achieved more
power and which has stipulated numbers of Fijian, Indian, and
European members. A proposed new constitution, which would
transform Fiji from a colony to self-governing territory, is in the
offing and remains the subject of debate among the Fijian, Indian,

and European communities, each of which wants to assure as secure a place for itself as possible.

Temporary deadlock: The proposed constitution is not, to be sure, all that is being debated. The report of a Colonial Office-appointed board of inquiry on economic development, presented in 1960, suggested a number of reforms which could pave the way for economic expansion. Some have been adopted, but two major suggestions have both been opposed by the Fijian community. One would do away with the earlier-described Fijian administration and merge the governing of Fiji communities with those of the rest of the colony. Conceivably this would tend to bring more Fijians into the cash economy system and involve more Fijians in wage-paying labor. The other would alter the Fijians' ownership of land, so long protected under British rule. The commission opined that land not actually needed or used by Fijian communities should be made available to members of any race for development which would benefit the colony's economy.

Bones of contention, to be sure. And there are others. Education, for example, is impeded because of what amounts to segregated systems for the Fijian and Indian communities. No law impels separate schools, but Fijians prefer their children to be educated in schools where the Fijian language remains dominant, and Indians insist on clinging to Hindustani in their schools. Neither group appears willing to compromise on English to the extent that their own languages would be completely submerged by it.

Languages and literacy: The literacy rate is high, particularly among Fijians—well over 90 percent. But school still is not compulsory, except in the case of Fijian communities where a primary school is not more than three miles distant. And schools, even those operated by the government, still are not tuition-free. Medical problems are far from completely solved, despite the justifiably famous Fiji School of Medicine, which attracts students from many Pacific islands to its courses, and trains ancillary medical personnel, as well as the medical officers who are prepared for hospital and government service rather than private practice. There is a great need for more paved roads. The demand for decent cheap housing in the towns is greater than the supply. There continues to be animosity among the races.

The British, it cannot be denied, have done one of their best jobs of colonial administration in Fiji—from the start, under Sir Arthur Gordon. But it cannot be denied, either, that one finds among their numbers individuals with the patronizing—and often prejudiced and bigoted—attitudes toward the Fijians and Indians that are not unlike those one encountered during the pre-independence era in many British African colonies. Racial prejudices, it must be added, are not exclusively British in Fiji. It is not difficult to find oneself listening to Fijians on anti-Indian kicks, nor are Indians with anti-Fijian feelings a rarity.

Pleasant pace: What is most amazing is that with all of its complexities and problems, life goes on rather pleasantly in Fiji. The third postwar development scheme has been under way since 1961, and in the earlier two some twenty-eight million dollars had been expended, mostly as a result of grants from Britain. Sugar continues to thrive as Big Business, bringing in more than twenty-six million dollars a year in revenue. Coconut oil and copra remain important and there are minerals as well—gold, for example, and manganese. Small industry is by no means unknown, as in many Pacific islands. Fiji produces a wide range of products, including cigarettes, beer, matches, soft drinks, and a good deal else. And the visitor will be interested to know that tourism is regarded as an industry with tremendous potential, with financial grants and taxation relief available to builders of new hotels, and a well-managed tourist bureau. Most gratifying, though, is the delightfully *simpático* atmosphere of Fiji. There is no more courteous an area in the Pacific. If the British, in Fiji, were to ask tourists to award "smile cards" as the French have done in France, they couldn't keep their printing presses inoperable for even a moment.

Islands of smiles: For in Fiji just about *everyone* smiles and courtesy appears instinctive. I suspect that if one were to run a popularity contest among visitors, that the gracious, good-looking

Fijian—of the major groups in Fiji—would come out on top. But the Indian is in a rather peculiar position. He knows he outnumbers the Fijian and that the culture he represents is one of the most brilliant and highly developed in the world. But he knows, too, that the visitor coming to Fiji is more interested in the Fijians. He tends, as a result, to stay in the background, and may need more drawing out than his Fijian compatriots. But he is, invariably, a pleasant chap, and Fiji in many ways would be much the poorer without him.

Add it all up and one cannot but be optimistic about Fiji and its future. This land which has overcome so many difficulties through good sense, compromise, and the acceptance of new ways, might well emerge, as has similarly complex Trinidad and Tobago, an independent nation of which all its peoples may be proud.

YOUR VISIT TO FIJI

The ideal Fiji visit is not a whizbang, dash-in-dash-out affair. Other South Pacific island destinations are far more easily taken in by the traveler in a hurry. Fiji, though, takes a bit of time to understand and, thereby, to savor. Considerable distances are involved in getting about. The international airport is at one end of the main island, the capital and principal port at the other. The leading resort is midway between the two. From still another harbor city, near the international airport, cruises depart for smaller outer islands. Still other islands of the group may be gained by air or sea.

And, perhaps most important, the pattern of life in multiracial, multicultural Fiji is not as quickly grasped as in other South Pacific areas. Situations are more complex than they often appear, and it takes a bit of time to get the feel of them. For even the most rushed of Round the Pacific travelers, a week in Fiji is not too long. And a fortnight is far more to be preferred if one is to relax and do more than stick pretty heavily to sightseeing. Just a few days? Well, of course, if that's the maximum you can spare. A taste, however tiny, is far better than none at all—in any country, including Fiji.

But first Fiji facts first. And that means we should start out with spelling and pronunciation in Fijian. They can be maddeningly confusing, and although I may add to this confusion rather than clarify it by an explanatory note, I'll try anyway. The point is that Fijian, for reasons I shall never understand, is not always written phonetically in English. Thus, at times one finds the name of King Cakobau spelled Thakombau—which is the way it's pronounced. One finds Nadi spelled Nandi—the way *it's* pronounced. Besides "c" being pronounced "th," and "d" being pronounced "nd," there are others, equally zany. Beqa is pronounced Mbeng-ga (*b* as in *mb* and *q* coming out as *ng-g*), and for Sigatoka say Singatoka (*g* as *ng*). All clear? I didn't think so. But don't worry, you're not alone. A quaff or two of *kava* and all will seem well.

Kava, the non-alcoholic but slightly numbing brew made from water and the powdered roots of the pepper tree, is similar to the drink consumed in the Polynesian islands, from which the Melanesian Fijians undoubtedly adopted it. But in Fiji it is known as *yaqona,* and one doesn't just gulp it down. It is drunk as part of a traditional ceremony, which visitors are expected to follow to the best of their ability. The yaqona ceremony is multi-purpose. In the old days, warriors never went into battle before a round of yaqona. And even today the ceremony is a part of every important public function—from the welcoming of visitors to a remote village to the installation of a new Governor of the colony.

The brew is prepared in a large multi-legged bowl known as a *tanoa,* which is usually carved from a single piece of wood. Some bowls are round, with as many as eight or ten legs, and some are turtle-shaped. A polished half-coconut shell (*bilo*) serves as a cup. The yaqona is always freshly prepared, at ceremonials. Indeed, while the powder and water are mixed, singers chant and drums beat in the background, as hosts and guests sit cross-legged. The beverage is served on a seniority basis, with the most important guest doing the honors first. Before accepting the bilo from the cupbearer, the guest claps his hands three times, takes the brew and chugalugs it down (all in one swallow), places the bilo on a holder provided for it, and again claps three times.

Traditional Fijian feasts, known as *magiti,* are invariably preceded by yaqona ceremonies, and followed by *meke*—the traditional dance—with musical accompaniment by an *a capella* choir of either men or women, or women alone. Fijians sing beautifully, and their dances—for long the way in which they passed legends from one generation to another to another—are imbued with tremendous dramatic power. (Americans lucky enough to have seen the troupe of the Fiji Military Forces during its 1965 U.S. visit will know what I'm talking about.) Dancers are men who wear skirts (known in Fiji as *sulus*) of wide leaves, and mask their faces in rather ominous-looking makeup. The women among the accompanying singers are either in long, missionary-inspired gowns of printed cotton or in gay cotton sulus accessorized with flowered leis. Fijian song-and-dance may not have the lithe, romantic quality of Polynesia, particularly Tahiti; but it is distinctively Fijian, and of great and memorable impact.

A Fijian feast? Don't turn one down. The food, far more Polynesian in influence than the dancing, is interesting, if not always delicious to uninitiated taste buds. It's liable to include turtle or chicken soup, pig roasted in an earth oven called a *lovo,* baked breadfruit, a seafood entrée or two (probably baked in leaves), and a variety of fresh fruits including the delicious Fijian pineapple and papaya.

Village life in Fiji is not unlike that of Polynesian islands, with the traditional communal politico-economic system still in effect, thanks to the earlier-described separate Fijian administration which the British have preserved. Chiefdoms remain hereditary, and still another carryover—the "what's mine is yours" tradition —is in part responsible for the dearth of Fijians entering businesses of their own. Custom dictates that one's family is entitled to any of one's possessions, and Fijians are only just beginning to break away from this practice which makes the accumulation of wealth—or, indeed, of stock in a store—precariously difficult. Fijian villages are neat, green, and attractive. Houses, known as *bures* (pronounced *burays*) are squarish, thatched affairs, many still with pounded dirt floors, and their inhabitants are smiling and hospitable.

A Fiji itinerary: Many factors enter into a Fiji itinerary—port of arrival, length of stay, personal tastes and interests, to name but a few. But here's a suggested itinerary which might well satisfy the average-length visitor interested in having a look at the highlights and the opportunity to relax while so doing. Assuming that one arrives by air, the starting point will be Nadi. From there, take off for Lautoka, and, after seeing it, depart on a cruise to the Mamanuca group of islands. Upon returning to Lautoka from the cruise, depart by car to the resort at Korolevu, halfway along the coastal Queen's Road to Suva, which would be the next destination. From Suva one could make excursions to such outlying islands as Ovalau, Vanua Levu, and Beqa. Or, with less time, simply fly back to Nadi for departure from Fiji. The sea traveler would be arriving in Suva, and might well arrange a similar program, taking in Suva and excursions emanating from it, upon arrival, continuing on to Korolevu, proceeding to Lautoka and a cruise, thence a short drive from Lautoka to Nadi, and a return to Suva by air.

Nadi (pronounced Nandi), the port of arrival for international air travelers to Fiji, is hardly Fiji at its loveliest. The air terminal is, as earlier mentioned, modern, spacious, and with every convenience, and a tribute to the way in which Fiji has exploited its South Pacific Hub location to develop as a major air terminus. There are, near the airport, some good hotels (see Creature Comforts) quietly isolated in their own grounds, which offer one the comfort and convenience needed for refreshment after a long flight. The countryside is a great mass of sugar fields, and the town of Nadi—a community of about three thousand—is an unprepossessing place with a rather ramshackle main street whose main attractions for the visitor are a host of Indian-operated shops selling duty-free merchandise.

Lautoka is Fiji's No. 2 town, and might well be called Sugarville, for a good many of its eight thousand inhabitants are in some way or other engaged in the sugar industry. Just outside of town is Fiji's largest sugar mill (which may be inspected), and from Lautoka's port the great bulk of Fijian sugar is exported to foreign markets. There is good accommodation, a somewhat more substantial city center than that of Nadi (with even more Indian-operated duty-free shops), good accommodation (see Creature Comforts), swimming at nearby Saweni Beach, and a neat and modern harbor from which pleasure-cruise yachts depart. To be taken in too: special programs for visitors in the village of *Viseisei,* midway between Nadi and Lautoka; noted for their male choir, the villagers put on an arousing song-dance-ceremonial show.

The *Stardust* is deceptively modest at first glance. It's not a great, multidecked cruise liner of the kind seen in the Caribbean or the Mediterranean. But it has everything one could desire for three splendidly relaxed, incredibly beautiful days. Originally built for the Australian Navy, the 112-foot yacht was converted to a pleasure craft in 1957, and its young Aussie skipper, Captain Dick Smith, sailed it through the South Pacific for three years before settling in Fiji, refitting, and going into the passenger business. There are accommodations for only twelve, in six cabins, four of which have private bathrooms, and the other two sharing a bath. Sleeping space is all in the lower deck. Above, on the main deck, are an attractive dining room up forward (where both breakfast and dinner are served), a comfortable bar-lounge-library (where each passenger mixes his own drinks at any time of day or evening, making a note of what he's had for billing at journey's end), and a mostly covered weather deck, at which lunch is served buffet style, as well as morning coffee and afternoon tea. There are chairs for relaxing and snoozing, an open aft-deck for deep-sea fishing and sunning, and still additional deck space for get-away-from-it-all periods or watching the stars—surely a trillion of them—in the evening. The crew, aside from Captain Smith, is Fijian and first rate, the service is delightful, dress is informal (no

jackets or ties allowed by the captain's express orders!) and the
food, prepared in a tiny galley by an ingenious chef who doubles
at times on deck duty, is the finest I've had anywhere in Fiji.
(Excellent Australian wine is on the house, at dinner.) Destinations? The Mamanuca Islands, at once exquisitely scenic and set
in waters which are calmer and with more sunshine than one can
find, year-round, anywhere in the South Pacific. Three days have
never before passed so quickly for me. One ties up at a different
anchorage each night. There's great swimming, hunts for shells
and coral, and superb snorkeling the first day at uninhabited
Malamala Island; a pre-sunset swim later that day at Ngaulito
Island, also pure beachcomber with nary a single resident; a visit
the next day to a picture-book village on little Yanuya Island—
going ashore in the *Stardust*'s motor launches, greetings by
youngsters on the beach, formal welcome at an elaborate yaqona
ceremony in the chief's house, chats with the villagers, a brilliant
dance performance with almost all of the village men participat-
ing, and—before returning to the yacht—a chance to buy shells
and coral at bargain rates from the villagers, and a dip in the sea,
from their idyllic beach. The last day out, after an evening of informal music and dancing offered by the versatile crew, is dominated by a midday stop at uninhabited Mana Island. The launches
take passengers to one shore and the captain leads the group
through the thickly forested little islet to its distant shore—and
still another memorable beach. There's more time for leisurely
swimming, sunning, and shelling while the chef prepares a sumptuous barbecue. That evening—the third—the *Stardust* is back in
Lautoka harbor as the sun is setting. The passengers have ex-
changed addresses, good-byes and handshakes are made to the
captain and crew, and a dozen of the most fortunate of people
are back in the real world. The tab—all-inclusive with the exception of minimally priced drinks from the honor-system bar—
ranges from $60 to $76 per person, two to a cabin, in most
cabins; $104, in the sole de luxe cabin; there's a 50 percent sur-
charge for single occupancy. Departures are twice weekly, usually
Sunday and Wednesday, and I suggest you book through your

travel agent, or Captain Smith (P. O. Box 269, Lautoka, Fiji) as much in advance as you're able. Note, too, that the *Stardust* has a new, 104-foot, thirty-passenger sister ship, and that other three-day "Blue Lagoon" cruises, to the Yasawa Islands, a bit more distant from Lautoka than the Mamanucas, are made regularly by the modern, 112-foot, twenty-passenger *Sayandra,* under Captain Theron S. Withers; rates about $80 per person, two to a cabin. And there are still others, out of Suva, and mentioned later on in this chapter.

Korolevu is a self-contained beach resort, about halfway between Nadi and Suva, on the coastal Queen's Road. It is a pleasant stopover point for those motoring from one side of the island to the other. There's swimming in the sea and at a pool alongside the sea, all kinds of excursion possibilities (including visits to nearby villages), tennis, lawn-bowling Australian-style, deep-sea fishing, excursions to the barrier reef for shells, sun, and snorkeling, nightly dancing, and on Wednesday and Saturday nights only a great buffet spread, with both Fijian and Western dishes, along with the yaqona ceremony, and the traditional meke dancing. If your itinerary does not otherwise include a feast, a yaqona ceremony and the meke, do your best to see it on Wednesday or Saturday night at Korolevu, more details of which follow in the Creature Comforts section.

Suva is the essence of Fiji. It is, of course, the capital and the sole metropolis, and its populace—some forty thousand—is a zesty mélange of Fijians, Indians, Chinese, Britons, Australians, and New Zealanders, not to mention a sprinkling of Tongans, Samoans, and migrants from still other South Pacific islands. And of course a visiting American or two, as well! I suppose those who say one South Pacific capital is much like another are not entirely incorrect. But I don't see it that way. There are similarities, of course—as there are with all cities of a geographical area. But Suva is quite special. Much bigger, neater, and more attractive than Tahiti's Pepeete; another world from sleepy little Pago Pago in American Samoa or Nukualofa in Tonga; infinitely livelier than

Western Samoa's Apia, but without the sophistication and the style of New Caledonia's Nouméa.

People-watching is reason enough for a Suva visit. One can easily idle away the better part of a morning watching the crowds pass by on the seafront Victoria Parade or one of the busy streets leading off it, through the center of the city into the residential hills. The policemen stand out, of course—tall, handsome Fijians in immaculate jackets and starched white sulus with the distinctive serrated hems one sees nowhere else in the Pacific. The lovely Fijian women pass by, many in Western dress, some in the longer, more traditional costumes. There are the Indian ladies, their straight black hair neatly gathered in a bun, their long saris of filmy gauze-like materials or brocaded silk, their gold jewelry. There are Sikhs, bearded and turbaned, just as in India. There are the Europeans—men in tan walking shorts, high white socks, and white, short-sleeved shirts; women in the flowered prints which are common to British-governed tropics all over the world. There are, too, Polynesians from neighboring islands—Tongans in lava-lavas with the plaited straw sashes unique to their kingdom, Samoans in gay flowered lava-lavas, Rotumans from the Fiji-administered but Polynesian island of Rotuma. And members of the not inconsiderable Chinese community, to complete the picture.

Suva was selected as the capital of Fiji by the British in 1877 and is, therefore, a relatively new city, built around a venerable Fijian village of the same name. The aforementioned Victoria Parade—surely one of the South Pacific's most scenic thoroughfares—fronts the sea, and the reef-protected harbor is one of the finest in the islands. But there is the town itself to be seen: its most imposing sector is at the eastern end of Victoria Parade. There one finds the somber and massive Government Buildings which front on the beautifully tended green of Albert Park. Across the way from the park, going seaward, is the colonnaded Grand Pacific Hotel (see Creature Comforts), and continuing east Victoria Parade becomes Queen Elizabeth Drive. Flanking it are the handsome Botanical Gardens—an ideal setting for the relatively small but interesting Suva Museum, with exhibits of Fijian culture and history, among which I would highly rate the beautiful handicraft specimens, the giant war canoes for which Fiji was the envy of neighboring islands (and which are no longer made), and some mementos of the short-lived Kingdom of Fiji which preceded the takeover by Britain.

Government House has an enviable setting in British territories around the world and Suva's is no exception. Its main gate is just beyond the museum (there's a statue on the grounds commemorating the Deed of Cession), and the mansion stands, high on a hill, within the confines of a handsome private park. At the other end of town is the aquarium, with some rather dazzling displays of marine life. On Prince's Street, near Prince's Landing, where passengers come ashore from liners, is the municipal market where the buyers and sellers—a composite of Fiji—are as intriguing as the wares on sale. And these range from fresh produce and seafood to all manner of handicrafts. The nearby wharves are worth a stroll, if one would see stevedores unloading copra, bananas, and other tropical cargo from adjacent island plantations. There are, too, the shops on Victoria Parade and on the thoroughfares leading off it—particularly Cumming Street, with its maze of tiny but interesting emporia.

Beyond town, one gains a fine view of urban area, harbor, and Rewa River Estuary from the Reservoir Lookout in the village of Tamavua. Saturday nights, particularly for those not enjoying a feast at the earlier-mentioned Korolevu, should be reserved for Loki's Fijian Bure—a giant Fijian dwelling at Tamavua where each Saturday at eight visitors are presented with Fijian music, dancing, and food—all authentic, and done with the charm and finesse which characterize the Fijians. Remember, too, that you may swim at the municipal pool near the town hall and that you can sample yaqona (sans ceremony) at the Fiji Visitors Bureau (Epworth House, Prince's Street), which gives each imbiber a certificate of membership in the Fellowship of Yaqona Drinkers.

I hope you will allow time for a brief excursion or two from

Suva, aside from the panoramic view from Tamavua. Earmark a morning for a cruise on the glass-bottomed motor launch *Oolooloo* for a look at Suva Harbour and the splendors of the undersea coral gardens beneath the harbor's barrier reef. Take the car-water bus trip up the Rewa River Delta to a Fijian village and a picnic lunch on a verdant nearby island. And then consider more extensive excursions to other islands of Fiji.

Excursions to other islands: Viti Levu is the only island of the Fiji group that is at all extensively equipped for tourists in any quantity. But it is possible to visit a few others of the group. The *Maroro,* an auxiliary ketch, cruises regularly to *Beqa* the home of the noted Fijian "fire-walkers," and arrangements can be made for visitors to see demonstration of the ancient art of stepping barefoot across a bed of hot coals, to emerge with nary a trace of burns. The same ship calls at *Kandavu,* whose women for centuries have called giant turtles in from the sea. *Vanua Levu,* the second largest Fijian island, may be reached by air; there are daily flights to Savusavu, on its lushly tropical south coast, and with a small beach resort—a few flying minutes distant—to the sugar town of *Lambasa* on the less lush and less rainy north coast. *Ovalau* is the site of now-quiet Levuka, the magnificently situated town which was Fiji's capital prior to 1877, when the government moved to Suva. There is no air service, but Ovalau is not far from the east coast of Viti Levu and one can reach it from Suva by means of daily bus-boat service.

WHAT TO BUY

There's a wide choice in Fiji. Local handicrafts, of course. But in addition, duty-free liquor, perfume, watches, cameras, tape-recorders, and other non-local luxury manufactured goods. There are, as well, East Indian scarves, saris, filigree jewelry, and sandals. Note, too, that tailors make up suits—using British woolens and other imported fabrics—quickly and inexpensively. And remember, too, that Fiji is a prime source of shells and coral—free

if you pick it off the beaches yourself, but even when purchased
far less expensive than in Australia, Hawaii, or the mainland
United States. In *Suva,* the aforementioned municipal market
should be one's first stop for local handicrafts. Also good is the
Reef Shop, which has an interesting selection—hand-turned pottery, wood carving, masi-cloth (the Fijian version of Polynesian
tapa cloth), ceremonial drums (*loli*), a variety of woven baskets,
fine mats, dolls, coral and shells, leis and shell jewelry. One finds
bits and pieces of handicrafts in many of the other shops. For
luxury products—Swiss watches, Japanese tape-recorders, Dutch
radios—almost anything in this line from cameras to stereo record
players—there are a great many sources, among them Burns
Philp, Miller's, Stinsons, Carpenter's, Morris Hedstrom, and
Prasad's. Caines-Janiff specializes in cameras of many makes, and
auxiliary photographic equipment. Proud's, a chain of Australian
jewelry-watch shops, has the same specialties in its Suva branch.
G. B. Hari & Co. has a custom-tailoring department (promising
suits in as little as eight hours), and a wide range of Indian and
duty-free merchandise as well. P. A. Ram Ritu Co. makes men's
suits in a day, and Kalyan & Co. specializes in custom-made
women's clothes, also within a day. A. J. Swann's Drugstore has a
wide variety of French perfumes and colognes. The Desai
Book Depot has a big paperback selection, airmail editions
of Australian and New Zealand newspapers, and American and
other foreign magazines. It has branches in Nadi and Lautoka.
The big firms like Burns Philp and Morris Hedstrom have
branches in *Nadi* and *Lautoka,* too, and there are countless
smaller stores with duty-free merchandise in those towns. They're
all clustered about each other, on the main street of each town,
and I hesitate to recommend one over the other. Best bet is to
make the rounds, looking over the types of merchandise that interest you, bargaining, and purchasing on the basis of the brand
name you're buying—always making sure that warranty certificates (and the names and addresses of foreign service depots) are
included. There is, as earlier mentioned, a duty-free shop in Nadi
International Airport, on the main floor, and, for in-transit and

departing international passengers, additional shops upstairs selling duty-free liquor and cigarettes. Many of the duty-free shops in Suva sell duty-free liquor but only for shipboard passengers; it is delivered to their ships, as the law prohibits its being consumed within Fiji. In the villages, particularly coastal villages, one does well to look for villagers selling shells, coral, and even handcrafts. The local beer (Fiji brand) is not as good as Australian (which is sold in cans), but it's not bad, and it's inexpensive. Fiji-made cigarettes include Craven A (English-style), Pall Mall and Piccadilly (filtered), Consulate (mentholated and filtered), and Crown.

CREATURE COMFORTS

With the exception of a pair of American-owned hotels in Nadi, most hotels in Fiji are British- or Australian-managed. None quite ranks with the best of Tahiti, and cuisine tends to run along British colonial lines, which means that with a few exceptions it can range from just okay to downright dreary. Service is invariably pleasant though, and one can be quite comfortable in the better hotels. The government is encouraging hotel construction, and with the constantly increasing popularity of tourism, new ones are going up. But there still is a shortage of rooms, and advance reservations are almost essential. **Nadi:** The Mocambo, American-owned and -managed, is modern, attractive, and high on a hilltop affording a splendid view of sugar fields, sea, and outlying islands. The main dining room is the best eating spot in the Nadi area, and there's also an informal coffee shop open round the clock (a blessing for passengers arriving in the dead of night—and many do at Nadi), a swimming pool, a pair of bars, barber shop and beauty salon, a shop with periodicals, tobacco, handicrafts, and duty-free articles, arrangements for sightseeing, cruises, horseback riding, thoroughly delightful service and pleasant—if not overlarge—bedrooms, all air conditioned and with bath. Singles from $9, doubles from $14.50. The Skylodge, under the same ownership as the Mocambo, is smaller and more in-

formal (coats and ties are not required in the evening), with a
pleasant dining room-coffee shop, a lively bar-cocktail lounge
with Fijian entertainment, a swimming pool, nine-hole pitch and
putt golf course free to guests, well-equipped indoor game room,
volley ball, flower-filled grounds, and imaginatively decorated
bedrooms, most all air conditioned and with bathrooms. Singles
run just under $9, all are air conditioned, very tiny and with
doorless private bathrooms—but still comfortable. Air-conditioned
doubles with bath from about $11.50 (minimum) to about $15.50
(de luxe). Opened in 1965, the triangular-design Tanoa boasts
40 rooms, all with bath and air conditioning, dining room, cocktail lounge, pool, and terrace—and fine views; singles about $8,
doubles about $12. **Lautoka:** The Cathay Hotel, under the same
management as Suva's Grand Pacific (of which more later), is one
of Fiji's newest. All of its rooms are centrally air conditioned
with private bath and balcony. There's a restaurant serving reasonably priced lunches and dinners, and breakfast is included in
the room rates: from $8.45 single, $14.40 double. Off the coast,
on an uninhabited isle of the Mamanuca group, the Castaways—a
get-away-from-it-all-retreat—is being planned. **Korolevu:** The
Korolevu Beach Hotel, midway between Nadi and Suva (the latter is sixty-four miles distant) and mentioned earlier in this chapter, is a self-contained beach resort, just about the only such
establishment in Fiji. Most of the accommodation is in individual
Fijian-style bures, each with private bath, many of them newly
constructed in 1966. There are, as well, conventional-style bedrooms in the main building; these too are all with private bath.
There's a bar-lounge with entertainment, a dining room with service that I found slow and indifferent, and with only mediocre
food; a bathing beach and swimming pool, and a variety of activities, detailed earlier in this chapter. Rates from about $9 single,
$10.50 double, European plan. A day's meals average about
$5.25; the Saturday and Wednesday night feasts described earlier
in this chapter are excellent and are about $4. Not far from
Korolevu, a major resort hotel is going up on **Yauca Island.**
Korotogo: Fifteen miles from Korolevu Beach and fifty miles

from Nadi, on Queen's Road, is the pleasing new Reef Lodge. The bedrooms are agreeably spacious, some have terraces, and all are with bath. There's a dining room, bar-lounge (with nightly dancing), and swimming pool, as well as a lovely beach and a reef for the exploration of coral and marine life and skin-diving. Boats and fishing tackle are for rent. Rates are exceptionally moderate, considering the modernity, the setting, and the facilities: from $6.70 single, $10.40 double, including breakfast. Lunch and dinner average less than $4 per day, and Reef Lodge guests are welcome at the Korolevu Beach Hotel's Wednesday and Saturday night feasts. **Suva:** The Grand Pacific is of the caliber of Hong Kong's Peninsula and Singapore's Raffles—elderly (although modernized and with a new wing), atmospheric, and British Colonial at its most appealing—and its most Maughamesque. Splendidly located on Victoria Parade, with the sea as its back yard and Albert Park just opposite its front lawn, the GP is all that one expects of a South Pacific hotel: a vast, high-ceilinged lobby-lounge with sulu-clad waiters serving cool drinks, a sea-view dining room (with excellent Chinese and Indian cuisine as well as British fare and nightly dinner music), spacious verandas of Old School proportions, a cocktail lounge, dancing alfresco in the Tapa Room, and a gift shop. Add to the foregoing excellent service, a honey of a new swimming pool, a centrally air-conditioned new wing, each of its rooms most tastefully furnished, and redecorated, modernized rooms in the main building to boot. The result is Fiji's best hotel. All rates include breakfast: Singles (main building) from a bit under $9; $9.70 in the new wing; doubles $14.50 in the main building, about $17 in the new wing. The Club Hotel, in the heart of downtown Suva, is functionally modern, with restaurant, cocktail lounge, and bar, and all rooms air conditioned and with bath. Most singles from about $9 (a few are less), doubles from $14 European plan. Hotel Suva, under amiable Australian management, is also centrally located, has a number of rooms with bath and air conditioning, a modestly priced air-conditioned dining room with good service, and the new rooftop Skyline Lounge which offers a fine panoramic view of Suva. Rates

include breakfast. Air-conditioned single with bath from about
$6.50; air-conditioned doubles with bath from about $9.50. Suva's
newest are the fully air conditioned Outrigger and the Hotel Fiji,
near the airport. Suva after dark? Well, there are the aforementioned hotel lounges, usually with music and entertainment, sometimes with dancing. There's the Golden Dragon, a cabaret with
regular dances and entertainment. There are films at five cinemas,
with nightly programs starting at eight, there are occasional con-
certs and plays by amateur groups—often they can be most enjoyable, and invariably they offer a good opportunity to mix and
mingle with a cross section of the populace. I suggest you keep up
with local activities by daily perusal of the most interesting Fiji
Times, whose masthead bills it as "The first newspaper in the
world every day," explaining that it is "published at midnight
from Monday to Saturday at Suva, just west of the International
Date Line, when the new day begins." **Vanua Levu Island:** Savusavu's hotel is the Hot Springs, with a hillside, over-the-harbor
location, only eight rooms, and not all of them with private facilities. From $6 single; restaurant. Outside of Savusavu Town-
ship, and seven miles from the airport, is Muanicula Estate,
which has three bures, each with private bath, and a restaurant.
Rates (including meals) are $9 single, $13 double. At Lambasa,
the Grand Eastern Hotel has its own swimming pool and dining
room, and all ten rooms have private baths. The rates, including
breakfast, are about $5 per person. **Ovalau Island:** Levuka's Royal
Hotel has a lovely midtown situation, overlooking the harbor, but
none of the rooms have private bath; the daily per person rate is
just under $8, including meals.

New Caledonia

La Nouvelle Calédonie

Entry requirements: Passports are required of all foreign visitors, and for many, visas (obtainable from French consulates) are necessary, too. However, American citizens in transit (carrying proof of onward transportation) need no visa if their stay is for ten days or less. A smallpox vaccination certificate is required of all visitors. **Best times for a visit:** The climate is fairly pleasant the year round, but the most ideal period is the southern winter—from June to September. These are the coolest and driest months—generally in the seventies in Nouméa, with from two and a half to less than four inches of rain monthly. From after Christmas through March is the hottest time of the year, and the rainiest—but even then the temperatures do not go above the mid-eighties. There can be an occasional hurricane during this period, and rains can be heavy, particularly on the east coast, which is the wetter, more heavily tropical side of the island; the west coast, site of Nouméa, is infinitely drier. Also relatively dry and sunny the year round is the Isle of Pines, a major visitor attraction. In other words, don't hesitate to include New Caledonia in an itinerary at any time of year, for you're likely to have good luck with weather on the west coast and Isle of Pines no matter when you go. *Do* be wary, however, of visits to the east coast during the wet months, particularly if you're on a tight schedule, for you may get rained in—and I speak from experience. **Currency:** The French Pacific franc (CFP Fr.), of which there are 87 to the U.S. dollar; a franc, in other words, being worth a little more than a cent (10 frs.=12 cents, 100 frs.=$1.15, 500 frs.=

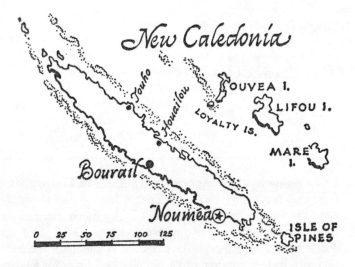

$5.75, 1000 frs.=$11.50). Hotels change money, generally at the same rate as the sole bank, the Banque de l'Indo-Chine. Paper money still is printed in the gargantuan sizes which Metropolitan France blessedly dispensed with years ago. Thousand- and hundred-franc notes—big enough to write long letters on—are terribly similar-looking, so check them carefully after you unfold your bulky wad to pay a bill. (This currency has the same value as that used in Tahiti, but Tahitian currency, for some odd reason, is not acceptable in New Caledonia.) **Film availability:** Quite plentiful supplies of both color and black-and-white film, including Kodak— but at prices more expensive than in the United States; black-and-white processing within a day. **Languages:** French, of course, is the official language, and the medium of instruction in the schools. You'll find it helpful, if you speak it, regardless of your fluency, especially on the east coast. But there's a good bit of English spoken in the leading hotels, restaurants, night spots, and shops of Nouméa, at the airports, and on the Isle of Pines—thanks in large part to the heavy trade, touristic and commercial, with Australians and New Zealanders. **Transportation:** Qantas has a regular jet service from Sydney, Australia, with the flying time a quick and delightful two and a half hours; other lines jet in as well. It is worth knowing, in advance of arrival, that international flights land at Tontouta Airport. Built during World War II, recently modernized and enlarged, and some thirty miles from Nouméa, the terminal is small but modern, with a bar, lounge, and post office which are open for all flights, and a branch of the Government Tourist Bureau. The road into town, while eminently scenic, is not everywhere as smooth as it might be, although it is being improved in bits and pieces. There are three types of transport into Nouméa: airport bus, private taxi, and air taxi (Transpac Airlines). I suggest you take the air taxi into town upon arrival, and depart via the road, particularly if you've not driven through that part of the island. The air taxi lands at the in-town Magenta Airport, which is used for all domestic flights of Transpac, New Caledonia's own airline. Transpac's little fleet of small but well-operated aircraft connects Nouméa with the east coast, the Isle of Pines, and the Loyalty Islands, which are a part of New Caledonia, and the airline doubles as a tour agency, running its own excellent packaged excursions. It works closely with the authorities, is doing a first-rate job of developing and promoting New Caledonian tourism, and employs a largely bilingual staff which is excellent at question-answering. Getting to New Caledonia by sea is time-consuming but not otherwise difficult. Matson Lines' *Monterey* and *Mariposa* call at Nouméa on their regular Pacific cruises. Coming from Europe—Marseilles, France—by way of the Panama Canal are ships of Messageries Maritimes, a French line; they go on from Nouméa to Australia. Messageries Maritimes also operate the SS *Polynésie,* in monthly service between Sydney and Nouméa, and there are luxury cruises out of Sydney to Nouméa and other Pacific points, most of which operate during the Australian winter months and during the Christmas period. Local transportation, other than the air service outlined above, includes taxis ($1 for as much as a two-mile in-town trip), and little blue buses (called Baby-cars), which depart every ten minutes from Central Square (near the Fountain Monument) to the beach area at Anse Vata, for 18 cents. Rent-a-car services use mostly French

cars (Citroëns and Peugeots) and rates range from $7 to
$12. **Tipping:** You won't be arrested if you tip, but you will
be violating local custom, and I suggest you do not spoil a
good thing—and go along. It's not at all difficult to form the
no-tipping habit! **Clothes:** New Caledonia is not *quite* as
casual as Tahiti in that men generally wear long trousers,
shoes, and socks at night. (In Tahiti shorts and sandals are,
in many places, acceptable around the clock.) But in New
Caledonia during the day shorts are in order for both men
and women. Ties and jackets are by no means essential for
men after dark, but women change from their daytime shorts
to dresses. This being a bit of France, bikinis are popular at
the beaches. **Business hours:** Shops close for lunch, generally
from 11 to 2. They open early, at 7:15, and close for the
day, Monday through Saturday, at 5:30. Most offices have
fairly similar hours, but the bank (Banque de l'Indo-Chine)
naturally keeps bankers' hours: 8:30–10:30, 1:30–3:30,
Monday through Friday. Along with Tahiti, restaurant, bar,
and cabaret hours are the most liberal in the South Pacific.
Cabarets, for example, don't open until 9 P.M., and bars stay
open round the clock if business warrants. **Further information:** Office du Tourisme de la Nouvelle Calédonie, Boîte
Postale 688, Nouméa, New Caledonia, for mail inquiries;
Syndicat d'Initiative, Square Olry, Nouméa, for on-the-spot
inquiries; Transpac Airlines and Tours, Nouméa, New Caledonia; Qantas Airways, Nouméa, New Caledonia; French
Government Tourist Office, 610 Fifth Avenue, New York;
18 South Michigan Avenue, Chicago; 323 Geary Street, San
Francisco; 9418 Wilshire Boulevard, Beverly Hills, and
1170 Drummond Street, Montreal.

INTRODUCING NEW CALEDONIA

Take a cigar-shaped island a couple of jet hours from Australia, name it after Scotland, populate it with Melanesians, Indonesians, Vietnamese, and with more Europeans than inhabit

any other South Pacific isle, import *la vie Française* (government, language, cuisine, culture), discover one of the richest and best-quality nickel deposits in the world, dot liberally with fun-seeking holidaymakers mostly from semi-austere New Zealand—and you come up with New Caledonia.

Now a zestful, prosperous French Overseas Territory, this island (and its dependencies, which include the Loyalty group and the lushly picture-book Isle of Pines), has not, perhaps, had the richest, most event-packed history of Southern Hemisphere areas, but as recently as World War II it was visited by more than a hundred thousand American military men, and for a period during the nineteenth century it was quite as notorious a penal colony as the New World's Devil's Island.

But today, half a world away, I find it exceedingly difficult to find anyone who knows where New Caledonia is, let alone what it is. Perhaps because it was not, fortunately, the scene of a bloody battle, ex-GI's who know it say little about it. And because it is so overshadowed, touristically, by legendary Tahiti, even prospective American tourists headed for the South Pacific tend to disregard it.

Franco-Melanesian mélange: New Caledonia and Tahiti do share a common mother-government and official language, and they both are South Pacific islands. But there the similarity between the two ends. New Caledonia is much larger in both area and population. Its own people are Melanesians and not Polynesians. Its capital is the biggest French city south of Marseilles— in contrast to Tahiti's Papeete, which remains small and unpretentious. Its booming if inflated economy, generated by "Le Nickel" Company's mines, makes it a far different proposition economically than Tahiti. And, perhaps more significant, its ambiance—thanks to its inordinately large European population— is French with a Melanesian underlay, whereas Tahiti's is Polynesian with a French (or perhaps I should say Franco-American) façade. (The population breakdown reveals the inordinately heavy European strength. Some twenty-nine thousand out of a total of about eighty-nine thousand persons living in New Caledonia are European or part-European. Melanesians number about thirty-seven thousand. The remainder are mostly Indonesian, Vietnamese, Tahitian, and Wallis Islanders.)

Depending on one's source, New Caledonia was discovered by a Frenchman, the navigator Bougainville, or by the ubiquitous Englishman, Captain James Cook. The likelihood is that Bougainville sailed past the island, without landing, in 1768, but that Cook was the first European to go ashore, in 1774, when he named the place after Scotland. Nearly two decades later, in 1792, a French expedition landed on the Isle of Pines (also named by Cook), and had a look, as well, at New Caledonia's east coast. Ensuing decades saw a motley assortment of navigators, runaway seamen, explorers, traders, and even Australian convicts attracted to the island. But none stayed until, in the 1840s, the first missionaries arrived. (A French priest, Monsignor Douaré, founded the first Catholic mission in 1844, aided by Marist fathers.)

Penal colony beginnings: All the while Britain had eyes on the island, but like France hesitated to move in, the cannibalistic proclivities of the islanders serving as a deterrent. But in 1850 the crew of a French ship was killed, and reportedly eaten. The French decided it was time for them to step in, and Rear Admiral Febvrier-Despointes took possession of the main island, in the name of France, on September 24, 1853, and of the Isle of Pines a few days thereafter. And well he did, for France's sake, for the British were, so annals of the period say, just about to do so themselves.

Paris, perhaps not knowing quite what to do with its new territory, utilized it in much the same way that it did French Guiana—as the site of a penal colony. The first prisoners arrived in 1864 and for the four ensuing decades terrifying tales of grisly conditions floated back to Europe, much as they did from Devil's Island, off the northern tip of South America. All told some forty thousand prisoners, a staggeringly high number when one considers the island's distance from the motherland, served time in New Caledonia, mostly at Île Nou, in Nouméa Harbor.

It was not until 1897 that convict transportation ceased; long-term convicts, freed prisoners, or their descendants were still on the scene well into the present century.

Elections and progress: But prisoners were but a portion of the colony's populace. There were, it is estimated, some seventy thousand Melanesians when the French arrived, and there are now about half that number; thanks, in this island as in others, to the questionable benefits of European civilization. At any rate, France (like the United States in Samoa during its first half-century) governed New Caledonia as a naval base until 1885. In that year a civil governor took over with the assistance of a local —and not very strong—parliament. More recently, things have gone reasonably well, insofar as Franco-Melanesian relationships are concerned. There were some rather nasty uprisings toward the end of the naval base period, and again during World War I.

But, without undue speed, the French have gradually allowed the Melanesians to participate increasingly in the administration of their country. The first major election of consequence took place in 1957, and more than half the voters were Melanesian— a most impressive proportion in a heavily European community. In true French style, or perhaps one should say true French style pre-de Gaulle, eight political parties were on the ballot, three of them coming out on top, with Maurice Lenormand's left-wing Union Calédonienne then, as now, the dominant leader. The advent of the Gaullist government in Paris led to a crisis in New Caledonian politics, in 1958, when le Général himself sent a representative to mediate interparty differences in Nouméa.

Later that year New Caledonia, like all French territories, voted in the referendum for a new French constitution, and the result was overwhelmingly affirmative. Afterward, a new election voted in an even stronger Union Calédonienne majority for the Territorial Assembly; the Governing Council (or Cabinet) was strengthened, and New Caledonia embarked upon a period of social welfare legislation which includes pre-natal care for mothers, family allowances, and workers' pensions. The idea, and most commendable it is, has been to improve the standard of living of the mass of people, but the program—which takes in taxes about a third of each worker's salary—has, at the same time, appeared to raise production costs and consumer prices. Much-wanted new industries, to supplement the nickel mines in a world where demand for that metal appears to be subsiding, are hesitant about coming in.

Governor Marc Biros, in office since early 1963, and not having an easy time with New Caledonia's economics, was succeeded in 1965 by Jean Risterucci, an energetic Corsican who had been Director of Overseas Territories, in Paris, serving as right-hand man and troubleshooter for his Minister. (The Governor, incidentally, has a dual job, for he is in addition French High Commissioner in the Pacific, and the chief representative of Paris not only in New Caledonia but with the Overseas Territories of French Polynesia and Wallis and Futuna, as well.)

World War II—and changes: Still, New Caledonia remains a magnet, for one reason or another. Up to the time of World War II its mines and copra plantations were largely worked by indentured labor, mostly from Vietnam and Indonesia. During the war, the system quite naturally came to a halt, and in its place newcomers to the pro-Gaullist island were scores of thousands of Allied soldiers manning hospitals for Pacific wounded, maintaining air and supply bases for Pacific battles, contributing several volunteer contingents of troops and, hardly unimportant, serving as an effective deterrent against Japanese invasion.

After the war, indenturing of labor was resumed and continued until 1951, when the political upheaval in Vietnam brought it to a halt, and repatriation was attempted. The hitch was that most of the Vietnamese in New Caledonia were from Communist-controlled North Vietnam, and it was not easy to get them all back home—even those who wanted to return. In 1959, those remaining were permitted to look for work wherever they wanted, or to go into business for themselves—and many have. More recently, repatriation became possible for both groups, Vietnamese and Indonesians, but with the increasing social benefits in New Caledonia, and the relatively high wages, many have elected to remain. There are, it is now estimated, some four thousand of each nationality now resident, and many live in Nouméa, preferring work not as laborers but as taxi drivers and shopkeepers, and disassociating themselves from their own community groups in favor of integrating with the broader community. In other words, the territory has inadvertently been presented with a substantial Asian community, living alongside Melanesians, French, and the not inconsiderable newcomers from neighboring Pacific islands.

Contemporary melting pot: Today's visitor is, then, caught up with a pleasantly hodgepodge melting pot. It would be absurd to say racial prejudice does not exist; it does, of course, and non-whites remain at the bottom of the barrel economically and socially, if not politically. But there is, happily, no color bar in public places including, as a matter of fact, the schools, both urban and rural. (There are both public and church-related— mostly Catholic, less Protestant—primary schools, state supported, as well as a handful of secondary schools; an academic— pre-University—college; a technical college, and an agricultural college.) No one seems to feel any hesitation about going anywhere, including the cafes (although it is worth noting that Melanesians have been able to drink hard liquor—legally—only since 1963).

More and more roads are being paved. A domestic airline constantly increases its routes and adds to its equipment, making communication easier among communities distant from one another. New construction constantly changes the face of increasingly modern Nouméa. There is a cosmopolitan atmosphere engendered by the presence of half a dozen member nations' peoples working at the Nouméa-based South Pacific Commission, and by the increased numbers of tourists from nearby New Zealand and Australia (not to mention the United States), all coupled with the relaxed and amiable Melanesian personality. Most of all, though, the feel of France is in the air—at once crisp and businesslike, at once smart and *au courant,* at once Gallic and cosmopolitan, at once gay and infused with the *joie de vivre* which eternally, troubles and crises notwithstanding, follow the *tricoleur* wherever it flies.

YOUR VISIT TO NEW CALEDONIA

It would be unfair of me, at this point, not to make clear my unabashedly Francophile sentiments. I am, and there's no point in denying it, a pushover for things French, not only in France, but wherever the French have settled. I remain convinced that no European culture travels as well as the French—no matter the destination. The British presence in its colonies and ex-colonies can be amusing, even at times reassuring—but always slightly absurd, with its Stiff-Upper-Lip, White-Man's-Burden, We-Suffer-in-Silence qualities, and its proclivity for warm beer, food often even more dreadful than in the mother country, dressing for dinner regardless of the intensity of the heat and humidity, and—aside from splendiferous uniforms for the military and the police —an almost complete absence of smartness or style. The Americans abroad are, of course, more difficult for an American himself to judge objectively but, if one can generalize, their presence even as civilians tends to resemble the ever-so-spotless and efficient but dully antiseptic and humorless qualities of officers' quarters at Army bases.

The French are something else again. They are, first off, far less color-conscious than the Anglo-Saxons—prejudiced and patronizing at times, but infinitely more disposed to marry outside of their race, to open their eyes and their ears and their intellects to the cultures and customs which surround them. They take seriously their roles as administrators, professional people, businessmen, housewives. But they give the impression of being somewhat relaxed about it. They may at times close their eyes to poverty, dirt, and neglect, but their senses are attuned to the best of their subject peoples' cultures, and these they pick up, show off, exploit, build upon.

All the while, though, they remain French to the core. They confer French citizenship upon every individual in every one of their overseas territories, instead of fabricating new designations for such peoples, as have the British ("protected persons") and ourselves ("American nationals"). But perhaps most important for the visitor, they insist upon living well. And here we all benefit. They will not do without their wine, their cheese, sometimes even their temperate-zone fruits. Unlike the British, and often the Americans, who rely on private clubs (closed to tourists) for recreation and leisure, they open restaurants and hotels and cafes. These are, of course, mainly for their own use, but New Caledonia is a perfect example of how their existence made possible the commencement of a foreign tourist industry, quite literally from scratch. Most of the public places in Nouméa were there for the city's own residents' comfort and pleasure.

And with the serious triggering of tourist promotion, New Caledonia found that the facilities provided for its own people were the nucleus of attractions for foreigners. This is true in even smaller French territories, where there are far tinier European populations. The Frenchman, no matter where he lives, eats well, drinks well, amuses himself well, dresses smartly—but sensibly. Nowhere in the South Pacific is there this marvelous sense of Frenchness, this heavily Gallic ambiance, this taste of continental Europe in the Pacific tropics—all there principally for the resident European populace (none bigger on any South Pacific isle), all there to be savored by the visitor as well.

I do not mean to infer, from the foregoing, that New Caledonia's unique European quality is its only lure, for we're dealing with a number of other factors in this territory. Most important is the main island, often referred to as Grande Terre. It's substantial in area, with a length of some 250 miles and a width of twenty-five miles, and its mountain ranges (two of them paralleling each other with peaks as high as fifty-five hundred feet) are among the most ruggedly dramatic in the Pacific, as one can't help but notice on almost any tour out of Nouméa. I have, earlier, referred to the varying climates of the two coasts, east and west, and it follows that their vegetation differs as well. The west coast, site of Nouméa, must pay a price for its relative dryness and is, therefore, far more arid and less luxuriant than one might expect in this part of the world. But the infinitely rainier east coast is something else again: as lush and luxuriant an area as one could find in the South Pacific. The same goes for the verdant Isle of Pines, and the Loyalty Islands as well. Still other dependencies of the territories are a group of four islets, known as the Huons, with no permanent populations; the eleven coral islets of the Chesterfield group, also unpopulated, and a scattering of other inaccessible islands.

New Caledonia's indigenous population of Melanesians is of interest principally because it gives the impression of being far less developed than that of also-Melanesian Fiji. One cannot imagine that in earlier days this was the case, but today Melanesian life in New Caledonia strikes one as infinitely inferior, culturally and otherwise, to that of Fiji. It may be that the missionaries did their work too well, and it is conceivable that the culture of the people on this island never reached the peak of the Fijians'. But most visitors to New Caledonia will almost certainly include Fiji as well in their itineraries, and find the contrasts of interest.

A New Caledonian itinerary: Nouméa itself, as I have tried to indicate, is the territory's most special feature. But I should consider a visit to the Isle of Pines a requisite as well (particularly for those who would enjoy explorations of the immense barrier reef which flanks New Caledonia), and, assuming weather permits, a journey to the lush and lovely east coast. The less-developed Loyalty Islands, particularly Ouvea Isle, might well be on longer itineraries. New Zealanders and Australians spend as much as a fortnight—sometimes longer—in New Caledonia which, for many of them, is the first truly foreign place they've visited. The New Zealanders in particular revel in the round-the-clock availability of liquor in the cafes, coming as they do from a land where bars close at six every evening. And they frequently cut loose in this relatively uninhibited Gallic atmosphere. Americans, who by the time they get to New Caledonia have invariably seen a bit of the world, will not be so thunderstruck, nor as compelled to stay as long.

Nouméa, boldly perched on a hill-flanked peninsula, is at once a slow-paced, elderly French Colonial town of the Old School, an urban center of sleek white stucco buildings whose shops are filled with the highest proportion of elegant consumer wares in the Pacific, and—most happily for the visitor—resorts with hotels flanking white sand beaches which are but minutes from the city center. Unless one is stubbornly obstinate, headquarters will be at one of the beach hotels, either on the Baie des Citrons or the adjoining Anse Vata Beach area. In either case, the water and the sands are but steps from one's hotel entrance. And from both the little blue "Babycar" buses—or taxis—whisk one downtown whenever its attractions beckon.

Well-organized bus tours are a good starter. They get one through the town proper, and environs (including the interesting Melanesian village and Roman Catholic Mission at *St. Louis*) in an afternoon. But then one does well to amble about independently.

The prettiest part of Nouméa proper is its gracious and capacious Square Central. The town's principal bus and taxi station fringes it, at the intersection of Rue Austerlitz and Rue Anatole France. The square extends east from Rue Jean Jaures for some two verdant blocks. A walk along Rue Jean Jaures on its northern flank takes one past the charming frame Town Hall, perhaps the town's best example of Colonial architecture. Near the square— and here one does well to be on hand *very* early in the morning— is the Public Market, an alfresco mélange of still-kicking fish from the sea, whining chickens in handmade cages, luscious tropical fruits and vegetables, and hawkers barking their wares in French to buyers and potential buyers representing the Nouméa melting pot: European, Melanesian, Indonesian, Vietnamese, Polynesian. Then a switch to nearby Rue Georges Clemenceau and Rue de l'Alma and the modern shops and department stores in the area they dominate.

The entire central district of the town is easily, and most pleasantly, walkable. Laid out in gridiron fashion, it is easy to get about, and on one's ambles other requisites should most certainly include the lovely Roman Catholic cathedral, atop a hill on a narrow street which could easily be in a French Riviera town; the Museum-Library, the Avenue Marechal Foch, along the Baie de la Moselle; the wartime headquarters of Admiral "Bull" Halsey, now the South Pacific Commission on Rue Anatole France, which is not far from the Melanesian Art Exhibition on the same street, and the main harbor area just west of Rue Jules Ferry. Île Nou, site of the old and unlamented penal colony, is opposite the main harbor; indeed, it serves as a splendid natural protection for it. There are no organized tours to Île Nou, but the tourist office might be able to assist you in getting over, and it could also direct you to a New Caledonia oddity; girls' cricket, played with much gusto by female cricketers whose billowy, flowered robes seem not at all to impede action: audiences at the matches are as much fun as the games themselves.

Then to the beach area: for swimming, sunbathing, snorkeling, chugging about in foot-propelled *pédalo* boats, day-long glass-bottomed boat excursions to the magnificent barrier reef and Lagoon (with lunch on Île Amedée), and—this is absolutely essential—a visit to the Nouméa Aquarium, one of the great marine-life museums of the world. Founded as recently as 1956 by the Catalas, a Franco-Dutch couple, both of whom are marine scientists, and operated privately by them, the aquarium is a wonderland of exhibits—all fauna from the New Caledonia barrier reef, and mostly collected by the Catalas themselves. One finds the cuttlefish, the pearly nautilus, and—among many other unusual and unusually beautiful exhibits—the only fluorescent corals to be seen anywhere on our planet, and of such splendor that they alone make a New Caledonia visit worthwhile.

West coast excursions from Nouméa do not, to be sure, take one through country as verdant as east coast territory. But one tour—a full day—is exceptionally worthwhile. It goes north to the Melanesian village of Petit Couli, at the base of the Central Mountain chain, then continues along to the somewhat substantial town of *Bourail* via a village called *Moindou* and the eye-filling *Momea Pass,* from which there's a memorable view extending all the way out to the lagoon and barrier reef. From Bourail the route is to the lookout point at *Roche Percée,* with a picnic lunch (and swim) on its beach. Before returning, there's a stop at the New Zealand Pacific War Cemetery, and a rest and refreshment stop at a point where one can have a look at a cagou, New Caledonia's answer to New Zealand's kiwi bird. Still another day-long trip takes one to a country village for a midday *bougna.* The bougna is the Melanesian's counterpart of the *tamaraa*— Tahiti's Polynesian feast. After a rum punch you'll lunch on pig, fish, or poultry wrapped in banana leaves and roasted over a hot-stone fire—all washed down with good French wine. Later, there's tea (if you haven't done too well with the bougna) at a stop at the aforementioned village and mission at St. Louis, en route back.

The Isle of Pines (*île des Pins,* in French; *Kunie* to the Melanesians) is a scenic half-hour plane trip from Nouméa's Magenta Airport, over the lagoon and the barrier reef. After landing at the island's thatched air terminal, there's a rather bumpy—but once again richly scenic—ride on an archaic vehicle called a bus, to Relais de Kanumera, the island's sole hostelry, and one that you will find it difficult to leave. I go into detail on the hotel later on in this chapter. Suffice it to say, at this point, that it's designed in Melanesian bungalow style, that there are two perfectly magnificent crescent-shaped beaches of white, white sand, palm-flanked and with exquisite crystal clear water, and that the swimming, snorkeling, deep-sea fishing (including excursions to the barrier reef), sailing, water-skiing, and *pédalo*-boating are all that one could desire. The Isle of Pines has a tiny populace of less than a thousand and its sightseeing requisites are so few— Melanesian settlements, tall and vast caves enshrouded in orchids and greenery—that one hasn't the slightest guilt about long sun-baths, time-consuming multi-course French lunches and dinners, amiable but aimless evenings over drinks in the bar—and naps in true beachcomber style.

The east coast: The east coast is New Caledonia at its most verdant, at its most Melanesian, and its least European. Far less developed than the area around Nouméa, on the west coast, and with no resort facilities comparable to those on the Isle of Pines, the east coast is virtually virgin tourist territory, being developed with intelligence—and a good deal of elbow grease. As I have earlier warned, this is the wettest part of New Caledonia, and one does well to consider traveling to and through it during the dry months. At other times, rains can be so heavy and visibility so poor that planes (small aircraft are used) cannot take off or land; roads, many of them unpaved, can be impassable; streams, most of them traversed by government-operated rafts for want of enough bridges, can quickly become unnegotiable.

You may, regardless of the time of year, want to throw caution to the winds, and set out anyway. And I couldn't really blame you, for this is beautiful country, and in such tremendous contrast to the more arid east coast that to leave New Caledonia without seeing it is to depart with only a partial picture of the territory. You can, of course, travel on your own, with a rented car, cutting through the mountains at *Bourail,* driving through one of the most scenic of passes in the Southern Hemisphere, and ending up on the east coast, first at *Houailou.*

Upon arrival the route to follow is north along the coast to *Poindimie,* and beyond to *Hienghene.* But on one's own, one can miss a good deal, and information sources en route are relatively scarce. By far the better way to see the region is by means of an escorted tour. I suggest one that will take you from Nouméa to Poindimie (the flight takes half an hour; the airport is a clearing with a tiny thatched hut) where you will be met, driven to *Touho* for lunch in what I consider to be the best restaurant I sampled in New Caledonia, and go on from there. You'll get to villages nestled in the mountains where the locals will take you through their homes (they are nothing like the *bures* of Fiji or the *fales* of Samoa, and their thatched roofs are invariably held in place with boulders), show off their shell collections, explain their cooking methods, demonstrate hunting implements, and introduce you to their families. You'll cross streams on man-propelled rafts chugging through swift currents; you'll drive past coffee and coconut plantations, through landscapes brilliant with flowers. You'll spend evenings at any one of several small but comfortable and modern hotels, making conversation with the European locals at the bar, retiring early, after fine dinners and glorious sunsets, rising for a swim and the continuing journey.

The Loyalty Islands: Both Ouvea and Lifou, in the Loyalty Islands group, are able—just able—to accommodate visitors. On each island there's a tiny hotel-bar-restaurant, a small local populace, perfectly splendid beaches where superb shells and coral are yours for the picking, village life even more simple than on the east coast of New Caledonia, and virtually no fellow tourists. Of the two islands (both are coral atolls), Ouvea's beach—fifteen miles of literally dazzling white sand with nary an occupant to mar the solitude—is the more spectacular. But one cannot go wrong at Lifou, either. Flights over, in both cases, are less than an hour long, and eminently scenic. A shell and coral collector who misses the magnificent (and free) loot on the Ouvea beach will never forgive himself; I don't know of any South Pacific isle regularly accessible by plane where he could do better.

WHAT TO BUY

New Caledonia is a surprise for shoppers. Thanks to its substantial European population, well-paid and reasonably affluent for the most part, there's considerable demand for the luxuries one finds in Paris boutiques, but one would not dream of coming upon them in such profusion and quality on a South Pacific island. Prices? One pays, for French luxury goods, about what one might pay in France. In other words, aside from French perfume which is an exceptional buy, expect to pay what you would on the Rue de Rivoli, which is less than on Fifth Avenue or Michigan Avenue, but still is not peanuts. The point is, though, that the selection of *haute couture* articles is first rate, and towers over what one finds in France's other Pacific island of note, Tahiti—where the resident European population is so much smaller. Have a look and I suspect you'll be treating yourself to some little *bibelot* or other that you hadn't expected to take home from the South Pacific. For women there are fine lingerie, shoes, fabrics by the yard and ready-made dresses, suits, blouses from top designers, gloves, costume jewelry, slacks, shorts, scarves, compacts, and other accessories. For men, there are dress shirts, neckties, sweaters, gloves, belts, and jackets. And there are children's things, as well. Where to go? Without question I would urge you to beeline for Claude France, 24 Rue de l'Alma, a large, modern specialty shop in the heart of the shopping district, with stocks ranging from perfume and cologne (Balmain, Dior, Chanel, Rochas, many others) to and through clothing—even including formal wear—and accessories for men, women, and children. You'll find products of name designers like Dior, Cardin, and Patou (their one-of-a-kind silk scarves make superb, light-to-fly-with gifts) and other, more reasonably priced articles as well.

Adjoining Claude France is the Librairie Pentecost, with what is probably Nouméa's biggest selection of English-language magazines and paperback books, including whodunits, as well as postcards. Exceptionally good for perfumes, colognes, and soaps, of which it has an enormous selection—from Caron to Givenchy—is the Roanne Shop, 38 Rue Georges Clemenceau. The Anne Boutique, 33 Rue Georges Clemenceau, is a charming source of accessories—straw beach hats, costume jewelry, scarves, as well as dresses, perfumes, and what the French call *frivolités* (alluring trifles is a fair translation). Gipsy, Rue du General Mangin near Rue Jean Jaures, features postcards and local handicrafts, at which I must say New Caledonia does not excel. In the new Bettina Arcade Building, Avenue de la Victoire at Rue du Docteur Auegan, one finds a number of shops—Bettina's for shoes, women's clothes, and accessories, perfumes, and twenty-four-hour dry cleaning and pressing; Lucien—women's hairdressing (phone 35-48 in advance for a rendezvous), and Vogue for men's wear. Katara and Mareva are both good for shells and coral, although you'll have no need for them after a trip to the Loyalty Islands— or, indeed, strolls along many other beaches, particularly on the east coast.

CREATURE COMFORTS

Hotels—Nouméa is making constant progress in the realm of accommodation, and it is not at all difficult to be comfortable. There are no jarring skyscrapers, fortunately, and most hotels are of moderate to small size, insofar as number of rooms go. The better ones, though, feature air conditioning and private baths, as well as restaurants, bars, and cafes in connection. All will book sightseeing tours, of course, take care of laundry and pressing fairly speedily, and, by and large, service is pleasant. Rates go from about $7 single, $10 double. Newest and the only true luxury hotel is the 78-room Château Royal, at Magnin Point just beyond Anse Vata Beach. Of French Colonial style, with a swimming pool, and an interior done by one of the SS *France*'s designers, it is financed by French, American, and Australian interests, is air conditioned, has a pool, restaurant, nightclub, three bars, tennis courts, shops, and hairdresser; singles from $10, doubles from $15. Also new is the 50-room Le Nouvata, in Anse Vata, with swimming pool, cabaret, restaurant, bar; rates—including breakfast—start at about $12 single, $17 double, with air conditioning about $3.50 extra. Completed in 1964 was the Nouméa Hotel, a former private club which was extensively modernized and enlarged. Facing the Baie des Citrons, it has thirty-two rooms, many with air conditioning, a restaurant and bar-cafe, and impersonal, if fairly efficient, service. Smack in the center of town (but with the disadvantage of not being on a beach) is the also new Caledonia Hotel, a twenty-five-room establishment with air conditioning, restaurant, and bar. Somewhat older but also good is Lantana, on Anse Vata Beach, with many air-conditioned rooms. On the heights of Mount Coffyn is the twenty-two-room Hotel Makona; each room has its bath and a view-affording balcony; there's a restaurant, and the Pub bar-lounge as well. **West coast:** Bourail's best is the fourteen-room Niaouli, with restaurant and bar. **East coast:** The Hotel de Touho, at Touho, is a bungalow-style affair with a superb restaurant across the road, but with only so-so facilities in its bungalows, and a beach where the tide appears to be out—but *way* out—enough of the time to make swimming far more of a rarity than it should be in the South Pacific. The Hotel de la Plage is a little four-roomer at Poindimie—spotlessly clean, comfortable, modern, with good food and service. The lounge-bar-lobby-restaurant is a single room occupying the main floor; the bedrooms—each with bath—are one flight up, and there's a fine beach nearby. The Chez Maître Pierre at Hienghene is another small place. It too is modern, though, and with a bar and restaurant.

Isle of Pines: I've already alluded to the Relais de Kanumera, a lovely bungalow-style place, with the main building devoted to dining room, bar, lounge, and with a terrace for drinks. The two beaches are sheer heaven, and there's free water-skiing (lessons included), *pédalo*-boating, excursions to the barrier reef, fishing trips, a smart little boutique, excellent French cuisine pleasantly served, and thoroughly delightful service. From $17 single, $39 double American plan.

Loyalty Islands: Ouvea offers the little Comptoirs d'Ouvea— two rooms, a restaurant-bar, and a magnificent beach; on Lifou, there's the Relais de We—and a wee place it is, with but two guest rooms, and a restaurant-bar.

Restaurants: Dining, it should go without saying, is a principal joy of this outpost of *la belle France*. Like France itself, it's difficult to come upon a bad or indifferent meal. And in the South Pacific this is a state of affairs not to be taken lightly. All of the impedimenta of French cuisine is present, from the imported wines and cheeses to the crusty bread baked thrice daily and the difficult-to-read, hand-lettered menus. *Breakfast* (*petit déjeuner*), unless one orders otherwise, is the familiar *café complet*—just-out-of-the-oven French bread or rolls (*petit pain*), butter, jam, and coffee. Snacks, like ham sandwiches made on lengthwise portions of French bread, are available in the bars and cafes, along with drinks, alcoholic and otherwise. Both lunch (*déjeuner*) and dinner (*dîner*) are proper meals, with the former often more elaborate than the latter. Best buys are the *table d'hôte* full-course meals, known in French simply as *le menu*. (These specials, always a favorite of the locals, are not always clearly indicated on the menu card—known in French simply as *la carte*. But don't hesitate to ask about them.) Choices? You'll find a wide range— *steak grillé* or *entrecôte* and *pommes frites* (steak and French fries), which are the Frenchman's mealtime mainstays, *crêpes flambées*—dessert pancakes, *salade de poisson* (seafood salad) . . . and, well, the range is wide, from *pâtés* and soups to the traditional *café filtre* (not to mention dishes made of the local octopus, flying fox, and coconut heart, as well as occasional Tahitian, Indonesian, and Vietnamese foods). The Melanesians' festive *bougnas* are best sampled on the earlier-mentioned bougna sightseeing tours. Wines, of course, are considered essential to the enjoyment of a lunch or dinner, and one finds vintage reds (St. Emilion, Haut Médoc, Château Barret), white (Chablis, Pouilly Fuissé, Riesling), and rosé or pink (Côte du Rhone, Rosé d'Anjou, Clairigny). Considerably less expensive, but rarely unpalatable is the *vin ordinaire* or *vin de table* of each restaurant—served in carafes, and invariably popular at non-festive meals. (But don't be afraid to ask for water, if you prefer it!) It is possible, in the cheaper restaurants, to dine or lunch well for about two dollars, *vin ordinaire* included. Better places, of course, charge more. In the top category are Biarritz, the Circle Civil (a private club on the Baie des Citrons whose dining room is open to the public), La Cascade in the Hotel Nouméa, and Cyranos. Moderate-priced places include the Esquinade, the Nouvata Hotel restaurant, Chez Nicolas, and La Potinière. Budget spots include Le

Cagou, La Pérouse Snack, Esplanade, and Pizzeria. The Asia is good for both Chinese and Vietnamese food.

Outside of Nouméa, the choice is pretty much limited to the dining rooms of the hotels, which generally do an excellent job. Particularly outstanding is the Hotel de Touho, in Touho. The Relais de Kanumera on the Isle of Pines is first rate, too, and even the little Hotel de la Plage at Poindimie does itself proud.

Bar-tearoom-cafe establishments in Nouméa—which will serve an *apéritif,* a cocktail, or a beer, not to mention soft drinks, tea, coffee, sandwiches, and short-order snacks on virtually round-the-clock schedules—include the King's Cross, Jean-Paul, the Pizzeria, the Bambino, and the Esplanade; all the better hotels have these facilities, too.

Nightclubs and cabarets are lively, fun, and not to be omitted from one's after-dark schedule. Entertainers, generally, are imports from still another French Overseas territory: Tahiti. The Santa Monica is a delightful, Polynesian-decor spot—darkish, intimate, and most pleasant. The Tahiti is much bigger and brassier, and a good place to catch the local young people relaxing. Others include the Tivoli and the Biarritz. And on Saturday and Sunday nights hotels can advise you of still additional places with special dances those evenings. Generally, there are no cover charges or minimums, and drinks average less than a dollar.

Private clubs welcome visitors who have secured temporary membership cards from the Government Tourist Office or the Syndicat d'Initiative. These include the Tennis Club du Mont Coffyn, and the Cercle Nautique (Yacht Club).

New Zealand

Entry requirements: A valid passport and, for American citizens, a visa, obtainable from New Zealand consulates. There is no charge for single-entry visas, but should your itinerary be taking you to New Zealand more than once on your journey, request a *multiple-entry* visa; a charge of two dollars is made for each entrance granted. Canadian citizens require no visas. All visitors need smallpox vaccination certificates. **Best times for a visit:** New Zealand is a temperate-zone country with the seasons, of course, the reverse of ours. It follows, then, that the farther *north* one goes, the warmer the climate. Broadly speaking, there are far fewer extremes of temperature than are found in the United States. Auckland's winter averages, for example, are in the fifties; its summer averages in the mid- to high sixties, with highs in the low seventies. The all-round best period is, perhaps, that from September through April—or, in other words, spring through summer. Winter sports enthusiasts, on the other hand, might well prefer to plan their visit during the Northern Hemisphere summer, which is New Zealand's winter—June through August. Be prepared for a fair bit of rain, particularly from May through October. **Currency:** The New Zealand pound, at par with the United Kingdom pound, and the equivalent of $2.80. The pound is divided into twenty shillings, each shilling valued at about fourteen cents. And the shilling is subdivided into twelve pence. One finds notes in denominations of ten shillings, a pound, five pounds, ten pounds, and fifty pounds. Coins are the half-penny, penny, shilling, and florin equaling two shillings. Half-crown coins (two and a half shillings) are being withdrawn from circulation, so if you come across one, hang on to it; it will become a collector's

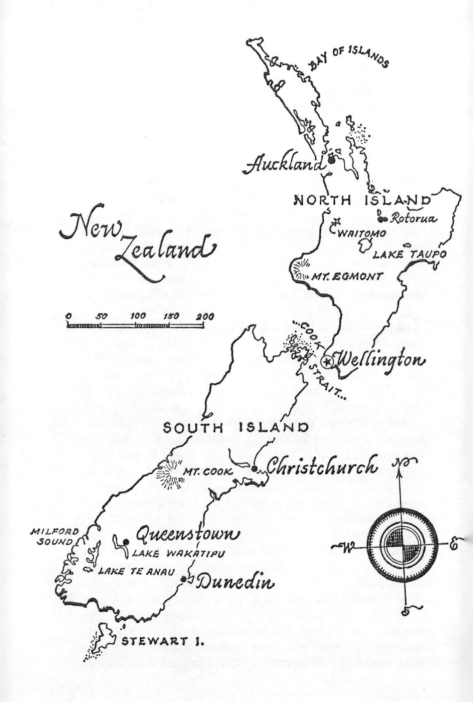

item. If you're not familiar with currency designations, here's a sample: £5/17/6=five pounds, seventeen shillings, and sixpence; a price tag marked 6/ or 6s. translates as six shillings, but 6d=sixpence. To further confuse you, note that a pound is often referred to as a "quid," and a shilling as a "bob." There is no coin or note to denote it, but prices are sometimes given in guineas, a guinea being twenty-one shillings—one shilling over a pound. (New Zealand will convert to decimal currency in July 1967, after which there will undoubtedly be a transitional period when both old and new currencies will be used; the New Zealand dollar will be the equivalent of half a pound—or U.S. $1.40.) **Film availability:** There are fair stocks of color and black-and-white film, generally Kodak, but prices are higher than in the United States. Black-and-white processing is rapid, but color can take a week. **Languages:** The official language is English and it's spoken by everyone including the Maoris, many of whom still speak their own language, a Polynesian tongue, as well. Spoken New Zealand English is generally far less distinctive—and less colorful— than Australian English, but it is rarely the Oxonian of England, as it is often presumed to be, and most New Zealanders, like their Australian neighbors, can be identified as Down Underers simply by their pronunciation of the teen numbers, thirteen coming out as thir-deen, eighteen as ay-deen, etc. **Transportation:** New Zealand emerged into the jet age a good half decade later than most of the rest of the world. With the opening of its $28 million Mangere International Airport (nine miles south of Auckland) in late 1965, it finally became a direct link in round-the-world jet routes. The new terminal building at Mangere offers a range of facilities, including duty-free shops. Although Auckland is the principal port of entry for flights from abroad, one may also enter, from Australia, at Wellington and at Christchurch, the chief city of the country's South Island. A number of airlines serve New Zealand from foreign points, including Qantas, whose jets land at all three cities, linking them with their round-the-world routes via the Australian cities of Sydney, Melbourne, and Brisbane. Within New Zealand, the principal airline is the

government-operated National Airlines Corporation, known
colloquially as NAC. Its largest aircraft, to date, are Viscounts, and standards of service—both aloft and on the
ground—cannot, in my experience, be compared with those
of international lines. It gets you there, though, if not always punctually. Certain areas not served by NAC—particularly in the touristically important South Island—are the
territory of the much smaller but much better operated
Mount Cook Airlines. Its largest craft are DC-3s and
its smallest are tiny three-passenger Cessnas with ski pon-
toons instead of landing wheels. Both pilots and stewards
take a personal interest in each passenger. (You're invariably invited up into the cockpit for the most spectacular
views.) Mount Cook Airlines really knows the New Zealand
Alps, has an excellent safety record, and is the ideal way
to get about the most interesting region of the country. It
operates a bus system in conjunction with its air service,
again of interest to South Island travelers. There is, as well,
frequent ship service between the North and South Islands.
There are other bus systems throughout the country, one a
division of the government-operated New Zealand Railways,
whose buses are far better than their trains. Main roads
are good—and they need to be, for one out of four New
Zealanders owns a car. Self-drive cars are available at sensible rates (Mutual Rental Cars are the leading firm and
represent Hertz), there are any number of packaged tours,
and within the cities there are public conveyances and
reasonably priced taxis. **Tipping:** New Zealanders do not,
as a rule, tip, and it does not seem to me that there is
any reason for foreigners to do so, except in the case of
special services. If you feel you must, keep it minimal, the
best rule being to regard a shilling (fourteen cents) as you
would a quarter at home. I doubt if you'll find any great
compulsion to tip; unusually good service is hard to come
by, and is to be found mostly in the better government-
operated resort hotels where much of the staff consists of
Australians on working vacations. **Clothes:** In the cities,
dress as you would in town, at home. At rural resorts,
women generally change for dinner and men wear jackets
and ties at that time, although dress is more informal

during the day. Remember that summers can be quite cool. You'll want conventional warm-weather togs, of course, but don't be without lightweight woolen suits, a sweater, and of course a raincoat, even at that season. And do not expect to encounter high fashion, New Zealand being a good bit behind Australia, and much else of the world, in this regard. **Business hours:** In major cities shops are generally open from 9 A.M. to 5:30 P.M. Monday through Thursday, and until 9 P.M. Friday, but are closed Saturday and, of course, Sunday. In Auckland, a few souvenir-type places open on weekends when cruise ships are in port. Bars close, countrywide, at 6 P.M. Guests registered in hotels may, however, live quite dangerously and drink until 10 P.M., or through room service for as long as it operates. **Further information:** New Zealand Government Travel Commissioner, 630 Fifth Avenue, New York; New Zealand Government Travel Commissioner, 153 Kearny Street, San Francisco; New Zealand Tourist and Publicity Department, Wellington, New Zealand (tourist bureau branches in Auckland, Christchurch, and the Australian cities of Sydney, Melbourne, Brisbane, Adelaide, Canberra, and Perth); Qantas Airways, Auckland, Wellington, and Christchurch, New Zealand.

INTRODUCING NEW ZEALAND

> *". . . No virgin lands he left unknown,*
> *Where future Englands might be sown . . ."*
> —From a poem entitled *Captain
> Cook,* by Alfred Domett, a mid-
> nineteenth-century Prime Minis-
> ter of New Zealand.

Particularly if he is an American, one expects, indeed one *wants* to be enthusiastic about New Zealand. It is, to begin with, an English-speaking land, and language, differences in accent and occasional word choice notwithstanding, is a strong bond between peoples. It is a dominantly temperate-zone country—and climatic similarities between lands tend to make it easier for their citizens to understand each other. It is democratic, with institutions—freedom of speech, press, religion, the ballot—that Americans value highly. It was, like the United States, a British colony before it achieved sovereignty. It is, like the United States, a relatively young nation whose early European settlers struggled not only with their natural environment but fought an indigenous people for supremacy.

Like the United States, it is seriously attempting to redress the wrongs between majority and minority groups. It is today—and long has been—a good friend of the United States, both as partner in international trade and commerce, and generally, as ally in matters of mutual political concern. And again, like the United States, it is geographically detached from Europe, the continent from which its culture is derived.

New Zealand and the United States: One can, of course, go on with still additional similarities. Both countries are dominantly Christian. Both insist on compulsory education. Both have exceedingly high standards of living. Both have been allies in two World Wars. Both have known periods of commendably progressive government, particularly in the area of welfare, social services, and—with New Zealand the pioneer here—medical care insurance.

But there are vast differences, far more complex than the obvious ones of area, population, and geography, but quite possibly related to these, and without doubt having to do with the sentiment expressed in the fragment of a New Zealand Prime Minister's poetic tribute to Captain Cook, quoted at the beginning of this section. New Zealand, even in the mid-twentieth century, continues to look upon itself as one of the "future Englands" which Captain James Cook so brilliantly charted. Whereas America, quite literally, became a melting pot of the world's people and set its goals on achieving a distinctive national quality of its own, New Zealand steadfastly cocked its collective eye toward

London, eleven thousand miles away. And still does. It is, consequently, far more homogeneous a land today than the United
Kingdom, and with a far more rigid and discriminatory immigration policy. It has been self-governing for more than a century and
a sovereign state, albeit within the Commonwealth, for more than
half a century, but more of its citizens than not continue to refer
to Britain as "home," even though neither they nor—in all likelihood—their great-grandparents were born there. In its almost
compulsive zeal to emulate the mother country—and many New
Zealanders still refer to it as just that—New Zealand has paid a
heavy price.

The British connection: Its people are conflicted over their
views toward Britons; the relationship is a kind of love-hate ro-
mance, there being at once the envy of the Briton and disdain
toward him for what is considered to be—and not always justly
—a patronizing air of the New Zealand "colonial." (One still finds
New Zealanders who do indeed term themselves "colonials," and
not in jest, either.) Of more significance is the blindness of the
New Zealander toward the non-Anglo-Saxon world, and the rich-
ness of other people's cultures. New Zealand has been so preoc-
cupied in keeping its European populace "British" that it has
deprived itself of the dynamism which comes of a heterogeneous
society.

Even the culture of its Maori minority—despite mostly super-
ficial trappings which linger on, rather pitifully—has been so
diluted that it is weak, colorless, and rather tawdry when contrasted to the still vibrant life of other Polynesian peoples on
neighboring islands.

Neighbors, near and far: Not even New Zealand's tremendous
involvement with other peoples in World War II really opened its
eyes. Unlike Australia, which has aggressively welcomed continental Europeans and gained tremendous vitality and dynamism
by so doing, New Zealand contents itself with an annual quota of
British immigrants and a relative handful of Dutchmen, the only
other Europeans interested in migrating whom it considers close
enough to the Anglo-Saxon mold. Closer neighbors? Aside from

its ANZAC relationship with Australia and the United States, its Colombo Plan membership—it participates in social and economic projects in Asian Commonwealth countries and trains students from them in its universities, its participation in the hardly effervescent Southeast Asia Treaty Organization, its stewardship over the nearby Polynesian Cook Islands and its administration for several decades of now independent Western Samoa (which it botched miserably for the first half of its stewardship) —New Zealand is only just beginning to develop an awareness of the Pacific islands and of Asia. (Excluding Australia, and Canada and the United States, if one terms them Pacific countries, it had full-time government representatives resident in seven Asian and Pacific nations in 1964.)

Facets of Asian life which have been familiar to Americans (and indeed many residents of Europe) since World War II are just now being discovered by New Zealanders. (A leading magazine, *New Zealand Women's Weekly,* came forth as recently as March 1965 with a revealing spread on the Japanese tea ceremony, by stating that "the Orient and its customs have long been a source of fascination for the Western World . . ." and went on to impart that "some of them are so sacred and hallowed that it is a great honour for foreigners to take part in or even witness them." Among these, it develops, "is the ancient tea ceremony in Japan performed on very special occasions, [which] Westerners are welcome to watch!") The exclamation point is the magazine's. Westerners, as a matter of fact, had been watching the Japanese tea ceremony at mass-production tourist teahouses a good decade before *New Zealand Women's Weekly* stumbled upon Japan, and I make mention of this article only to indicate the current state of New Zealand's involvement with its neighbors.

The tired look: Identification with a part of the world so long considered "foreign" is one thing. Acceptance of current ideas from the West which it so cherishes and with which it has so long been identified, is still another. And it is here that New Zealand is most to be deplored. It is today dull and, despite its athletic skills and proclivities, tired. It appears, in many respects, a good decade behind Australia in almost every facet of contemporary life and living, and even more behind its beloved England. It seems to have virtually no awareness of life as it is lived today in continental Europe, and what it imports from the United States, in the realm of fads and fashions, come late, and often would have been better not coming at all. It seems content with mediocrity in many spheres. Architecturally it has not—unlike Australia—any distinguished tradition on which to build. (This may be because it lacked the great early convict-architects of its neighbor.) Its cities' elderly buildings are easily forgettable, and its new construction is no better than most of what is going up today everywhere—which is pretty bad. It has never learned style, in any sense. (A New Zealand edition of *Vogue* manages to come out quarterly, and bravely does its best to appear chic.) Furniture in the stores is of appalling design. Clothes, even relatively easy-to-copy articles like men's and women's knitwear, are tacky. Hotels, except for a handful of merciful exceptions to the rule, are rather pitiful excuses for hostelries. Restaurants, rarely eaten in by New Zealanders, exist principally to keep travelers from starvation. It was illegal, as late as early 1965, for country club members to be served liquor in their clubhouses. Bars close, countrywide, at six in the evening (except for residents of hotels). Trains—still without dining cars and with wooden seats in second class—are tolerated only because the fares are cheap. The jet aircraft, in a country at once geographically isolated and dependent upon trade to survive, did not appear in New Zealand until 1965, by which time it was commonplace even in the underdeveloped lands of Africa and Asia.

There is not, so far as I could find, a serious magazine of opinion. (Australia has a number, in contrast.) Not even daily newspapers, competently edited though many are, devote any appreciable space to thoughtful, reflective criticism beyond that of day-to-day matters. New Zealand's most noted writer, Katherine Mansfield, lived mostly in England, as does the contemporary thriller writer, talented Ngaio Marsh. There are some good art galleries and museums, orchestras and theaters, but they tend toward the conservative and the status quo. Indeed, it is not difficult in the case of art galleries to ask about their locations and receive blank stares from locals who have never been to them.

Self-satisfied, defensive: The New Zealander's tendency is to be self-satisfied and defensive, and one is told, more often than not, that no more can be expected of so "small and isolated" a country. But one cannot have it both ways. A country cannot expect to be equated with a civilization (that of the modern West) and at the same time to have excuses made for it, particularly a country as highly developed as New Zealand.

How does such a state of affairs come about? Why does a modern nation, which was built out of the wilderness in a century and a half, come to the point where it is content with second best? Some New Zealanders, and other critics, blame the country's progressive social legislation for the current lack of get-up-and-go. (Finance Minister H. R. Lake stated in a 1965 Parliamentary debate that New Zealanders are the world's most heavily taxed people; a member of the National Party's administration, he blamed the high taxes on the policies of previous Labor governments, which instituted the country's noted "cradle-to-grave" social security programs.) The government medical scheme and a commendably wide range of welfare services are given as the excuse for contemporary apathy. But the Scandinavian countries—with small populations not too unlike New Zealand's, and with similar terrain—have comprehensive welfare programs, too. They have their problems but general acceptance of the dull and the mediocre are hardly among them; indeed, they continue to pioneer in new directions. They have the one advantage which New Zealand lacks —proximity to the rest of Europe. New Zealand's closest major neighbor is Australia, some fourteen hundred miles distant. Its isolation, coupled with its smallness and its carefully controlled, homogeneous populace, seem to be ganging up on it, with the result that it appears to feel it must do things in a small way because it *is* a small place.

A backward glance: I doubt, if that was the way its early citizens approached matters, that it would have made the progress it has, for its developing period was in many ways more difficult than Australia's. New Zealand settlers found terrain much harsher and an already resident people far less disposed to welcome them than were Australia's relatively docile aborigines. Indeed, as W. H. Oliver has written in *The Story of New Zealand*, "New Zealand's history, since the arrival of the Europeans, has been a history of struggle; a struggle between Polynesia and Europe . . . ; a struggle between groups and interests within the European population . . . [which] journeyed out to New Zealand from the eighteenth century on, out of curiosity, out of greed, out of an ambition for security."

The Maori migrations: It was, of course, the relatively late arrival of the colonists from Europe that created so much difficulty. New Zealand's earliest known inhabitants were a people believed to be Polynesian, who became most known for their skill in stalking an enormous (and now extinct) wingless bird known as a moa, which was quite possibly a progenitor of the smaller ostrich and emu. The moa hunters were more or less replaced, in toto, by the arrival of still another Polynesian people, the Maoris. They came in giant canoes—quite amazingly—all the way from what is now French Polynesia, their homeland being known in legend as Hawaiki and now believed to be the island of Raiatea, now a stopover point on flights between Tahiti and Bora Bora.

The earliest of these Pacific Vikings probably arrived in New Zealand in the twelfth century. Later still others came, and it was about 1350 that what is known in New Zealand history as the Great Migration took place. Succeeding centuries saw the Maori making the adjustment to a largely temperate zone environment from the tropics where they had lived, and evolving a culture related to but in many ways dissimilar from those of their brothers still resident in the hot-climate islands.

The Maoris had New Zealand all to themselves for a substantial period. In 1642 Abel Tasman, the Dutch navigator (for whom the Australian state of Tasmania was ultimately named) charted several hundred miles of the coast, and gave the country the name by which it still is called. He was the first European to see New Zealand and it was well over a century before another arrived. That was Captain James Cook, who mapped the New Zealand coasts in the course of three voyages starting in 1769. The decades following saw whalers, sealers, and traders using the small but bawdy community of Kororeka as a kind of unofficial European headquarters.

Early Europeans: It was not long before Kororeka, some of whose part-time residents were from America's New England, had achieved a dubious fame as the "hell-hole of the Pacific." The first missionaries arrived in 1814, but even the introduction of Christianity among the Maori was not enough to calm things down. The early work of the Kororeka crowd—whose introduction of firearms and firewater tended to counteract the missionaries' endeavors—helped make things far too lively, and the British Government decided it was time to step in. They sent Captain William Hobson out to negotiate with the Maori. In 1840 he was able (in the best traditions of Imperial Britain) to get the leading Maori chiefs to cede the sovereignty of their country to the British Crown, by means of the Treaty of Waitangi, the original of which may still be seen in the National Archives at Wellington. The Maori were given full status as British subjects and guaranteed protection of their lands. New Zealand, by virtue of the Waitangi Treaty and of Captain Cook's having formally "taken possession" on his 1769 visit, had become a proper British colony. (For some years earlier, it had been considered a part of the colony of New South Wales, in Australia.)

Model colony: The timing seemed perfect. That same year, settlement from England got under way in a substantial fashion, and one might have thought things would go swimmingly. But the Treaty of Waitangi did not swiftly transform New Zealand into a bed of roses. Although today the Treaty continues morally binding on the government, with its terms extended into a number of important laws, it was not able to avert the bloody wars between *Pakeha* (the white man) and Maori, mainly over the sale of land. British troops, sometimes with certain Maori chiefs as allies, fought against the rebels for several decades, mostly on the North Island (which is where most Maoris live today).

Concurrently, though, settlement continued, and it could not have been more different from that of Australia. Whereas the latter country began life as an overseas prison, New Zealand's settlement was something else again. It was creative, unique, precedent-setting, and largely the fruition of an idea of an Englishman—Edward Gibbon Wakefield—who had himself been a convict, and who, while in prison, put his ideas in writing. In essence, what he favored was the settlement of new areas by free men rather than prisoners, with inexpensive land the lure, and fees from its sale going toward the erection of community institutions like churches and schools. Wakefield and some friends organized the New Zealand Company, and despite opposition from missionaries on the scene (who were worried—and rightly so—that immigrants would threaten Maori interests) and the British Government (which was not originally disposed to open up New Zealand to Europeans), the New Zealand Company ships brought over carefully selected groups of newcomers, making sure that the essential professions and trades (farmers, artisans, physicians, clergymen, and—not to be overlooked—capitalists) were all represented. Wellington was established by the Company in 1840, and by 1850 there were half a dozen New Zealand communities, all of them started by the New Zealand Company save two: Christchurch, established under the auspices of the Church of England, and Dunedin, with Free Church of Scotland sponsorship.

By 1852 the colonists were able to convince London that they should be self-governing, and they received a constitution. Two years later Parliament met for the first time in Auckland. In 1865, Wellington—at the southern tip of the North Island and therefore more conveniently accessible to South Islanders than Auckland—was made the capital. In 1867, by which time the Maori wars were almost over (they ended in 1871), Maori people were given the right to elect four members of the lower chamber, the House of Representatives, and a few years later two of them took seats allocated to them in the upper house, known as the Legislative Council (abolished in 1951).

Pioneering legislation: Free education became compulsory in 1877, women received the vote in 1893, and before the twentieth century was born, New Zealand had pioneered in still other areas, with a wave of social and industrial legislation, including the 1894 Industrial Conciliation and Arbitration Act, and the 1898 Old Age Pensions Act. In 1907 the country achieved what was known as "dominion" status—which meant that to all intents and purposes it was on its own (although it was not until 1931 that the Statute of Westminster formally recognized its complete autonomy and equality with the United Kingdom and fellow Commonwealth members).

All this while the country developed economically. The South Island, fortunately never bothered by the Maori Wars which took place on the North Island, prospered with agriculture, grazing, and a pair of fabulous gold rushes. The country began to develop wealth through its shipments abroad of wool and wheat, and with the arrival of the refrigerator ship and the cream separator they were able to add dairy products and mutton to their export list.

The lure of the country remained, and migrants continued to come from Britain and even from Australia. World War I interrupted progress as it did in many countries. New Zealand forces fought valiantly in Europe, occupied Western Samoa (and governed it as a League of Nations Mandate and a UN Trusteeship Territory until it became independent in 1962).

New Zealand's "New Deal": Later, the Great Depression of the 1930s brought hard times to New Zealand as it did everywhere, and what Franklin D. Roosevelt's New Deal attempted with so much success, as a remedy, in the United States, the Labor party undertook in New Zealand, with even more daring. Remaining in office for four terms, after going in, in 1935, the Labor Government resumed where the earlier Liberal Government had left off at the turn of the century. There were liberalized old-age and sickness pensions, government low-rent housing, the introduction of the forty-hour week and closed union shop, a government hospital-medical care program financed by taxes, and family allowances to parents, with weekly stipends for each child.

The exciting, innovating Labor period and the World War II era which followed were undoubtedly modern New Zealand's greatest hours. The forces of this small country—Army, Navy, Air—were deployed on every front in the global war, from the Solomons to North Africa. Labor stayed in power until 1949 when the opposition National party took over until 1957. Labor then returned for three years, but since 1960 the National Party has been back in office. Under Prime Minister Keith J. Holyoake it controls a majority of the unicameral eighty-seat Parliament, and supports the United States in Vietnam with—as of March 1966 —an artillery battery and surgical team. The opposition Labor party, under N. E. Kirk, favors only noncombatant Vietnam aid.

New Zealand, like such Commonwealth countries as Australia, Canada, Jamaica, and Trinidad and Tobago, is a constitutional monarchy, Queen Elizabeth II being its sovereign, as well as the sovereign of the United Kingdom and the other monarchies within the Commonwealth. She is represented in Wellington by a Governor-General, currently Brigadier Sir Bernard Fergusson, of the United Kingdom. (Unlike Canada, Trinidad and Tobago, and Jamaica—whose Governors-General are Canadians, Trinidadians, and Jamaicans, respectively, New Zealand prefers Governors-General from the U.K., and probably always will, so strong are its ties to Britain. This strongly pro-British sentiment is even revealed in the flag flying from Government House in Wellington; one sees the Union Jack of the U.K. rather than New Zealand's own flag, even though the Governor-General is representing the Queen as sovereign of New Zealand and not as Head of State of the United Kingdom. The Canadians, in contrast, fly their own flag at Government House in Ottawa. The Australians still do not fly theirs at Canberra's Government House, but I suspect they will, long before New Zealand does.)

Maori-white relations: It is, quite possibly, in its attempt to integrate the Maori with the European, or Pakeha, that the government is doing its most commendable current work. Its job is not nearly as staggering as is the United States Government's in relation to the Negro American, but it is decidedly an uphill battle, made no easier by the bigotry and prejudice of many Pakehas and by the difficulty found by many Maoris in making the jump from a long-disadvantaged society to that of the prosperous majority. White man's bullets and diseases killed off a good many Maoris in the last century, but in recent decades their birth rate has been high and they now constitute some 7 percent of the total population, there being an estimated 194,000. The great majority are in the North Island, where their lot is—probably because of their numbers—much more difficult than in the South Island, where one can still find Pakehas who have never seen a Maori.

The government has long since outlawed a color bar—at least legally. "Regardless of any racial or cultural differences," states a publication of the Department of Maori Affairs, "Maoris have a natural and legal right to full equality with all other New Zealanders." Schools are open to all students, although Maori-only schools (with less than a third of all students) continue to operate for those Maori families who want their children to attend them. Public places—hotels, restaurants, theaters, and the like—are open to everyone, and one sees Maori customers, at least at those which they can financially afford.

Housing and jobs: Despite a prevailing derisive attitude on the part of many whites, intermarriage is increasing. Urban areas have attracted many of the traditionally rural Maoris since World War II. Jobs, though, particularly in work above the menial labor level, remain a stumbling block, although a number of Maoris have distinguished themselves in the professions. Housing has been a problem, too, but the situation is improving by means of government-assisted developments which are helping integrate the Maori into the white community.

The ancient culture of the Maori, as I indicated earlier, has been dissipated to a great extent, as a part of the price not only of integration but of exploitation. Now of course, the Maori is trying to retain what is left, and still gain equality with the whites.

Neither retention of the old culture nor assimilation with the new is proving easy. But it would appear to at least one observer that with so much of the best of the old already extinct, further integration is worth the effort. What is meant by integration in New Zealand? The government put it this way in a Department of Maori Affairs publication: "We regard the integration of Maori and Pakeha as the making of a whole new culture by the combination and adaptation of the two pre-existing cultures." And it went on to elaborate: "A well integrated, racially mixed community would be composed largely of people who have achieved a cultural balance suitable to their particular environment and the makeup of the local population. Activities would be shared by both Maori and Pakeha and participation would not be determined entirely on the basis of race but of personal interest and ability as well. The community would be tolerant of diversity and would not attach handicaps to particular cultural choices." A high goal to be sure; if ever achieved it would even exceed the melding of the races which Brazil has attempted with some success.

U.S. and Aussie contrasts: But even at this point the Maoris of New Zealand are eons ahead of the patronized American Indian (what relatively few descendants there are of those we didn't kill off), miles ahead of the Negro of the American South, in many ways more accepted than the Negro of the U. S. North, and not to be compared with the Australian aborigine, whose shameful treatment for two centuries is only just now being reconsidered. A Canadian Indian, Chief Golden Eagle of the Crees, who is with the Indian Affairs Department of the Canadian Government, spent four months in New Zealand during 1965 to observe Maori-Pakeha relationships on a United Nations fellowship. "Integration is certainly on the way," he reported to the press, "but the existing suspicion between the races is likely to continue for several generations." He opined that the "chief fault lay with the Pakeha." But it may well be that more aggressive leadership and a more positive stand against racism are needed on behalf of the Maoris, at least if the reaction of the president of

the New Zealand Maori Council, Sir Turi Carroll, is indicative.
He released to the press, prior to the 1965 visit of the all-white
rugby team from apartheid-governed South Africa, a statement on
behalf of the council urging that "politics should be forgotten"
during the tour, and explaining that "the Maori people love their
rugby too much to allow a side issue to mar their enjoyment of
the tour. . . . As hosts to the visitors and admirers of their
prowess, they will be bound to treat them as honored guests."
The statement concluded with the assurance that "we Maoris will
always be strongly opposed to racial discrimination," but made
clear that it believed the issue of Maoris on a New Zealand team
visiting South Africa—an anticipated problem—had nothing to
do with the New Zealand visit of the lily-white South African
team. I cannot conceive of a substantial and organized non-white
minority of any country graciously welcoming a segregated white
South African group. Could it be that New Zealanders, both
Pakeha *and* Maori, have reached the point where such considerations of human dignity are fine—if they don't interfere with the
national pastime?

YOUR VISIT TO NEW ZEALAND

New Zealand, when compared with its nearest important neighbor—Australia—is small, of course, in contrast. But it's by no
means as tiny as you might think. There's a thousand-mile stretch
from the tip of its North Island in the subtropics to little Stewart
Island, just across Foveaux Strait from the South Island. With an
area of nearly 104,000 square miles, New Zealand is somewhat
bigger than the United Kingdom and a little smaller than Italy,
and the American state of Nevada. The majority of the approximately 2.6 million New Zealanders live on the North Island, which
is the seat of both Auckland, the largest city but not the capital,
as often supposed—and Wellington, which *is* the capital.

It is on the North Island that one finds areas of fantastic thermal activity, as well as a sprinkling of snowy volcanic peaks, a good deal of rich pasture land, and the bulk of the Maori populace. The South Island, separated from the North by Cook Strait, has a pair of principal cities (Christchurch and Dunedin), and terrain which makes it one of the most superbly beautiful islands of the world. The Southern Alps extend from north to south for almost the entire length of the island's western flank, and the fiords of the southwest are among the loveliest to be seen anywhere. In between, one comes upon immense glaciers and splendid lakes.

A New Zealand itinerary? Time spent on the scene is, of course, the deciding factor. But it is to be devoutly hoped that you will not commit the blunder of a shockingly high percentage of visitors and limit your visit to the North Island. If time is so much of the essence, see the South Island and reserve the North for a subsequent trip. For to go to New Zealand and miss the South Island is utterly senseless. There is nothing to rank with it in the Southern Hemisphere, not even lake-and-mountain districts of southern Argentina and Chile, in South America.

Specifics? Naturally, the ideal visit will take in, as a minimum, the most representative locales of both islands. On the North Island these would include—in my view—Auckland, the Waitomo caves, the thermal region embracing Rotorua (center of Maori life), Wairakei, and (if there is time) Lake Taupo, Tongariro National Park, and Wellington. Soaring Mount Egmont is worthy of a visit, if one has additional time, and the far northern region, in the vicinity of the Bay of Islands, is also of interest. On the South Island, aside from Christchurch, the island's principal hub of transport, one should take in the Mount Cook area, Milford Sound, Queenstown, Lake Te Anau in Fiordland National Park and, if there is time, Dunedin. To undertake most of the foregoing, a *minimum* of two weeks is recommended; a few days in excess of that will make the going a bit more leisurely. It is, of course, possible to pick and choose from among highlights of both islands in even less time. But—and I repeat—if one's stay is to be so short that a choice must be made between the North and the South Islands, choose the South!

NORTH ISLAND

Auckland, with its environs, is home to about one out of every five New Zealanders. With a population in the neighborhood of half a million, it is the country's largest city by far. To say that it is also New Zealand's most sophisticated urban center —and this is the case—is not to imply that it comes anywhere close to Australia's leading cities. It is trying, though, in its slow, cautious way, to put its best foot forward to the visitor. The overall picture of the downtown area is one of an agreeable natural setting by no means improved upon by the works of man, but there are, to compensate, not one but two harbors, any number of the parks upon which New Zealanders dote, a pair of museums which most certainly should be visited, several fine over-all vista points, and some popular beaches on the fringes. The core of the city, centered about Queen Street, the main business thoroughfare which emanates from the harbor, does not appear any more distinguished to a newcomer than, say, a fairly substantial town in the English provinces. Indeed, it might be far less so, for urban England away from London has in recent years made considerably more strides in the ways of taste, style, and comfort than has Auckland.

Auckland, which served for a period as the capital after Captain William Hobson concluded the Waitangi Treaty with the Maoris a century and a quarter ago, straddles an eight-mile-wide isthmus, with Waitemata Harbour to the east and Manukau Harbour on the west. There are mountains, including extinct volcanoes (some threescore of them) all about, and the one to which I suggest you head for a panoramic picture is 643-foot Mount Eden. Then, unless you would have still another view from One Tree Hill, amidst Cornwall Park, I should visit the 190-acre Domain, a handsome park replete with playing fields, gardens, and, most important, the War Memorial Museum, a pleasing neoclassic building with what is probably the finest of Maori collections anywhere in the world. Nowhere, not even in the Maori-populated Rotorua area, is one able to perceive the one-time greatness of the Maori civilization better—its genius at the design and building of the great canoes which sailed the Pacific, its prowess at wood-carving and allied decorative arts, its architecture, clothing, social and governmental organization. There are, as well, excellent collections of ethnological materials from other South Pacific regions—Polynesia, Micronesia, and Melanesia. The War Memorial Museum is the site also of a planetarium of special interest to those of us from another hemisphere, where the heavens are studded with constellations of a different variety.

To be seen, too, is the city's chief repository of the culture of the European New Zealander—the Auckland City Art Gallery. Here, in recently renovated galleries, one finds paintings which convey a picture of New Zealand life from early colonial days through to the contemporary period, where sculpture complements oils and watercolors, prints and etchings. Here, too, is the country's largest and best collection of foreign art—the chief contact point with the art of the West for those New Zealanders who would see firsthand what its practitioners are producing. The contemporary sculpture, incidentally, is first rate, with Degas, Rodin, Maillol, Moore, and Epstein among those represented, and it is at this museum that one finds an encouraging awareness of the arts of New Zealand's Asian neighbors. I saw, during my visits, special shows from both Iran and Japan.

You will, before you leave Auckland, probably want to see the pretty floral clock—so reminiscent of those in Switzerland—in Albert Park, and the adjoining Auckland University. And if your visit is a weekend one, you may see New Zealand's nearly extinct national bird, the sad-looking flightless kiwi, at the Auckland Zoo, between noon and 4 P.M. on Saturdays and Sundays. New Zealand's Governor-General, the Queen's representative, has an official residence in Auckland, used during his visits there from Wellington. It is not open to the public, but the turn-of-century-period Town Hall is, and you might want to have a look at its concert chamber and dining hall. To get beyond the city, the

Waitakere Scenic Drive is a good bet. It takes one to and through the Waitakere Mountains, and en route there are views of the city and its two harbors. The Ellerslie Racetrack is another favored destination. There are, as well, the beaches, miles and miles of them, which flank the city both to the east and the west, and which are accessible by public bus service. Nearby islands are easily accessible as well. There is regular boat service, for example, to Rangitoto Island, at the entrance to Waitemata Harbour, where the lures are the area's highest volcanic peak, nine hundred feet in height, swimming, and round-the-island bus tours. And there are twice-daily harbor sightseeing cruises in summer.

Waitomo Caves: Waitomo, the site of extraordinary grottos wherein dwell countless thousands of glowworms, is inevitably visited in the course of a journey between Auckland and the thermal region of the North Island. There is an elderly Tourist Hotel Corporation hotel near the three principal caves, and a visit to the largest, Waitomo, can be comfortably undertaken in half a day. The descent is made by foot to a great pool, way down in the depths, at which point visitors silently step aboard rowboats for the highlight of the guided tour—a row through the darkened cavern whose ceilings are covered by an intricate blue-gold web of the glowworms. The lesser caves, Ruakuri and Aranui, are more distant from the hotel. All three of the limestone caves, with their stalactites and stalagmites, are in themselves remarkable, glowworms or no.

Rotorua is the North Island's most tourist-frequented destination, after Auckland and Wellington, and is in desperate need of truly first-class accommodations. It is a smallish, hardly prepossessing city, with its two lures the thermal activity and the concentration of Maori residents. There is, you are warned, a pervasive, always-present smell of sulphur in the air, which takes a bit of getting used to. The locals are, of course, accustomed to it, although not all newcomers become enamored of it. For those anxious for sweeter-smelling areas, the thing to do is beeline for the requisite attractions in the area.

In the heart of town, these would include the natural hot-water swimming pools in the Government Gardens (Ward and Blue Baths for recreational swimming, Main Baths for therapeutic bathing). All are open day and evening, and a dip is often ideal after a long day's sightseeing. Outside of town one is faced with a wealth of choices, for this is an area quite literally bubbling with geysers, boiling pools, mud volcanoes, and assorted other freaks of nature. Wherever you go, watch where you're walking, for nature's creations are strange and weird as well as beautiful, and many are *hot* and liquid.

I would call a half-day trip to *Waiotapu,* some twenty miles from town, the most essential Rotorua excursion. Here are to be found all manner of hissing, gurgling, and erupting phenomena —steam vents, mud pools, deep craters, a steaming waterfall, and the lovely Lady Knox Geyser, which erupts with ladylike regularity at 10 A.M., as high as seventy feet and for as long as an hour and a quarter. Equally important is a trip to *Whakarewarewa*—but two miles from town and known colloquially (and fortunately) as Whaka. The lures here are a fantastic concentration of thermal wonders, which visitors are guided through by Maori residents of the adjacent village, in itself of interest particularly because of the natural pools which residents use for bathtubs, and the heated-by-nature earth which they employ for cooking. There's a model *pa,* or village, where the carving in public buildings is most impressive. With an additional hour or two at your disposal, you should head posthaste to the town's airport and book an hour or even a half-hour sightseeing flight. James' Aviation's small but modern craft will fly you right over the thermal area, and there's no better way to fully appreciate the strangely compelling beauty of the region, including—if you'll not have time to see them from the ground—the Wairakei geothermal area and Lake Taupo.

Another full day free? Occupy it with a bus tour to *Waimangu.* Included will be visits to a crater lake, Lake Rotomahana with its steaming cliffs, and hot springs hissing at the water's edge. There will be a visit, too, to what little remains of the village of Te Wairoa, buried by an eruption of Mount Tarawera in 1886. En route back the route is via the pretty Blue and Green lakes. It is entirely likely that there will be a Maori "concert party" in the Rotorua Town Hall auditorium during your visit. Take it in, most certainly, but do not expect the kind of thing you'll probably have seen in the Polynesian islands of the Pacific. The caliber of performance varies, of course, but the Rotorua concert parties indicate how sadly diluted the Maori culture has become as a result of prolonged contact with the white New Zealander and the attempt—only partially successful as yet—to be integrated in the dominantly European society of the country. I'm sure you'll find the Maori people you meet charming and personable, as a rule. You'll also find them the palest Polynesians extant (possibly because of centuries of life in a temperate zone climate, possibly because of much mixture with the European for so long, possibly a combination of both). But I suspect you'll agree, also, that what remains of their traditional culture—at least as seen in and about Rotorua—is but a pitiful remnant of what must once have been tremendously vital and beautiful. Indeed, if I were a Maori leader in Rotorua, I would rather the visitor saw no concert party at all than what was presented during my visit.

Wairakei, not far from Rotorua, lies within that portion of the thermal area where the thermal steam has been harnessed for electric power in the remarkable Wairakei Thermal Valley. One sees for miles on end fountains spouting into the air at the thermal steam-generating plant. Wairakei is blessed with a good Tourist Hotel Corporation hotel, at which there's a thermal swimming pool, golf, tennis, and nearby beauty spots like the Huka Rapids and Falls, and the Karapiti Blowhole, which has for centuries been shooting great globs of dry steam into the air.

Lake Taupo, just five miles from Wairakei, is New Zealand's largest (it's some twenty-five miles long and as much as fifteen miles wide) and is perhaps best known for its trout fishing. They're big ones, there are a lot of them, and the avid angler does well to allow for as much fishing time at Taupo as is possible. (Tackle and boats are available on the spot.) The little town of Taupo is at the head of the lake and from it, when the weather is really clear, one can see the mountains of the Tongariro National Park, some sixty miles distant.

Tongariro National Park is dominated by a trio of volcanic peaks—Tongariro, Ngauruhoe, and Ruapehu, which at 9175 feet is North Island's highest, and a haven for summer climbers and winter skiers. The Park is the site of the Château, one of the Tourist Hotel Corporation's better hotels. There's a fine golf course, and one can keep busy on excursions, either by foot (half an hour to a full day) or by motor, to nearby rivers, pools, hot springs, gorges, waterfalls, and—for a great thrill—the crater lake atop Mount Ruapehu.

Mount Egmont, in Egmont National Park, a hundred miles west of Tongariro National Park, in the coastal Taranaki district, is perhaps the most beautiful of the North Island volcanic peaks, and is set amidst pretty pastureland. The best good accommodation nearby is in the town of New Plymouth.

The Bay of Islands area, at the North Island's northern tip, is New Zealand at its most tropical and its most historic. The region is a maze of islands and inlets, with fine beaches, little Russell (on the site of the once infamous whalers' settlement of Kororeka; Waitangi, in whose Treaty House British sovereignty was proclaimed in 1840; great deep-sea fishing, and—a real bonus—a fine new Tourist Hotel Corporation hotel.

Wellington: New Zealand chose the site of its capital wisely and well. It is at the southern tip of North Island, making it accessible to South Islanders as well as those who live to the north. (The nearest South Island port, Picton, is just across the narrowest part of Cook Strait.) But the situation is more than convenient. Wellington is the most handsomely located of any of the country's major cities. It is built on a series of hills which form a kind of semi-circle around its brilliant Port Nicholson Harbour, and the first thing the visitor wants to do is to ascend to any of a trio of first-rate observation points to take in the panorama. The most fun to reach is at Kelburn, which is gained by a San Francisco-type cable car from the lower station at Lambton Quay. Still other splendid views are afforded from the Mount

Victoria Lookout, 648 feet high, and from Mount Wakefield, with almost one-thousand-foot elevation. I should make it up to at least one of these on a clear night as well as on a sunny day. The only other comparable vistas in the South Pacific are those of Hobart, Tasmania (from Mount Wellington behind it) and Tutuila, American Samoa, from the new cable car leading to the educational television station above Pago Pago. On the surface, Wellington is something else again, and in a sense typifies urban New Zealand, which so often is more attractive from a distance than from close up.

This being the capital, you will, of course, want to see the Parliament Building, incredibly uninviting though it is; the rather quaint all-wooden Government Building, a Victorian structure nearby; the Newton Park Zoo (with an enormous animal and bird collection, including the kiwi); the sixty-two-acre Botanical Garden, and two important institutions, neither of which should be neglected. One is the National Art Gallery and Museum (with interesting New Zealand paintings and sculpture in the Gallery section, excellent Maori and other Pacific exhibits in the Museum section and, adjoining, the Carillon Tower and new Hall of Memories, memorials to the 26,600 New Zealanders who died in the two World Wars and the Boer War in South Africa). The other is the unique Alexander Turnbull Library, internationally noted (and justifiably so) for its research program in Pacific history and geography. The library, though not actually a museum, has a small but interesting series of displays, with the *chef d'oeuvre* the original parchment on which is hand-inscribed the historic Treaty of Waitangi.

The commercial district revolves around Willis Street, and there is swimming right in the heart of town, at Oriental Bay. Even more swimming? A thirty-mile Marine Drive encompasses beaches and fine view-points along the nearby coast, and Wellington's pride and joy is a new heated indoor swimming pool which is far more attractive than its name: the Freyberg Tepid Pool. There's horse racing (for which New Zealanders have a passion) at Trentham, in the Hutt Valley about twenty miles from town.

Wellington is very interested in amateur theater; groups perform frequently in the auditorium of the Town Hall, and the capital is the headquarters of the New Zealand National Orchestra, National Ballet Company, and National Theatre. Shipping plays a substantial role in Wellington's economy—a third of the country's imports and exports pass through its port, but government employs about one out of five Wellingtonians, of which there are, in town and suburbs, over a quarter of a million.

SOUTH ISLAND

Christchurch: The metropolis of South Island is no more exciting a city than is any urban center in New Zealand. But if one doesn't take too seriously its claim to being the most English city outside of England, it can be pleasant enough for a short visit, and would be even more so if it had a top-rank in-town hotel. Christchurch, on the Canterbury Plains of South Island's east coast, is the focal point for South Island tourists. Ships put in almost daily from Wellington at its port, the nearby town of Lyttelton, and from Australia as well. The modern international airport was the first in New Zealand with jet service, when Qantas 707s started flying in from Australia in the spring of 1965. And that same airport will be of especial interest to the American visitor, for not far from the terminal building is the advance headquarters of Operation Deepfreeze, the U. S. Navy's Antarctic program. Deepfreeze personnel pass through the Christchurch depot to and from their Antarctic tours of duty, and their ships sail for the American base at McMurdo Sound from Christchurch's port of Lyttelton.

The town of Christchurch, as mentioned earlier, was a planned settlement. The Church of England founded it in 1850, picking and choosing settlers from each social class, and with all of the essential occupations and professions represented. The idea was to create a bit of England in New Zealand's South Island, and although I don't mean to infer that the plan was unsuccessful—

far from it—I don't think you'll think you're anywhere but in
New Zealand when you visit Christchurch. The center of the
town, Cathedral Square, is bordered by ugly commercial establishments and dominated by a Victorian Gothic cathedral which
is one of the most unattractive neo-Gothic structures of substance
that I have seen anywhere. (It was started in 1864 but crises arose
—mostly financial—and it wasn't finished until 1904.) Nearby,
the aesthetics improve at the old Provincial Chamber Building,
an 1876 building with a fine arched ceiling and pleasingly elaborate decor which is Victorian Gothic at its decided best. The
University of Canterbury, also on Gothic lines, is handsome, and
the entire Botanic Gardens complex is eminently worthy of a visit.
The gardens themselves are the most beautiful in New Zealand,
and certainly among the loveliest in the Southern Hemisphere.
Fringed by the Avon River, which meanders delightfully through
the town, they embrace a vast archery lawn, a rose garden, natu-
ral-style gardens in which pools and trees are important features,
and a hothouse set amidst a brilliant-hued maze of flower beds.
Hagley Park, a five-hundred-acre domain, adjoins the gardens,
and with its playing fields, lake, and riding trails is as beloved of
Christchurch residents as is New York's Central Park; indeed,
Christchurch has had to fight as much as New York to keep the
park a park.

But there's more to the Botanic Gardens area. Aside from the
earlier-mentioned University of Canterbury, there is Christ's College—a boys' preparatory school—with *its* Gothic quadrangle.
And at the entrance to the gardens is the Canterbury Museum,
with the Maori collections one sees in a number of New Zealand
cities, but also with a charming reproduction of an early Christchurch street, with interiors of houses and shops of a century ago.
A few hundred yards from the Museum, through the gardens, is
the McDougall Art Gallery, with a smallish but good collection
of paintings and sculpture, tastefully displayed.

Town panorama? Nothing like Wellington, I'm afraid, but the
Summit Road does lead to the tops of the hills which surround
the city, and one does well to make the excursion, stopping at a

iew of Perth, capital of the State of Western Australia, from King's Park.

e United States Embassy, Canberra, Australia.

w Australians are found all over their adopted country; here, an Italian
staurant on Todd Street, the main thoroughfare of Alice Springs,
orthern Territory.

The English house in which Captain Cook was born, transported, brick by brick, by grateful Australians to a park in Melbourne.

Australian wines are among the world's finest: a winery in South Australia.

Ayers Rock, the world's largest monolith rock, in Australia's Northern Territory.

Australian aborigines, inventors of the boomerang, still know how to throw it; here, a demonstration at Ross River, near Alice Springs.

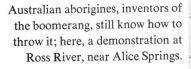

The splendid ruins of the convict-designed and -built church at the long-disbanded Port Arthur penal settlement, Tasmania.

A view of central Adelaide, capital of South Australia, from one of the series of parks which encircle it.

Australian universities have handsome campuses; the University of Western Australia, Perth.

Rural Australia: shepherd, sheep dog, flock, at a New South Wales sheep station.

Australia's architectural heritage
is typified by these Georgian houses
in the tiny village of Richmond,
Tasmania.

Sydney new and old: gracious
town houses, a towering
skyscraper-in-the-making.

Australian state legislative buildings
are imposing; here, the Parliament of
the State of Queensland, Brisbane.

tearoom which takes itself very seriously (as well it might, being in the style of a baronial manor house) and calls itself the Sign of the Takahe. There are, as with every New Zealand city, quantities of good beaches in the neighborhood, and not one but a brace of racetracks—trotting at Addington, and regular racing at Riccarton. Christchurch, incidentally, is the site of the biannual Pan Pacific Arts Festival. And there's one other matter of import: the Canterbury Public Relations Office has on file a list of families who like to informally entertain foreign visitors of similar occupations or interests in their homes. If you'd like to take advantage of this standing invitation, do so through your hotel desk. But don't tarry. The glories of South Island await.

Mount Cook, all 12,349 feet of it, is at once New Zealand's highest peak, and its most splendid destination. There is no point arguing which is most beautiful—the mountains of New Zealand's South Island, with Cook as their crowning glory, the Alps of Europe, the Rockies of North America, the peak-fringed fiords of Norway, or the Andes of Argentina and Chile. I have my own opinions, but I'll leave it for you to make up your mind. The important thing is to get to Mount Cook, and savor its magnificence.

The New Zealanders have a long way to go before their tourist plant, nationally, is anything approaching first class, but they cannot be bested when it comes to Mount Cook, its facilities, and the various means of access to it. One can fly, via Mount Cook Airlines' excellent DC-3 service from Christchurch, one can drive privately, one can take public buses, or one can join any one of a variety of package tours. And this is no dash-in-dash-out destination, unless time is at a premium. For the Hermitage at Mount Cook is the Government Tourist Hotel Corporation's finest hotel. Would that New Zealand—particularly its cities—had a couple dozen more like it!

Mount Cook, since 1953, has been the nucleus of one of our planet's most extraordinary national parks. Within its confines of 173,000 acres lie all but five of the twenty-seven New Zealand mountains which exceed ten thousand feet in elevation, and—

as a bonus—there are 140 additional peaks higher than seven thousand feet. More than a third of the park's territory is permanently surfaced by snow or glacial ice. Mount Cook itself has known a good many more climbers than, say, Everest. (Sir Edmund Hillary, incidentally, climbed the New Zealand Alps before he made the historic ascent of Everest with Nepal's Tensing Norkay.) But the total who have reached the summit—approximately 350 since the first ascent was made in 1894—still is relatively small.

You may, of course, have a try yourself, or you might want to settle for a trek over one of the glaciers in the vicinity of the Hermitage Hotel. Tasman Glacier, for example, is eighteen miles long and as much as two miles wide—one of the largest to be found anywhere outside of the polar areas. And there's a road leading from the Hermitage to Ball Hut—a ski lodge right on the glacier, where the icy surface is some seven hundred feet thick. Treks can also be made to other glaciers in the vicinity—Hooker, Godley, and Murchison, all about seven miles from the hotel.

A visit to the area in the New Zealand summer (November to January) is the ideal time for the nature-lover, for there are more than three hundred species of native plants in Mount Cook National Park, and the Park administration has labeled them on cleverly laid-out trails, leading from the hotel, which rents stout hiking boots and heavy socks for hikers. The Bowen Track can be negotiated in twenty minutes, and the Kea Point walk can be done in an hour and a half; others take twice that time to a full day.

Nothing can compare with one's own exploration, by foot, in an Alpine area. But even more exciting is seeing the Mount Cook area by means of the three-passenger aircraft operated by the skilled pilots of Mount Cook Airlines. The planes depart from an airstrip in front of the hotel and their destinations are the glaciers themselves—Tasman, Fox, Franz Josef. (The Franz Josef area, incidentally, can now be a separate destination, thanks to the new Tourist Hotel Corporation hotel there.) They are able to land without effort on the icy surface because their landing gear consists of skis as well as wheels, and they can choose the more appropriate of the two, depending on the terrain. For as piddling a fare as ten dollars one is transported from a luxury hotel over indescribably magnificent peaks and valleys to the great white wastelands of the glaciers. There is nothing quite like it. In summer, despite the altitude and the ice, the weather is mild and bracing (a light sweater is all that one need wear), the ice hard packed, the glare of the sun eerily brilliant, the horizon one of pristine peaks on all sides, the silence all-enveloping.

The ski planes were created originally for skiers (they'll take skis and equipment aboard as well as passengers), but non-skiing sightseers quite properly latched on to them shortly after Harry Wigley, Mount Cook Airlines' imaginative and resourceful director, inaugurated them a few years ago, and veterans of flights are awarded amusingly designed certificates of membership in the Unique Order of Plane Ski-Daddlers. The ski season at Cook extends from late June to September. There are tows on the grounds near Ball Hut for beginners, and the snowfields of the glaciers are a favorite with the more experienced. The hotel rents boots, skis, sticks, and other equipment, and there are instructors on hand as well.

But what of the traveler—and there are such—who neither hikes nor skis nor cares for longish bus tours to huts on glaciers? He need not even leave the Hermitage. The view from the lounges, public rooms, and indeed many bedrooms, is of Mount Cook itself.

Lake Te Anau is South Island's largest, and lies at the entrance to vast Fiordlands National Park. A four-armed body of water embracing more than 132 square miles, it is surrounded by a briskly beautiful region of peaks and woodlands. There is a smallish but good Tourist Hotel Corporation hotel overlooking the water, a number of lake cruises to occupy one and, in addition a glowworm grotto (discovered as recently as 1948) not dissimilar to the more famed caves at Waitomo, on the North Island. Daylong excursions may be made to Lake Manapouri, smaller than Te Anau but a gem and only thirteen miles distant; by launch, to

South Fiord and Gorge Falls and—again by boat—to Glade House on the banks of the Clinton River at the base of the six-thousand-foot-high Earl Mountains.

It is from Glade House that one may—if one feels up to it—commence a thirty-three-mile hike to Milford Sound, along a route known as the Milford Track. The journey takes seven days and is recommended only to the sturdy, with some experience of climbing and hiking. But there are easier ways to gain Milford Sound. One ran fly from Te Anau (or Queenstown) or one can go from Lake Te Anau by bus. I heartily urge that the approach be made in the last-mentioned fashion, with the exit from Milford Sound by air.

Indeed, it is because the approach to Milford from Te Anau *is* so beautiful that I suggest a layover at Te Anau. It deserves visiting if only to serve as a takeoff point for Milford. A half-day's drive, it takes one through the splendid Eglington and Hollyford Valleys, along the shores of placid Lakes Fergus and Gunn, beneath the 8210-foot peak of Mount Christina, and into the dark vastness of the ingeniously engineered Milford Tunnel—three-quarters of a mile in length. From the tunnel, one works one's way through Cleddau Canyon on a twelve-mile journey—down some twenty-three hundred feet past 9042-foot Mount Tutoko, to sea level and Milford Sound.

Milford Sound: A visit to Milford Sound is as essential as a stay at Mount Cook for minimal appreciation of the South Island's splendor. This is the loveliest of the island's awesome fiords. It is one of more than a dozen that wind their way in from the coastal waters of the southwest, meandering through an incredible wonderland of lakes, mountains, and their valleys—which were, eons ago, the beds of immense glaciers. At Milford, the Tourist Hotel Corporation has placed—with an eye to aesthetics, at just the right spot—the Milford Hotel, second only to Mount Cook's Hermitage in excellence. The view from the great picture windows in the lounges and from the front bedrooms is the almost perfectly triangular Mitre Peak, which juts directly into the waters of the sound, and is complemented by lower, only slightly less dramatic peaks surrounding it.

One can, of course, spend one's entire visit simply taking in the grandeur from the hotel. But I suggest getting a bit more close up, by means of the now-classic ten-mile launch cruise down the sound, passing Pembroke Glacier, 504-foot Bowen Falls, and, of course, Mitre Peak itself. Walks of varying duration may be made from the hotel, and, particularly if you do not utilize its services to fly back to the Outer World, I suggest one of the scenic flights over the region, offered by Southern Scenic Air Services. Their best, of forty-five minutes' duration at a cost of about twelve dollars, takes one over the Pembroke and Donne Glaciers, Mounts Madeline and Tutke, Lake Quill, the relatively little-known but lovely Sutherland Falls, and, before returning, you fly *over* the route of the Milford Track, taking it in the easy way.

Alternatively, one can see the region from the air utilizing the flight as a means of departure for either the earlier-mentioned Lake Te Anau or for Queenstown.

Queenstown is a pretty little community nestled at the foot of the Remarkables Mountains, straddling the shores of fifty-two-mile-long Lake Wakatipu. It had its start as a center of the 1862 Gold Rush but lives today on the proceeds of what amounts to a year-round Tourist Rush, which will be considerably more lucrative when a planned new hotel is completed, probably in 1967 or 1968. Until such time, the visitor is advised to make his visit relatively brief, taking in the memorable view from nearby 5314-foot Coronet Peak (gained by a new skiers' chairlift which climbs fifteen hundred feet from a modern restaurant, lower down, but still at a thirty-eight-hundred-foot elevation), chugging about the lake on a new four-ton hydrofoil boat trip, making the interesting half-day boat excursion to the Cecil Peak Sheep Station (that's ranch to you, pahdnuh), lunching—or better yet, dining—at the delightful little Skyline Chalet on a peak fifteen hundred feet above town and lake, and possibly taking in the one-time Gold Rush settlement (including a museum devoted to the Good Old Days) at Arrowtown, three miles distant.

Dunedin, the No. 2 city of South Island, is as proud of its

Scottish heritage as Christchurch is of its impeccable English origins. Deftly straddling seven hills overlooking finger-shaped Otago Harbour, Dunedin, like its bigger neighbor to the north, was a planned community, its auspices being the Free Church of Scotland. There is still to be detected a Scottish burr in the accents of some residents, there is much obeisance to the kilt, the tartan, and the bagpipe, and there is a good deal of pride taken, with justification, in the city center, which is a well-designed octagon, and goes by that name. The Octagon's principal landmarks are two properly imposing places of worship—the First Church (Scottish) and St. Paul's Cathedral (Anglican), the Town Hall, and—this will not surprise you—a statue of Bobby Burns. There are a trio of museums: the Dunedin Museum, devoted mainly to Polynesian exhibits; an Art Gallery, heavy on New Zealand painting (more of which may be seen at the Public Library's changing picture exhibits), and—for the flavor of early Dunedin—the Early Settlers' Museum. To be taken in, too, are the neo-Gothic Otago University campus; Larnach's Castle, a private house built some ninety years ago now open to the public and with a fine view; the pleasant in-town Botanical and Queens Gardens and the out-of-town Glenfalloch Woodland Gardens; the beach and Marine Aquarium at nearby Portobello on the Otago Peninsula, and—most unusual—the albatross colony which is believed to be the only one in the world where the albatross has nested close to human habitation.

The Cook Islands comprise a South Pacific cluster northeast of New Zealand's North Island, not far from the Samoas. They are populated mostly by some twenty thousand Maoris who have been under New Zealand control since the turn of the century, and voted in 1965—in a UN-conducted plebiscite—to remain so, but with self-government. *Rarotonga* is the principal island, but even it is not yet truly in the tourist business, although transpacific liners make stops in its harbor; there are flights from Western Samoa, and plans for regular weekly air service from New Zealand. Hotel facilities are minimal.

WHAT TO BUY

Once one leaves the art galleries, and museums, the better Government Tourist Hotel Corporation hotels, and a relative handful of private houses, the state of aesthetics in New Zealand is among the lowest of the world's developed countries. Elegance, style, charm, and whimsy are generally absent from the New Zealand scene. Consequently, the prospective shopper from abroad finds himself in a unique position; he need devote no time *or* money to an activity which in most countries, developed or otherwise, is of some consequence. New Zealand, with its great wool industry, turns out quantities of monumentally unattractive knitted and woven goods, which cannot compare in style or quality with those of Australia—and which are by no means reasonable in price. So I would not suggest you bother looking for a sweater for Uncle Jim or a skirt for Cousin Ethel, particularly if Australia is on your itinerary. There is a good deal of jewelry made from native greenstone, used for centuries by the Maoris. And most of it is expensive and not of pleasing design. The same goes for many of the articles made from *paua,* a mother-of-pearl-like shell which, though not cheap, has a gaudy look about it, although you might feel otherwise. There is, to be sure, a good deal of Maori woodcarving. Take a look at the great canoes of the Maoris in the big-city museums, and at the superb decorative woodwork of the Maoris in their villages, and you weep at the souvenirs they turn out. At least they are presumed to turn them out. Some are not hand-carved, most are overpriced, commercial-looking, and in no way comparable (at least in my view) to what is available in the islands of Polynesia and Melanesia. There are a variety of objects machine-fashioned from the many beautiful New Zealand woods, and most of these, I regret to report, have a pitifully five-and-ten look to them, with overglossy lacquer finishes. And they're not cheap either. Sheepskin rugs are available, and indeed attractive, at least in the natural shade. Some, though, are dyed in primary colors and the result is that they look like the manmade fiber rugs we might buy for our bathrooms. You will, of course, want to have a look for yourself, and the best sources are the chain of Disabled Servicemen's Shops, which are to be found on Queen Street, High Street, Princess Wharf, and the airport, in Auckland, and also in Wellington, Christchurch, and Dunedin, as well as a few smaller towns. Another Auckland source is the Maori Art & Souvenir Depot, in Queen's Arcade. The Sheepskin Rug Shop, 6 Little Queen Street, Auckland, is the best source for, naturally enough, sheepskin rugs, and it packs and ships abroad. And there are souvenir departments in the leading Auckland department stores—Milne & Choyce, John Court, and Smith & Caughey. Milne & Choyce, incidentally, has an Elizabeth Arden beauty salon and a men's barber shop, John Court has a beauty salon, and there's a men's barber shop at Smith & Caughey. In Wellington, aside from the Disabled Servicemen's Shop, try A. Green Jewellers, Stoneham's, and F. C. Wood, for souvenirs, and the Government Printing Office retail shop (opposite Parliament) for books and other publications on New Zealand. And in Rotorua, there's Eric Scholes' Gallery Shop, for souvenirs, paintings, and sheepskin rugs.

Remember when leaving the country that you may take advantage of the duty-free shop at Auckland's Mangere Airport, for liquor, cigarettes, French perfumes, watches, cameras, and other appliances. Note, though, that you must pay for what you buy in any foreign currency (including traveler's checks); New Zealand currency is not acceptable.

CREATURE COMFORTS

The visitor can better understand the hotel and restaurant situation in New Zealand if he is aware of two factors. The first is that hotels in the towns and cities have, by and large, been owned and operated by the major breweries, more as an outlet for the sale of their beers than as places of accommodation. The second is that New Zealanders are not a restaurant-conscious people. They're homebodies, pure and simple, and until very recently they ate in public places only when traveling on business or on holiday. Only in recent years have they begun to learn that city-dwellers in other developed countries eat in restaurants *for pleasure,* even though they have homes of their own equipped with kitchens. And that visitors from abroad, or even from other parts of their own country, might enjoy good restaurants with attractive surroundings and appetizing cuisine. The cities now, as a result, have a handful of good eating places. But, except for some modern motels on the outskirts and a couple of major exceptions to the rule—big new hotels going up in Auckland—city hotels remain largely substandard, even though a few have refurbished and spruced up. (The urban situation should change for the better as a result of a government program of financial assistance to hotel owners and developers, announced in late 1965.) The situation at country resorts is something else again. Here, where the breweries are not on the scene, the government has not been reluctant to step in, and the New Zealand Tourist Hotel Corporation operates ten hotels in favored tourist areas, some of them, of course, much better than others. Pending the opening of planned new hotels in places like Auckland—and new out-of-town motels, fine for motoring New Zealand businessmen but not so convenient for foreign tourists—the best of the Government Tourist Hotel Corporation hotels are the best in the country. Otherwise, one cannot count on a great deal, and simply must, in the best British tradition, make do. In addition, it is essential to realize that not even the better places are large, in the sense of those in bigger countries. Especially from November through April, rooms with private baths particularly are at a premium and *it is extremely important that one book as far as possible in advance.* Note, too, that the Tourist Hotel Corporation hotels offer a choice of American or European plan; American plan is more sensible, for there's generally no place else to go for meals. In the cities, some hotels are European plan, some bed and breakfast, some American plan, and some offer a choice. As for food, it, like accommodation,

is generally at its best in the Tourist Hotel Corporation hotels—
where it can be excellent—and at its most British Provincial
Worst in the town hotels, where correspondingly indifferent dining
room service is frequently the case. Remember, too, that public
bars close at 6 P.M., with the interval between five and six—
known as the six-o'clock swill—the time when shop and office
workers jam them, imbibing as much as is humanly possible before closing. Beer, incidentally, is the New Zealander's favorite
alcoholic beverage. It is served cold and is not at all bad. Whiskey,
though always obtainable, is far less popular. Registered guests
in hotels may order drinks at any time, in their rooms. And at the
Tourist Hotel Corporation places, there are cocktail lounges for
guests, which are generally open until about 10 P.M., and at
which mixed drinks and cocktails are excellently prepared. Meal
hours at all hotels and restaurants are fixed and *rigid*. And one
must not expect to be able to dine late. Dinner is generally over
at seven-thirty, although on some occasions this is extended. At
some of the better city hotels, guests who check in in the evening
are allowed, if they so request with their reservation, to eat what
is known as "late dinner" rather than go to bed hungry. But this
frivolous gesture is made only on week nights. I arrived, for
example, in Auckland—a metropolis of half a million souls, the
largest in the country—at eight o'clock on a Sunday evening, and
after scouring the city to find a restaurant open, had to settle for
tea and tiny sandwiches, *in my room*. Unless one wants to be
served a cup of tea and a biscuit at 7 A.M. it is necessary to hang
on the outer door knob the "No Morning Tea" sign usually provided; this practice obtains in all hotels. *A few food pointers:*
The evening meal, big as it may be, is called "tea" in private
homes, "dinner" in restaurants and hotels. "Hogget" is a cut of
lamb. "Silverside" of beef is corned beef; local delicacies like
fresh trout, strawberries, oysters, and the like, rarely appear on
menus. Resort hotels usually include morning coffee, afternoon
tea, and pre-bedtime snacks in their American plan rates. After-
dinner coffee at hotels is invariably served in the lounge (i.e.,
lobby) rather than at the table. And don't try to get roast beef

rare; it's virtually impossible. Steaks—made to order—*can* be obtained rare.

Auckland: Until the nine-and-three-quarter-million-dollar, 332-room, multifacility Auckland Inter-Continental opens, the newly renovated Royal International is about the best available. Rooms are spacious and rather giddily decorated, and all of them have private bath; service and food are fair. The location is central and rates begin at $10.50 single, $16.10 double, European plan. The De Brett, while smaller, has private baths with all its rooms, which are quite comfortable, dining rooms, bars. From about $13 single, $16 double, European plan. The Great Northern has a relatively small section of newly renovated rooms with private bath, dining room and bars; rooms with bath from $10.50 single, $21 double, with breakfast. The modern White Heron Lodge, while not central like the downtown hotels, has attractive rooms, all with bath, dining room and bars. Rates, European plan from $12.60 single, $16.80 double. Auckland restaurants, aside from the hotel dining rooms, are none too exciting, but you might try the Gourmet for continental-style cuisine, Lutèce, with a French flair; Troika, Russian-style specialties, and La Bohème, continental. **Waitomo:** The Hotel Waitomo, near the caves, is a part of the Tourist Hotel Corporation chain—elderly but comfortable enough, with a fair dining room, pleasant cocktail lounge, and a majority of rooms with private bath. Singles from $18, doubles from $35, American plan. **Rotorua:** This tourist mecca *really* needs a top-caliber new hotel. Meanwhile, though, there's the elderly Grand, with a new wing whose rooms all have private bath, a terribly stiff and proper dining room with dreary food and service to match, an amusingly Edwardian lounge, and a nice little bar where the martinis are first-rate. Menu cards and stationery make sure you realize the Grand has known moments of glory. It was, they state, "Patronized by Members of the Royal Family T. R. H. The Duke and Duchess of York, 1927." (In other words, the late King George VI and Queen Elizabeth the Queen Mother.) Rates are American plan only, from $12.50 single, $25 double. Though not a onetime royal retreat, Brent's Hotel gives the impression of being some-

what livelier than the very grand Grand, and it has a sizable
proportion of rooms with bath, a dining room and cocktail lounge,
dancing and entertainment nightly. American plan only; rates
from $11 single, $22 double, with bath. **Wairakei:** The Wairakei
Hotel, one of the better Tourist Hotel Corporation places, is
heated by thermal power, has a thermal swimming pool, its own
non-thermal twelve-hole golf course and tennis courts, a first-class
dining room and cocktail lounge, and a number of rooms with
bath. American plan rates from $18 single, $35 double with bath;
European plan optional. **Lake Taupo:** The Lake Hotel is modern,
almost all of its rooms have private bath, and one can trout-fish
from one's window—almost. Rates including breakfast are the
same single or double, from $8.40. Also on Lake Taupo, but on
the southern shores, at Tokaanu, is the smaller Tokaanu Hotel; it
caters mostly to anglers, and has a thermal swimming pool;
American plan singles from $16.80; doubles from $32.20; European plan optional. **Tongariro National Park:** The Château Tongariro is one of the better Tourist Hotel Corporation hostelries,
and its only need is for more rooms with private bath; it has
attractive public rooms and a lovely setting, good food in both
dining room and cafeteria, congenial cocktail lounge, nine-hole
golf links, tennis courts, bowling green, skiing from July through
September, and trout fishing, to boot, with equipment available
for hire, be you skier or angler. American plan only, from $18.20
single, with bath; $35 double with bath. **New Plymouth:** The
Royal Hotel is small but most of its rooms have bath; a good
overnight spot for visitors to nearby Mount Egmont. **Wellington:**
The Waterloo has been tastefully redecorated with attractive bedrooms (all with private bath), one of the country's best-looking
dining rooms, pleasant lounges, bars, good service; rates are for
bed and breakfast from $11 single, $19 double. The St. George
has private baths in all of its rooms but is sorely in need of
refurbishing, particularly in the case of its rather tacky public
rooms. Food, if you stick to simple things, is okay, though; there's
a congenial bar-lounge, and service is among the best I've had in
New Zealand; rates are American plan only, from $13 single,

$26 double. Others include the Royal Oak, all rooms with bath, from $8.40 single or double, European plan only, and the Grand, newly renovated, and with bed and breakfast rates from $9.45 single or double with bath. Away from the center of town, but very good, is the modern White Heron Lodge; all rooms have bath, TV, radio, coffee-making equipment, there's a swimming pool, American-style coffee shop, and Mermaid Restaurant; they serve until 11 P.M., a shockingly late hour in New Zealand, and there's nightly dancing in the Mermaid Restaurant Tuesday through Saturday—another fairly wicked departure from the norm. Also out of town is the new Tourist Village—a new (1966) hotel-motel complex; European plan only, from about $9 single, $12 double. Wellington restaurants, aside from those in the hotels and the Mermaid in the White Heron, include the Zodiac, which serves what it calls a "smorgasbord" luncheon (just fair), and has entertainment with dinner several nights weekly; the Normandie, with a French menu, Orsini's, with continental-style food, late-hour dinner service (to 11:30 P.M.) and dancing. At the Monde Marie, there's folk dancing nightly, and inexpensive dinners and lunches. **Christchurch:** The in-town hotels are quiet, conservative, and elderly. The Clarendon overlooks the Avon River, most of its rooms have bath, there's a so-so dining room and a cocktail lounge; American plan only, from $13 single with bath, $26 double with bath. Warner's, also central, has an ambiance not unlike the Clarendon, with similar amenities; American plan only, from $12 single, $24 double, with bath. The United Service Hotel is in about the same category, but not many of its rooms have bath; from $13 single with bath, $26 double with bath. The new Russley Lodge, away from the city center, $9 single; $14.80 double with breakfast, and the new 225-room White Heron Lodge, also out of town, averages $15.40 double. **Mount Cook:** The Hermitage is my hands-down choice as New Zealand's finest hotel. The Crown Prince in the Tourist Hotel Corporation chain, is handsomely designed, tastefully furnished, superbly situated with views of Mount Cook from its public rooms and many bedrooms, with first-rank service com-

parable to the finest anywhere, excellent cuisine, a delightful cocktail lounge, and a choice of de luxe accommodation in the main
building or less elaborate rooms in two adjoining lodges. Main
building rooms with bath go from $18 single, $35 double. Rates
given are American plan; there's an optional European plan as
well. **Franz Josef Glacier:** The Franz Josef Hotel, opened in 1964
by the Tourist Hotel Corporation, is built largely of local stone
and timber, snuggles in a forest setting beneath splendid Alpine
backdrop, has a number of rooms with private bath, a fine dining
room, cocktail lounge and public rooms. Rates from $18 single
with bath, $35 double with bath, American plan; European plan
optional. **Lake Te Anau:** The Te Anau is one of the smaller
of the Tourist Hotel Corporation group; a fair proportion of
its rooms have bath, the restaurant sets an excellent table, the
cocktail lounge is inviting, and so is the setting, on the lakefront.
Singles with bath from $18, doubles with bath from $35, American plan; optional European plan. **Milford Sound:** Hotel Milford,
with its inspired situation—Mitre Peak is seen from its front
rooms and lounges—is handsome, well-appointed, with good food
and drink, and fine accommodations; singles with bath from $18,
doubles with bath from $35, American plan; European plan
optional. **Queenstown:** Well, there's O'Connell's. The rooms tend
to be tiny, but some have bath. The dining room is generally
mobbed, the food dull, and the service slow and/or indifferent.
The bar is pleasant, though, and the location convenient and
central. Singles with bath from $13, doubles with bath from $26,
American plan only. And there's Foster's—small, but with great
views of Lake Wakatipu and the mountains, and all rooms have
bath; single or double (same rate for either) from $11 per person
American plan only. Plans are under way for a new seventy-room
hotel which should be completed in 1967 or 1968. Three cheers!
Dunedin: Choose from either the elderly Grand (with the biggest
proportion of private baths in town) or the City; both are central
and American plan; Grand rates go from $12 single, $24 double
with bath; the City is a bit cheaper. **Bay of Islands:** Waitangi Hotel, completed in 1964 by the Tourist Hotel Corporation, and just

right for its tropical setting with pool, outdoor dining patio, restaurant and cocktail lounge, golf course, private beach, facilities for deep-sea fishing and yachting, and attractive rooms, all with private bath; from $18 single, $35 double, American plan. **Cook Islands:** Rarotonga Hotel—small, with no private baths, a dining room and ocean swimming; $6 per person, American plan.

The Samoas

WESTERN SAMOA

Samoa I Sisifo

Entry requirements: A valid passport, a visa (obtainable through New Zealand consulates), and a valid smallpox vaccination certificate. Make application well in advance of departure, for the consulates do not issue visas without the approval of the Western Samoan Government in Apia. **Best time for a visit:** There is relatively little variation in temperature throughout the year. December, the hottest month, averages out at a bit more than two degrees over July, the coolest month. The average, year-round, in Apia, the capital, is eighty-five; and the thermometer never goes over the mid-nineties. But there are, of course, dry and wet seasons, although rain during the wet period is not necessarily of the Sadie Thompson variety. The wet period extends from November through April and the dry months are those intervening, May to October. There hasn't been a true hurricane for three-quarters of a century but there are occasionally severe storms. **Currency:** The Samoan pound, which is at par with the New Zealand pound (which is at par with the United Kingdom pound) and worth $2.80 U.S. There are twenty shillings to a pound, each being worth about fourteen cents. And there are twelve pence to a shilling, so that a Samoan penny is worth a bit more than a U.S. one. After New Zealand converts to the decimal system of currency, Western Samoa is expected to do likewise. You'll find New Zealand currency used

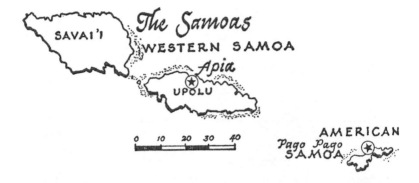

interchangeably with Samoan, and you can, if you wish, use U.S. currency in most places, there being a good deal of interchange between Western Samoa and its neighbor, American Samoa. But I would suggest that you follow the "In Rome, do as the Romans" precept, and convert your funds into the currency of the country. **Film availability:** You're liable to come across what you need, but I definitely suggest you have your own supplies with you. **Languages:** Samoan and English, with government documents and publications, and newspapers, published in both languages. English is widely spoken and taught in all schools. German-speaking visitors will find that that language is understood by old-timers who were educated during the pre-World War I period, and by the small but still influential residue of the old German community. Samoa is pronounced *"Sah-moa"* in Samoan, *"Sa-mo-a"* in English; you'll hear it Samoan style in Western Samoa, but most Americans in American Samoa—and many Samoans, too—use the English pronunciation. **Transportation:** Western Samoa's Faleolo Airport, until it enlarges its runways, cannot take aircraft larger than DC-3s, and as a result air service is limited. Meanwhile, Polynesian Airlines flies DC-3s between Western Samoa and American Samoa, as well as Tonga, Rarotonga in the Cook Islands, and Fiji Airways connects with Suva and Nadi in Fiji, by means of Herons. Faleolo Airport, grass-covered, flanking the sea, and with minimal facilities in its simple terminal, is twenty-three exceptionally scenic miles from Apia, and the airlines generally provide inexpensive transport into town. Getting to Western Samoa by sea is best accomplished on Union Steamship Company of New Zealand's *Matua* and *Tofua,* which ply regularly from Auckland to Fiji, Tonga, and American Samoa, as well as Western Samoa's port of Apia. They remain in port about two days, unloading their own cargo and taking bananas aboard. Passengers not disembarking permanently may utilize that time for sightseeing ashore and continue back to Auckland or intermediate ports. Ships ply weekly between Pago Pago, American Samoa, and Apia. Getting about Western Samoa's main island, Upolu, is no problem. The hotels, airlines, and Union Steamship Company assist visitors in arranging for sightseeing tours, or one may book cars or taxis directly with Gold Star Transport (Beach Road, Apia). Taxi rides within Apia average about forty-five cents. There is no air service between Upolu and Savai'i, the other principal island—only small launches. **Tipping:** Little to none; when done, in minimal amounts. **Clothes:** Very casual. Jackets and ties are unknown during the day (the Head of State received me in white sports shirt and lava-lava) and required after dark only for special receptions and important dinners (I suggest you ask if you're not specifically advised, when invited). Women visitors dress just about as informally as they please during the day; dresses of course in the evening. **Business hours:** Shops close at noon Saturday, and all day Sunday. During the week they're generally open from 8 A.M. to noon, shut up for lunch, and reopen from 1:30 P.M. to 4:30 P.M. **Further information:** Secretary to the Government, Prime Minister's Department, Apia, Western Samoa; Gold Star Transport, Apia, Western Samoa; Burns Philp (South Sea) Co., Ltd., Travel Department, Apia, Western Samoa.

INTRODUCING WESTERN SAMOA

Gertrude Stein, had she ever been asked, might well have opined that a Samoa is a Samoa is a Samoa. But there are *two* Samoas, and the one in question is quite possibly the least known, at least to Americans, and many of their Northern Hemisphere neighbors, of any of the major Pacific island groups.

It is, at the same time, one of the most unusual nations on earth. Although it has been a completely sovereign state since New Year's Day 1962, it

— is the only country which has achieved independence since World War II which has voluntarily chosen *not* to join the United Nations.

— is the first fully independent Polynesian state of modern times.

— is populated by a people surpassed by none in their friendliness toward strangers, but it has established diplomatic relations with but one country.

— was governed, within a single century (the last one) by four foreign powers and two world bodies.

— is where Germany began developing its immense Pacific Empire in the nineteenth century, to lose it all, bloodlessly, in the second decade of the twentieth.

— is where the United States engaged in unabashed nineteenth-century imperialistic activity, which culminated in the dividing of the then one Samoa into two—Western Samoa and American Samoa.

— is one of the world's smallest countries, but still has over fourteen times the area of neighboring American Samoa, and about six times the population.

How did all of this come to pass on these exquisitely beautiful islands in the mid-Pacific? The Samoans, hospitable though they are, had invited no visitors. They had evolved a culture suitable to their environment—a kind of elemental communistic village life, wherein they provided for themselves in a non-cash economy by means of a bountiful nature combined with the crops they grew and the fish they caught.

Enter the beachcombers: But visitors they had, a long line of them, beginning with the Dutchman Jacob Roggeveen in 1721, and continuing with assorted Frenchmen and Britons through the early nineteenth century, when beachcombing Americans and Germans joined other whites in settling down, taking Samoan wives, and asserting themselves, both politically and commercially, in their localities. Then came the missionaries. The pioneers were those of the London Missionary Society. John William, of that group, arrived in 1830 and shortly thereafter the Samoan language appeared in print, for the first time, in religious tracts.

Within half a century Samoa was a Christian land, and a literate land as well. The London Missionary Society (now called the Congregational Christian Church of Western Samoa, and its most populous denomination) led, but there were Wesleyans, Roman Catholics, and later, Seventh-Day Adventists and Mormons. Before too long, Samoans themselves were setting out for other islands, themselves missionaries.

All the while, motivations other than spiritual were occasioning other visits. By 1840 chiefs had made a trade treaty with a British naval captain, and a U.S. expedition under Commander Charles Wilkes had negotiated similarly with the Samoans, the while exploring and surveying the Polynesian islands—many of them for the first time—and researching, also as pioneers, Polynesian flora and fauna. Wilkes' surveys remain the basis of nearly all Samoan land measurements to this day.

Germans, Britons—and Yanks: Then came others of a more permanent nature. The first British consul set up shop in 1847 and that year the first European store was opened in Samoa. In 1853, the first U.S. commercial agent entered the scene and was followed, a few years after, by the first German consul. All of this activity was centered in the harbor community of Apia, which the Europeans simply took over for themselves, not only as residents, traders, and representatives of their home governments, but as administrators as well. Their laws obtained in Apia, with Samoans in control only beyond the town's borders.

The real beginnings of German colonization in the Pacific began with the arrival in Apia of a trader named August Unshelm, in 1856. Within half a decade he had opened branch posts in neighboring islands, and it was his commercial activity which slickly paved the way for the German colonies which were to evolve over the next half century throughout the Pacific. Unshelm's successor, August Weber, doubled as German consul and as trader, and upon taking over in 1861 promptly proceeded to multiply his commercial network, with literally hundreds of subtraders on as many islands. Locally, his great coup was the acquisition of seventy-five thousand acres of land in Samoa which he wanted the German Government to take over as a colony. The Franco-Prussian War at home made this grandiose scheme impossible. German colonization continued later, and a strong German presence had made itself felt in Samoa. The Hamburg firm that Weber and his predecessor represented, J. C. Godeffroy, was dissolved after the Franco-Prussian War but it was succeeded by a giant in name as well as influence, and at the risk of taking too much space I'll spell it out here: Deutsche Handels und Plantagen Gesellschaft der Sudsee Inseln zu Hamburg. Locals, for decades to come, referred to it simply as "The Long Handle Firm" or D.H. & P.G.

Rivalries and intrigues: Meanwhile, back in the hills behind Apia, there were other complications. The Samoans had been fighting like hell among themselves, with intrigues of various sorts arranged between them and in connivance with the constantiy more rivalrous Germans, British, and Americans. By 1872 the high chief of the island of Tutuila (now the principal island of American Samoa) offered a visiting U.S. warship captain naval base rights at Pago Pago in exchange for protection. The offer was spurned (it was, of course, later accepted), but the British and Americans between them continued to work for peace in the region.

It came, in 1873, and so did one Colonel A. B. Steinberger, a special agent of the United States Government, and one of the most remarkable knaves the Pacific islands have ever known. Steinberger helped arrange the peace, a Samoan king took over what was to be an independent state, and Steinberger went home. He was back again, the next year, bearing gifts for the chiefs and intent on staying on to help Samoa on its way as a free state. Once ashore, he declared himself an independent spirit, connected in no way with the U. S. Government, and after drafting a constitution for the new Samoan monarchy, got himself appointed Premier under King Malietoa. In effect, he became a dictator, and even got Malietoa to give way to another claimant to the throne, presumably on a take-turns arrangement.

The "Big Three" and Steinberger: All the while, the Big Three consuls on the scene watched unhappily. Of the three the German—whose country had the most ruthlessly imperialistic plans of all for Samoa—appeared the least perturbed with the Steinberger machinations. The British and American consuls set themselves to investigating, and the denouement came when they found that Steinberger, an American who had gotten himself to be Premier of Samoa, was actually on the payroll of a German trading firm, working for an ultimately German Samoa. The British and the American consuls got a British warship to evict Steinberger from Samoa in 1876, and upon his ultimate return to the States he sued the British for damages (they settled by compromising), and his efforts resulted in the American consul being recalled from Samoa.

Well, that was the end of the free Samoan state. It collapsed upon "Premier" Steinberger's departure, and the multinational intrigue continued. Britain declined protection to the Samoan chiefs. And Washington, upon being asked to provide same in 1877, did likewise. (It did, however, accept the right to set up a naval station at Pago Pago.) By 1889 the confusion had not abated and the major Western powers, in Apia, were quite literally at each other's throats, along with the respective high chiefs who were either their enemies or their allies.

A hurricane—and peace: A hurricane, of all things, saved the day—at least temporarily. On March 16, 1889, seven warships of the three nations were in Apia Harbor. They were so intent on watching each other's movements that they ignored bad-weather signals, and the hurricane that followed swallowed up three German ships and a similar number of U.S. vessels. (The remains of one still can be seen in the harbor.) Only Britain's *Calliope* escaped. But there were fifty-four American dead, and almost a hundred German lives were lost. The Big Three calmed down as a result, and the Berlin Treaty, later that year, provided for still another independent Samoa with consuls of the three powers to govern the city of Apia. But within half a decade a Samoan civil war had broken out. In 1899 the Berlin Treaty had to be scrapped and a new one created. Finally, the destiny of isolated, underdeveloped little Samoa—which had been content living its own life in its own style for many centuries—was settled. Or at least settled until the advent of World War I. The 1899 agreement provided that Britain would withdraw from the Samoan scene, that Germany would take over Western Samoa, and the eastern Samoa isles were to become American Samoa.

As a result of her early trading interests in Samoa, Germany was able to enter the twentieth century with ten Pacific colonies, Western Samoa being a key one. All that was to change during World War I. The German Pacific was defenseless. Australian troops literally walked ashore on all but one of the German islands below the equator and took over. The exception was Western Samoa, where New Zealand forces were deployed. After the war, the new League of Nations turned Western Samoa over to New Zealand, which operated it as a mandate until after World War II, at which time it became a Trusteeship Territory, still administered by New Zealand, but under the aegis of the United Nations Trusteeship Council.

New Zealand on the scene: For its first decade and a half as a colonial power (for that, in effect, was the situation) New Zealand did an absolutely abysmal job. Its representatives on the scene, mostly military men, knew Samoans only as island "natives" to be governed. The fact that Samoans, as Polynesians with an enviable culture of their own, were of the same ethnic group as New Zealand's own highly developed Maoris, appeared to go unnoticed. And while the New Zealanders were not cruel, ruthless colonists in the manner of their German predecessors, they turned deaf ears to the Samoans' demands for self-government. The more they ignored the Samoans and the more callous their treatment of them, the more resentful was the Samoans' reaction.

It was not surprising, therefore, that the originally small Samoan nationalist group, known as the Mau, increased in strength with each year. The occasional New Zealander on the scene who showed any sympathy with Samoan aspirations was deported. Wellington sent "investigators" whose missions proved fruitless. There were anti-New Zealand demonstrations, mass refusals to pay taxes, riots and deaths.

Had the League of Nations been strong it would, of course, have removed New Zealand as the administering power. An election at home was to change things, just as they looked blackest. In 1936 a Labor government was voted into power, and it immediately took steps to right New Zealand's manifold wrongs in Western Samoa. Mau leaders were invited to participate in local government, and the attitude of New Zealand changed as if overnight. Life resumed calmly, quietly, and amicably, and successive New Zealand governments, Conservative as well as Labor, supported the excellent policies of Administrator Sir Alfred Turnbull, who was at his post until 1946.

Self-rule—and independence: Progress was substantial enough so that after World War II, when the Mandate was transformed into a UN Trust Territory, a measure of self-government was introduced. This was expanded in the early 1950s, at New Zealand's suggestion. In 1957 New Zealand turned over control of vast estates it had taken over from the Germans after World War I to the Western Samoans' own Trust Estates Corporation. In 1960, 174 delegates (all but ten of them Samoans) met to write a constitution for the emerging independent nation; in 1961, in a UN-conducted plebiscite, Samoans voted overwhelmingly for sovereignty, and in January 1, 1962 the Independent State of Western Samoa came into being. Western Samoa is neither a republic nor a kingdom. I think it might best be described as a constitutional monarchy, with an elected Head of State taking the place of a King. What it has done, in effect, is to emulate, with imaginative Samoan twists, the governments of New Zealand and Britain. It did not have a solitary Royal Family to work with, however, so it elected, to begin with, co-Heads of State from among a group of four Samoan "Royal Sons," from noble families called *Tamaiga*.

The initial two joint Heads of State were to hold office for life unless they resigned or were removed from office by the Parliament. However, if one died before the other, the survivor was to continue as sole Head of State, until death, at which time the Parliament would elect a successor, presumably from among the four Royal Sons group. In 1963 one of the co-Heads (Tupua Tamases) died, and His Highness, Malietoa Tanumafili II, became the country's first sole Head of State. Handsome, personable, New Zealand-educated, and the father of seven, His Highness served as a member of the New Zealand delegation to the United Nations in New York before Samoan independence, and he was co-chairman of the Working Committee on Independence and later of the Constitutional Convention. Queen Elizabeth II designated him a Companion of the British Empire in 1959.

Power of the chiefs: As Head of State he has a good many powers, and not just ceremonial ones. He, the Prime Minister, and the Cabinet comprise the Executive Council; he appoints the Prime Minister and Cabinet from among the Parliamentary majority, must assent to all legislation before it becomes law, and has the power to grant pardons, reprieves, and to commute court sentences.

The third of the four Royal Sons, Fiame Mataafa, became the country's Prime Minister, and the fourth, Tuimaleifano, is a High Chief. Western Samoa's Parliament is unicameral, with forty-one Samoan and five European members. The latter are elected by individual vote of the European community, but the former—the Samoan members—are elected by the five thousand *matai,* or local chiefs, of the country. The method is hardly the most democratic of ways, as the government is well aware, but the matai are the traditional mainstay of the Samoan way of life, and the young country feels that their serving as electors will help preserve stability during its early years. (So powerful is the matai's role in each clan or family group that the country has one of the tiniest police forces of any in the world; there's virtually no need for the equivalent of cops on local beats in Western Samoa.)

Despite New Zealand's enlightened administration since the mid-thirties, Western Samoa remains a poor, underdeveloped country, almost solely dependent on agricultural crops—copra, cocoa, bananas, some coffee and rubber—for its income.

Concentration on the domestic: It wants, therefore, to keep as much money at home as possible, and for that reason has not gone to the expense of opening diplomatic missions in any country other than New Zealand, which serves as its diplomatic and consular agent abroad. It has not joined the United Nations, either, partly because of expense, partly to avoid the possibility of UN members seeking to influence its policy. And it has not joined the British Commonwealth, in part because of its special relationship with New Zealand, which it believes might no longer feel obligated to contribute to Samoan development.

There have been criticisms that Western Samoa has been moving forward too cautiously and without the required boldness, but help has been received from its former occupier, Germany; from its neighbor, the United States; from various Commonwealth countries other than New Zealand, and from the UN, which has been helping it plan a far-reaching economic program. As announced in 1965 this will embrace extensive land development, the creation of a proper handicrafts industry, the opening of food processing plants, and a plunge into tourism—which for some reason is considered a dirty word locally and is known by the euphemism, "visitor industry."

Conflict of cultures: A major problem for the country is the conflict of cultures. Samoans have learned to enjoy what money can bring them, but many still have not been able to make the change from village life, where their family will always care for them, to the demands of the Western system, which insists upon the earning of wages on a regular, organized basis. The country is today not without prophets of doom.

But at least one visitor remains an optimist. Wages may be higher in neighboring American Samoa (to which several thou-

sand Western Samoans have immigrated), but there is a buoyant
spirit that appears all-pervasive in Western Samoa—the kind of
feeling that comes when a people is at last on its own, making its
own progress or its own mistakes. Western Samoa has seen
enough of the blunders of others committed on its own territory
to benefit by them. It planned for its own independence carefully, indeed ingeniously, attempting to draw upon the best of its
own ways with the best of the West's. It is willing to give up the
international limelight and the world recognition which would
come from UN membership and a chain of foreign embassies,
to concentrate first on its own front yard. How this beautiful
little nation—with a populace less than that of Albany, New
York—moves from youth toward maturity is bound to have a
profound and meaningful effect on its island neighbors. Much of
the world still does not know Western Samoa, but the eyes of the
Pacific are upon this Polynesian pioneer.

YOUR VISIT TO WESTERN SAMOA

A developed tourist industry has advantages—and disadvan-
tages. The former include extensive facilities, such as hotels and
transport, which would mean in the case of Western Samoa that
the ordinary visitor could easily have a look at Savai'i, the bigger
but less developed of the two major islands. But Savai'i has no
hotels and no air service. The only access is by small launch.
The only way a visit is possible is to arrange for accommodation
in one of the villages, and to book passage over and back on
the launch. For most of us this is out of the question, so that
leaves the principal island, forty-five-mile-long Upolu. But don't
think that because Upolu is the site of the capital city and sole
town of substance that it's spoiled rotten for the visitor. On the
contrary. The relative dearth of tourists is what gives this island
so much of its charm. Nowhere in the Pacific is the visitor more
warmly welcomed, on no island are smiles wider or hospitality
more gracious. The good-looking Western Samoans are outra-

geous charmers and make even a brief visit to their richly verdant country more than worthwhile.

Anthropologists claim that today's Samoans are the purest survivors of the early Polynesian peoples and that traditional Polynesia is nowhere better observed than in the Samoas. With all of the European influence—for better or for worse—that these islands have known, it goes without saying that Western ways have made inroads. But the Samoans, aside from embracing Christianity, cling stubbornly to *f'aa Samoa*—the Samoan way. And *f'aa Samoa* revolves around the village, with the result that all of Western Samoa has but one city—and it was developed largely by Europeans. Within each village are the family or clanlike groups known as *aiga* (pronounced *eye-ing-a*), whose members are related either by blood, marriage, or adoption, and can embrace several generations. All are under the immediate authority of the matai, who bears the title of chief or orator. (The orator in Western Samoa is similar to the "talking chief" of American Samoa; he serves as spokesman/adviser/patronage-dispenser for the head chiefs.) The aiga is a kind of paternalistic communistic enterprise, with everyone responsible to the matai. Members farm as directed, fish as directed, make tapa, or weave mats as directed. The results of the group's labor are jointly shared, and in return for their efforts they know they always have a home and that they'll be cared for when ill or aged. The matai does his best to promote their welfare in the village community, whose chief, or *alii,* is elected from among the matai who, collectively, constitute the village council.

Samoan villages are invariably attractive, neat, and inviting. Houses, called *fale* (*fah*-lay), are unique in Pacific island design, and in my view the most ingenious of them all. Generally oval in shape, they have floors of crushed coral or stones, and thatched roofs over handsome, decoratively carved beams which are joined together with handmade coconut-fiber cord. The outer walls are no more than the Samoan equivalent of wide-slatted venetian blinds, woven mats serving as the slats. They are closed only if the weather is inclement, so that breezes are never prevented from doing a job of ventilation. As a result, the passerby gets a good glimpse—whether he wants it or not—of Samoan family life. (Needless to say, there are times when he does well not to stare.) Although some Samoan homes now have Western-style furniture, many Samoans still have not even taken to chairs. One sits cross-legged, American Indian fashion, or with one's legs under one. (Legs extended into the center of the *fale* are considered bad manners, although this is usually overlooked in the case of visitors.) At bedtime, finely woven mats are taken down from their storage place in the rafters of the *fale,* and a pile of them perform the functions of a mattress. Conventional sheets and blankets are used.

Smiles and handshakes are commonplace, as would be expected in such a gregarious society, and camera bearers are free, within the bounds of common courtesy, to snap away. Village houses are invariably set around a central court, usually grassy, called a *malae.* The most imposing house is the chief's and it is called a *maota.* There's always a guest house, too, kept available for village visitors, and there are separate edifices for cooking, which is done in ovens, or *umus.* These consist of above-ground beds of heated rocks. At feasts—*fia-fias*—taro, breadfruit, and bananas go directly over the rocks, and over these go pork and fish, then coverings of banana leaves. Food is served on banana-leaf "plates," and eaten with fingers or folded-leaf scoops.

Sanitation, I must point out, makes eminent good sense insofar as the village environment itself is concerned. But prospective swimmers and sunbathers are not at all charmed by the arrangement. Each village, at least those on or near the sea—as so many are—has a pier of its own jutting into the water. At its end is a privy, and, well, instead of a modern flush system, there's the vast Pacific Ocean.

Western Samoan villages can contain as many as thirty households, with one to several dozen members in each household. Aside from the aforementioned fia-fias, or feasts, the ceremony of drinking of *ava* (known in other Polynesian islands as *kava,* and in Fiji as *yaqona*) is common in Samoa and is accompanied by an elaborate ritual only somewhat similar to the other islands'. While the drink is being prepared (in Samoa, this is done by a young woman known as a *taupo;* she serves as a sort of ceremonial assistant to the chief until her retirement at marriage) with ground pepper tree roots and water, in a wooden bowl known as a *tanoa,* there are introductory speeches from the talking chief. The drink is eventually served to each guest in order of seniority, in polished half-coconut cups. In Samoa, one first pours a sprinkle of ava under his mat as an offering to the gods, then lifts his cup, the while intoning *"manuia"* to his hosts. When they come through with *"soifua"* it is, at long last, time to drink up. Women guests, thirsty though they may be, do not drink at all. A tap of the bowl with the fingers, as a sign of respect, is as far as they can go. Ava has many fans among Western visitors, but even those who come to like it admit that it is an acquired taste.

Apia is by no means a showplace but it's neat, pleasant, terribly difficult to get lost in, delightful to stroll about, and, with the only proper accommodation in the country, the sole point of departure for excursions. The core of the town is Main Beach Road, which fronts the crescent-shaped harbor. Aggie Grey's Hotel is at the lower end and the government-owned Casino Hotel (which, hopefully, will be replaced by a brand-new luxury hotel 'ere long) is at the other end. In between are a number of the town's many churches, the handsome Public Library with an interesting façade based on traditional designs, the Post Office and Bank of Western Samoa, the elderly Government Offices in a rambling white frame building, the spanking new New Zealand Commissioner's office (the country's only foreign government mission), and an assortment of mercantile establishments.

The wreck of the German ship *Adler*—destroyed in the hurricane of 1889—still is to be seen in the harbor. Additional commercial activity continues on Vaea Street, leading off Main Beach Road, and a requisite is Mulinuu, a bit away from the center of town, and the site of the Parliament of Samoa, designed in traditional *fale* style, even to details like a thatched roof and open walls. (Visitors are welcome to attend sessions; if one is on, try and spot the mace-bearer, whose uniform is the Samoan lava-lava, and who will be glad to pose for pictures if he's not busy.) A new law-courts building, Western in design, is across the road from Parliament; it too admits visitors.

And to be noted, too, is the monument to independence, erected by alumni of government schools, and with inscriptions in both Samoan and English. There is swimming on the handsome beach at *Laulii,* just a few miles from town.

Vailima is the house in which Robert Louis Stevenson lived with his wife from 1890 until his death in December 1894. It is superbly situated amidst beautifully tended gardens high in the hills, about three miles from central Apia. The central portion of the house dates from Stevenson's time, with the wings somewhat newer additions. Vailima was the official residence of the New Zealand High Commissioner in pre-Independence days. When independence came, the house was vacated. (The High Commissioner was appointed the first New Zealand Commissioner—or ambassador—to the new nation, and moved into a private house.) Vailima was earmarked as the official residence of the Head of State, but the country started out with joint Heads of State, and neither of them moved in. It remained vacant, except for state receptions, until one of the co-Heads of State died. At that time his survivor, His Highness Malietoa Tanumafili II, moved in with his large family. The room in which Stevenson worked, with the chair in which he wrote and other mementos of his residence, have been preserved as they were. The house is open only to visitors who have secured special permission from the Secretary to the Government in the Prime Minister's Department, Apia. But any visitor may make the five-hundred-foot ascent, by foot, up steep Mount Vaea, where Stevenson and his wife are buried. Carved on his grave is his own "Under the wide and starry sky" epitaph, and the words he wrote honoring his wife, "Teacher, Tender Comrade, Wife."

Excursions from Apia: The *barrier reef* that flanks much of the coast and the lagoons within are requisites for the skin-diver, swimmer, and for any visitor interested in shells, coral, and tropical fish. The marine life is brilliant. *Lefaga* is an on-the-beach village of great charm. Indeed, the film *Return to Paradise,* with Gary Cooper, was filmed there in 1952. The drive en route is a lovely one—as what Western Samoan drive isn't?—and ideally, can be a pleasant half-day's excursion. *Mulifanua* is the biggest of the country's copra plantations and one of the biggest of any in the South Pacific. A twenty-five-mile drive from Apia, it is at the end of a route which embraces a bevy of exceptionally lovely villages as well as the Christian Congregational Church's Training College at Malua. *Mafa Pass* takes one past nearly twenty miles of Pacific Ocean beaches and fronting villages, to Falefa Falls, and thence inland through the forest to Fuipisia Falls, 180 feet high and in a lush, photogenic setting.

Poutasi is a splendid drive, affording a panorama of great plantations and mountains, and the distant islands of Savai'i (largest in Western Samoa), Manono, and Apolima. There are, of course, countless other destinations. Take a picnic lunch from your hotel, plenty of film, some cold drinks, and your coolest and most comfortable clothes. Don't hesitate to stop at any village that strikes your fancy. You'll be welcome at all of them. Parades of children will follow you about, mothers will smile shyly from the doors of their fales, an occasional police officer—in immaculate khaki under a London bobby-type helmet (the same as worn by New Zealand police) will pass the time of day with you. If you're lucky you'll see fine-mats being woven, tapa cloth being made from bark, fale roofs being thatched. You'll drive past youngsters en route home from school (girls in cotton uniform dresses, boys in uniforms which incorporate the lava-lava instead of shorts). You'll revel in the splendor of the seashore, the mountains, and the lagoons. You'll laugh with the Samoans in their villages. You'll want to take more pictures than you've film for, and you'll wish, when you leave the country, that there was some sort of fountain in which you could drop a coin to be assured of a return visit.

WHAT TO BUY

Having retained so much of their traditional culture, the Samoans remain excellent craftsmen. Western Samoan prices are
cheaper, by and large, than those of American Samoa, workmanship is frequently excellent, and the range wide. You'll find
miniature ava bowls carved from a single piece of wood, miniature
fales and canoes, ceremonial clubs, tapa cloth (some imported
from Tonga), all kinds of woven-mat products including place
mats, baskets, shells, and coral, a variety of shell necklaces,
earrings, and bracelets, and records of Samoan music. Aggie
Grey's Curio Shop, adjoining the hotel by that name, has an
excellent selection; no bargaining. Vendors of handicrafts congregate in front of the Burns Philp Store, and with them bargaining is the rule.

CREATURE COMFORTS

When we consider that Apia is the capital of a country which
is just beginning to think about tourism as an industry, and
which for so many years has had its principal Western influence
from New Zealand—which is itself a beginner in the hotel and
restaurant fields—it does not do at all badly in these departments.
There are two hotels of substance. Aggie Grey's, run by a charming Samoan lady by that name, is synonymous with South Pacific hotelkeeping. It is a rambling frame structure with a lovely
rear garden, fresh-water swimming pool, and a series of quite
comfortable bungalows surrounding it—all of them with private
baths, and supplemented by older main building rooms, and a new
1966 wing. There's a bar-cocktail lounge on the lower veranda and
a pleasant dining room with not-bad meals on the upper veranda.
Service is pleasant; indeed, the waitresses at the drop of a hat
will go into their dance routines as soon as dinner is over, and
gentlemen guests are always welcome as partners. Bungalow

rates are about $10 per person per day, American plan; main building accommodation is cheaper. Aggie or her staff can help arrange sightseeing and guide service. The government-owned *Casino Hotel* dates from the German period—long and rambling, high-ceilinged, spacious and spotless lobby, big bedrooms (some with bath), and a number of New Zealanders, who are working for the Western Samoan Government, as permanent guests. Singles with bath are about $10, doubles with bath about $15, American plan; less, of course, for rooms without bath. (The government plans on replacing this hotel with a new hundred-room one, utilizing Samoan architectural motifs.) Night life is minimal in Apia. The hotel bars are for guests only, but are quite good about serving anyone who looks like a short-term tourist, whether he's in residence or not. (Liquor is sold only to permit holders on a point system; visitors and European residents may get permits easily, but it's tough for the Samoans. In 1963 there were only 1250 permits extant—to give you an idea. As a result, many Samoans make their own, at home, and the press is urging new legislation.) There are a few private and semi-private clubs (Five-Star and Polynesian are open to the public; Apia and RSA are private but members can take guests). There are the movies, and there are occasional fia-fias, the earlier-described Samoan feasts with traditional food, singing and dancing, which you do well to look for and—by hook or by crook—attend.

AMERICAN SAMOA

Entry requirements: For visits up to thirty days, U.S. citizens need only proof of citizenship (this need not be a passport, but it might just as well be if one is traveling elsewhere in the South Pacific, where passports are required), a valid smallpox vaccination certificate, and onward transportation (airline or steamship ticket). Foreign tourists' entry requirements are similar, except that valid passports are obligatory. Note that if a trip to the Independent State of Western Samoa is to be combined with one to American Samoa, there is a need not only for a passport but for a Western Samoan visa, obtainable from New Zealand consulates. **Best times for a visit:** Somerset Maugham may not have been overexaggerating in *Rain*. It *is* possible to undergo Sadie Thompson-type downpours, particularly during the rainy season, which extends from November through April. (Pago Pago averages some two hundred inches of rain a year—just about twice that of Apia, capital of Western Samoa, which is but a few air minutes distant.) The driest period is that of the remaining months, May through October. Temperatures vary little the year round, with maximums in the low to mid-nineties, and minimums in the seventies. The humidity is pretty much the same regardless of month, averaging about 83 percent. Heaviest storms occur during the December–March period. Evenings generally are cool and delightful. Don't hesitate over a visit even during the wet season; you may be fortunate enough to experience not a drop of rain for several days, or you may have only an occasional shower. **Currency:** The U.S. dollar. (U.S. postage is used also, and mainland rates apply, so this is a bargain spot for the dispatch of airmail postcards, six cents, and letters, eight cents!) **Film availability:** Generally good stocks of Kodak color and black-and-white are available. There is black-and-white processing as well. **Languages:** Samoan and English, with a good deal of the latter. Improved educational facilities are helping increase English-language fluency a good deal. **Transportation:** The handsome new airport at Tafuna, nine miles from Pago Pago, is one of the most beautiful in the Pacific. Its terminal is imaginatively designed in modified Samoan fale style, and there are refreshment facilities and a duty-free shop. There is a nine-thousand-foot runway. Pan Am jets fly in from the West Coast and Hawaii, and from Sydney; that line also flies DC-7s between Tafuna and Nadi, Fiji. Polynesian Airlines' DC-3s link Tafuna with Faleolo, the international airport of Western Samoa, near Apia. Round trip fare is about $26. Ships that call at Pago Pago include

Matson Lines' *Mariposa* and *Monterey,* one of which calls
every three weeks en route to the U. S. West Coast from
the south. Union Steamship Company of New Zealand's
Tofua, out of Auckland, calls regularly, and there are occasional passenger-carrying freighters. There is weekly service on small ships between Pago Pago and Apia, Western
Samoa, but I would suggest going by plane. There is no
regular air service among the islands of American Samoa,
but a small ship does ply regularly between Pago Pago
and the Manua Group islands. Taxis charge three dollars
for a ride from the airport to town, about fifty cents for
in-town rides, and five dollars per hour for chartered sightseeing drives. You can spot a taxi, even without a sign,
by its license plate; all cabs have the prefix "T". Individual
drivers can arrange tours, as can the hotel, and licensed
tour agents, among them the travel-tour department of
B. F. Kneubuhl, one of the oldest general trading companies
in the South Pacific. **Tipping:** There is no tipping in American Samoa. Bravo! **Clothes:** As light and cool as you can
produce. During the day even the Governor works in a
short-sleeved sports shirt, tieless, like everyone else. **Business
hours:** Pago Pago shops are open from 8 A.M. to noon, and
1 P.M. to 5 P.M., Monday through Friday, and 8 A.M.
to 1 P.M. Saturday. They're closed Sunday. The sole bank,
Bank of American Samoa, is open from 8 A.M. to noon,
Monday through Friday. **Further information:** Office of
Tourism, Government of American Samoa, Pago Pago,
American Samoa; Office of Territories, United States Department of Interior, Washington, D.C.

INTRODUCING AMERICAN SAMOA

It's tiny. No question about it. The entire area of American
Samoa is seventy-six square miles, and the population still is less
than twenty-five thousand. (By contrast, next-door Western Samoa

is a veritable giant, with some 130,000 people and its eleven hundred square miles.) But, since Secretary of the Interior Stewart Udall, the most creative man in that post since the New Deal's Harold "Old Curmudgeon" Ickes, sent Idahoan H. Rex Lee out to be Governor, in 1961, the eyes of the Pacific have been focused on this "unincorporated territory."

No one had given American Samoa the attention it deserves since Margaret Mead researched her classic *Coming of Age in Somoa* there—and that was in the 1920s. But Lee, used to tough problems after his distinguished service with the Interior Department's Bureau of Indian Affairs, set out to make changes, in what even the conservative *Reader's Digest* had termed "America's shame in the South Seas."

Navy days—and neglect: The pre-Lee years of American Samoa had been anything but happy ones. I've dealt with them at some length, as they relate to neighboring Western Samoa, in the section on that country. Until 1899 there was but one Samoa. It was in that year that a treaty signed by Germany, Britain, and the United States dissolved the highly unsuccessful Samoan kingdom (which had had a disastrous ten-year trial as a result of an 1889 treaty signed by the same powers) and created the two Samoas. Western Samoa comprises those islands west of the 171st degree of west longitude; American Samoa (still occasionally called Eastern Samoa) is that group to the east of the 171st degree. Even earlier, though, the harbor of Pago Pago had been ceded to the United States for use as a naval and coaling station, but it was in 1900 that the American Navy Department actually stepped in as administrator.

It stayed for half a century, and during all that period, while one short-term naval officer followed another as Governor, American Samoa was considered a military installation. The resident Samoans were looked upon as little more than peripheral. The Navy dealt with things like education, health, and sanitation only when it was felt that their complete neglect would impair operation of the base. Indeed, in 1922, the Secretary of the Navy said: "Government aid (to American Samoa) should be discouraged as far as possible and the people encouraged to do more for themselves." But there was not much encouragement.

Aside from the Navy brass, the only other outsiders on the island were the missionaries, doing their best to run some schools and their churches (the London Missionary Society and Roman Catholics date from the 1830s and 1840s, Mormons from the 1880s), and a handful of general traders who were successful through the years in getting the government to keep new competition away. "Everything was taken out [by the traders]," Governor Lee has said, "and nothing put back in. Nothing was done by them to encourage education—or anything else."

Change in the fifties: In 1951, the fueling operations at the naval base having become virtually obsolete, President Truman closed the station and transferred the administration of the territory from the Navy to the Department of the Interior. One would have thought that things could only get better after five decades of disdain and neglect. But the result was an almost complete vacuum in the American Samoan economy. For the base had been its sole industry, and the gap that resulted made for hard times. Really skilled administration was needed more than ever, but none was forthcoming. The early Interior Department Governors—even including a Samoan—could get nowhere near the help and attention that was needed from Washington. Deterioration—economic, political, social—set in. At a time—the decade of the fifties—when the European colonial powers were giving their possessions more attention than they'd ever received, America was letting its poorest territory become even poorer.

That's why the Lee administration is one of the most dramatic of modern South Pacific adventures. Within half a decade American Samoa has embarked, on a scale unprecedented in the entire region, on a revolutionary rehabilitation program. Indeed, it is the changes that have been and are being made that make this little speck on the map so exciting to visit today.

Enter Governor Lee: Lee had two advantages before he even arrived on the scene. First was the wholehearted support and carte blanche blessing of Secretary Udall. Second was solid Washington experience, a knowledge of the workings of Congress, and valuable contacts in places that count. He found, on his arrival, that the schools were in a disgraceful state—in a place where half the populace was under eighteen. The sole high school had room for only a third of those qualified to attend. Most teachers in the schools throughout the territory had difficulty communicating in English—the language of instruction—and had had little more than the equivalent of a Stateside fourth- or fifth-grade education. (The relatively few who got through with decent educations were leaving for greener pastures in Hawaii and the mainland.)

Even on so small a place as Tutuila (the main American Samoan island) the paved road was virtually unknown. Electric power worked at times, was uncooperative more often. Only a single outside industry had been attracted to replace the vacuum created by the demise of the naval base. Pago Pago, in the mid-twentieth century, was little changed from the ramshackle hamlet which was the setting of Maugham's *Rain*. To make matters more urgent, some two hundred delegates of the six-nation South Pacific Commission were to hold their first conference on American soil in little more than a year. And no one, up to that point, had known quite how to handle them, or, presumably, cared about the impressions they were to receive.

Governor Lee got busy. With his boss, Secretary Udall, and the White House behind him, he got Congress to appropriate $10 million for his first year's program, which was quite a jump from the average of $1.5 million for previous years. All in all, since that time more than $26 million have been appropriated for American Samoan development.

New look, new concepts, results: First came a spanking new airport with a nine-thousand-foot runway capable of taking jets —to make communications with the islands commensurate with our era. (Still later came a new terminal, a pair of modified jumbo Samoan fales, with a variety of facilities and an actual Ceremonial Great Fale, as well.) Then came a strikingly designed and much-needed community auditorium (later named by the chiefs in honor of the Governor). Sorely overcrowded Pago Pago High School got

an addition of three modern buildings. Paved roads (the first outside of town in Tutuila's history) were laid, linking Pago Pago
with the new airport and flanking a good bit of the bay. And
a cluster of apartment houses went up—not luxurious perhaps by
Stateside standards, but modern and functional so as to make
Samoan employment attractive to Stateside personnel. All of these
facilities were ready, thanks to emergency construction help from
Navy Seabees, in time for the South Pacific Commission conference.

Then Lee went on to other projects, and of them education
has been the most truly revolutionary. Lee found himself faced
with a dilemma. How to modernize an appallingly ineffective system that was largely staffed by ill-prepared Samoan teachers—
several hundred of them? He had a choice of replacing them with
Stateside teachers, which would be enormously expensive, would
necessitate new housing and facilities, would put a sizable group
of Samoans out of work, and might very well disturb the socio-
cultural pattern of the islands. His alternative sounded crackpot
and harebrained to many: an educational television system which
would not *supplement* live-teacher instruction in the classrooms
(as it does on the mainland) but would virtually *replace* it, with
Samoan teachers acting only as on-the-spot administrators of lessons, discussions, and the like, and instruction coming from TV
sets in each classroom, via a central educational TV center run
by a relative handful of TV experts, who would turn their posts
over to Samoans as soon as they became qualified.

TV in the tropics: Governor Lee engaged the National Association of Educational Broadcasters to survey the situation locally and then presented his plan to Congress, which came through
with an initial $1.6 million for three channels, and the assurance
that more would be coming if they worked out. After months of
deliberation and experimentation, engineers decided that the best
place for the TV transmitter—essential to the program—would be
atop sixteen-hundred-foot Mount Alava, behind Pago Pago, and
that the station would best be linked to town by means of a
cable car. That was completed in 1964, along with the quarter-
million-dollar Telecasting Center—as modern a TV studio as one

can find anywhere, with a million dollars' worth of the most up-to-date equipment, and a staff of mainland experts in educational TV.

Then came schools themselves. Forty ramshackle establishments in the villages are being replaced by half as many consolidated schools, all simply but handsomely built on traditional fale lines, with a TV receiver in each classroom. (The first order was for three hundred and the winning bidder was Motorola.) There will be new schools, too, on the small islands of the territory's Manua group, and even one (sans TV, alas) on unique, privately owned Swain's Island. The station's signals will extend as far as Western Samoa and Tonga. Governor Lee has offered their facilities both to Tonga and Western Samoa, with which he has established excellent relations. Both expressed interest, their only reservations being curricula, for both Tonga and Western Samoa follow the New Zealand pattern, and American Samoa's is, of course, that of the United States. Each consolidated school is staffed by Samoan teachers under the supervision of a mainland educational TV expert. In each of the villages these mainlanders are moving into the villages, the first outsiders to do so in the territory's history, except for missionaries. The system will be extended into the high schools as well, and a brand new school —a striking series of a dozen-odd fales, each giant-sized and holding a number of classrooms—is being constructed, too.

The system's initial expense is, of course, high, but operational expenses will be minimal for years to come, and the great benefit expected of the system—admittedly experimental—is the way in which it should be able to improve the educational standards of an underdeveloped area in a decade or less, instead of the several decades which would be required by conventional methods. Additionally, the system—if a success—would have applicability in countless other underdeveloped areas of the Pacific, as well as Asia, Latin America, and Africa, where the need for a well-educated people is equally great.

Samoa for the Samoans: But there are other facets of the new American Samoa. A new and more liberal constitution was drawn up in 1960, before Lee's arrival. But since he has been on the scene the basic laws of the document have actually been enacted into statutes, so that the two-house legislature—Senate composed of fifteen matai (chiefs) elected by village councils; House of Representatives composed of eighteen elected individuals—actually has some effective power for the first time in its history and, concurrently, the power of the Governor is greatly reduced. (It is interesting to note, here, that American Samoa's legislature is more democratically chosen than Western Samoa's; in that country's one-house Parliament only matais have the vote; in American Samoa members of the lower house are elected by popular vote.)

Tuna and tourism: Economic development is seeing great strides. The one tuna processing plant on the scene since 1954 (operated by Van Camp) has been supplemented by another, of comparable size, operated by Star-Kist. In addition, the American Can Company has set up a factory where tins for both plants are made, providing jobs for still additional Samoans. (The tuna, incidentally, are caught by Japanese, Okinawans, and Taiwanese, rather than Samoans; their tuna boats come down and fish in Samoan waters for limited periods.) The Governor envisions even more food canning and processing plants in the future. Additionally, Lee, who has given the people a feeling of self-confidence by making it possible for them to participate more fully in their government, also is encouraging them to open businesses of their own, to compete with the handful of big traders who have had a virtual monopoly for decades.

Even more exciting is American Samoa's debut in tourism. Until recently, its only pleasure visitors had been the one-day-ashore visitors on passenger liners. With the introduction of jet service still more tourists came by air—only to find severely limited accommodation available. However, by 1964 Governor Lee had arranged for the first proper hotel in the territory's history. But he did it the hard way. Rather than let outsiders come in and finance it entirely, staffing it with their people and leaving only lower-level jobs for Samoans, he insisted that it was to have a basis of Samoan financing. The result was the unique

American Samoan Development Corporation, in which twelve hundred Samoans have pledged a quarter of a million dollars, some having as little as a single ten-dollar share.

The rest of the money came in loans from the Bank of American Samoa and the Bank of Hawaii, in addition to a million dollars from the United States Area Redevelopment Agency in Washington. The hotel provides a hundred jobs for Samoans directly, and another hundred indirectly, and the hope is that it will be possible to train Samoans for management jobs not only in the hotel but in other phases of what is expected to become a rapidly expanding tourist industry. "The purpose of the federal investment here would be negated," Governor Lee stated, "if the 'New Samoa' found the local Polynesian people no longer the masters of their own homeland—limited to service as busboys and charwomen and cooks in an alien economic community."

The Lee programs and reforms, by and large, have met with tremendous enthusiasm from the Samoans. There have, of course, been opponents of his moves from entrenched personages, both Samoan and otherwise, with the bulk of the opposition coming from the wealthy traders—most of whom have, through the years, married Samoan women, but who still appear to regard the mass populace patronizingly, and who, understandably enough, would prefer to see the boat not rocked and their privileged positions weakened. (They are particularly unhappy over the new income tax, which they believe discriminates against them.)

Blueprints for progress: There still is much progress to be made. The villages of American Samoa, like those of Western Samoa, still have no modern sanitation systems, using drop-latrines at the ends of piers jutting into sea or lagoon. A privy-construction program is under way and should do away with the widely prevalent intestinal parasites with which most Samoans are bothered, at the same time making the territory—and its beaches —infinitely more appealing to the visitor. Filariasis (caused by certain mosquitoes, and occasionally leading to elephantiasis) is almost under control by means of a mass-pill campaign, and so is

tuberculosis. School lunch programs are attempting to correct mal-
nutrition among children. Funds already have been earmarked for
a much-needed new hospital to supplement an old frame one
which is a relic of Navy days. (There has, fortunately, been a
nurses' training school in operation for decades.) Other problems
appear, too. Currently, the American Samoan has the status of
an "American national." He is not, in other words, a full-fledged
U.S. citizen, but his status does give him the protection of the
U. S. Government and the right to travel to and through the
United States without restriction. It does not allow him to vote
in national elections or serve on juries. (A few Samoans, mostly
ex-servicemen, have become naturalized citizens during their service period.)

"Nationals" to citizens: Consequently, there is the hope, on
the one hand, that the time will come when all Samoans will be
U.S. citizens, but on the other, that if they do their land will not
disappear from under them. This conceivably could happen, because restrictive covenants in land deeds have been declared un-
constitutional under the U. S. Constitution, and in American
Samoa the law strictly stipulates that land can be owned only by
full- or half-blood Samoans—and no others. Even more immediate
than full citizenship is a move for the appointment of an American
Samoan delegate—as is the case with Puerto Rico—to the federal
Congress.

There is concern, too, that the modernization of the territory—
drawing people from their traditionally communistic and paternalistic village life to a cash economy and to the material possessions which cash buys—is not only diluting the Samoan culture
but placing the people in an in-between never-never land where
the conflicts before them are difficult to resolve. Even now, for
example, tin roofs are cheaper, easier to erect, and therefore becoming more popular than the beautiful thatch roofs of the fales.
A movement is afoot—led, indeed, by the Governor—to preserve
the thatch, but tin may be symbolic of the price American
Samoa may have to pay for progress.

YOUR VISIT TO AMERICAN SAMOA

Make no mistake about it: American Samoa is incredibly beautiful. Indeed, I know of no South Pacific island any lovelier. Much bigger Western Samoa is undeniably handsome, as I have tried to make clear in the section on that country. But its natural beauty has not quite the striking and dramatic brilliance of its smaller neighbor, particularly its main island of Tutuila.

Tutuila is home to all but a few thousand of American Samoa's inhabitants and is the only island developed for visitors. Some twenty-five miles long, it varies in width from two miles (where fiordlike Pago Pago Harbor cuts into the coastline) to six miles. Superb purple-green mountains—heavily wooded—extend almost the entire length of the island, and there are, as a consequence, breathtakingly beautiful valleys whose extremities dip right into the azure sea. The chief peaks are the famous Rainmaker (Mount Pioa, 1717 feet), Alava (site of the TV tower, 1609 feet), and the highest, Matafao (2141 feet).

Most of the villages flank the south and west coasts, although some are a bit inland on the southern mountain slopes. Basically, the villages are quite like those I've described in Western Samoa —fales—oblong thatched houses on platforms of ground coral or small stones, with open walls whose woven-mat blinds are lowered only in rain or wind. Like their counterparts in the other Samoa, the fales are clustered around a central green, or *malae,* with the chief's house the most imposing and the highest elevated, and a guest fale only slightly less impressive. Cooking, done in heated rocks above the ground, takes place in separate thatched buildings, and the only real differences between these villages and those in Western Samoa is the frequent U.S.-style baseball game one is likely to encounter on Tutuila. One tends to find more tin roofs on fales here, too, and a bit more adherence to Western-style clothes, although most women still wear long two-piece *puletasis,* and men lava-lavas.

The American Samoan has seen far more visitors than the Western Samoan, and he has known half a century of misrule from Americans, so that his welcome is not apt to be quite so spontaneous as that of the Western Samoan, nor are grins as likely to appear on his face as quickly. The New Deal, if that it may be called, of the Lee administration is helping to do away with feelings of distrust, but they cannot disappear overnight, and the visitor must be understanding. There is usually no problem with photographing Samoans in their villages, so long as one exercises common courtesy and asks permission before clicking, particularly when the lens is focused on fale interiors. The most willing subjects, as everywhere, are young children. The best roads are along the south coast, but the rugged, sparsely populated north coast is well worth looking at as well.

Sightseeing tours, by private taxi costing about ten dollars per day, are easily arranged and can be custom-made to suit the passengers. You will want to stop at villages all along the way, and I should certainly make it a point to stop at one of those which is the site of a new consolidated "television" school. That at *Lua* is particularly interesting, and should you go during the school day, ask the principal or one of the teachers if you may peep into a classroom or two and watch the kids watch their lessons coming from the TV screen. It's quite an experience.

Other villages which might well be on your itinerary: *Anua,* where much of the local woodcarving is done; *Laulii,* whose locals have one of the island's finest dance troupes and where you should try to take in a performance of the *suva,* as it is called; *Vaitogi,* where legend has it that the children's songs drew sharks and giant turtles to the shoreline, and *Leone,* with its impressive harbor.

Pago Pago (pronounced Pango Pango with a soft "ng") is of course visitors' headquarters. It stretches itself, snakelike, along the waterfront for several miles, and its central portion is built about the malae, a grassy square dominated by the white frame Government Headquarters (site of the Governor's office and other Executive Department offices) across from which is a fale at which handicrafts are sold. To be seen in Pago Pago are the striking new Lee Auditorium, the Broadcasting Center, which is headquarters for the earlier-described Educational TV network, and—via a six-minute cable car ride—the magnificent panorama from the observation deck at the TV transmitter building atop 1609-foot Mount Alava. No other South Pacific isle affords such an unbelievable view and, with good weather, that view includes Western Samoa and Manua. The tuna canneries are open to visitors, should they interest you.

On weekdays central Pago Pago makes for an interesting stroll, with the stores of the big traders, the United States Post Office (replete with Zip Code Number 96920 affixed to the sign above the entrance) and, most interesting, the passersby on the streets. On Sundays church is the big event. Samoans have beautiful voices and one does well to take in a service at one of the many, many churches. On that day of the week, women wear white or pastel puletasis and men don white lava-lavas, over which they wear white shirts, dark ties, and light jackets. The showplace of Pago Pago is, of course, the new Pago Pago Inter-Continental Hotel, overlooking the bay on the promontory known as Goat Island. Arrangements can be made for deep-sea fishing (barracuda, sailfish, marlin, tuna) and boat trips around Tutuila and to the other islands for the adventurous, and hikes into the mountains. And lucky is the visitor who can take in a *fia-fia,* or feast, with Samoan food specialties (suckling pig and *pulusami,* which is baked coconut wrapped in taro leaves are among the choicest tidbits), dancing, singing, and much merriment.

WHAT TO BUY

American Samoa is one of the very few places in the world from which U.S. travelers may bring home two hundred dollars' worth of merchandise duty free. (The American Virgin Islands and Guam are the only other territories in that category.) From every other destination outside of the fifty U.S. states, the maxi-

SOUTH PACIFIC POLICE

A Fijian guard, in serrated-edge sulu, at Government House, Suva.

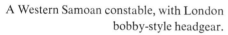

A Western Samoan constable, with London bobby-style headgear.

A Tongan policeman, with Aussie-style slouch-hat.

13

Intercontinental's Southern Cross, Melbourne, Australia.

14

The Hermitage, Mount Cook, New Zealand.

Bures of
Korolevu Beach Hotel,
Fiji.

Aggie Grey's Hotel, a landmark in Apia, Western Samoa.

16

A lady kangaroo poses, with assistance, with the head of an uncooperative "joey" protruding from her pouch; a sheep is shorn in a shearing shed; an emu—proud if not beautiful.

A koala, munching on eucalyptus leaves.

Bright-hued parrots being fed by tourists at Queensland's Corrobin Bird Sanctuary note one perched atop a youngster's head foreground.

mum allowable, duty free, is one hundred dollars. If you've other destinations on your itinerary, remember that your total duty-free allowance remains two hundred dollars; one hundred dollars' worth can be from American Samoa, though. Best sources for non-Samoan merchandise in the duty-free category are the shops at Tafuna Airport and in the Pago Pago Intercontinental Hotel. At them you'll find French perfumes and colognes, transistor radios, miniature TV sets, cameras, and other luxury goods, as well as liquor and cigarettes which are for departing visitors only and may not be consumed in the territory. Samoan handicrafts—wood carvings, wooden ava (kava) bowls, shell jewelry and leis, woven mats, place mats, fans, and tapa cloth also are on sale at these shops, at the handicraft center on the malae, all of which is alive with vendors on days that passenger ships are in port, and where bargaining is expected. Except on ship days, when vendors lower their prices to rock-bottom level at the end of the afternoon, I found prices more expensive than in Western Samoa, but this may not necessarily be so during your visit, and in any case the best advice is to buy what you like, when you see it; it may not be available later on in the trip.

CREATURE COMFORTS

Time was when Pago Pago had nothing to offer in the way of accommodation except a glorified boarding house known as the Rainmaker Hotel. A onetime military barracks, it bulged at the seams with guests, many of whom had to bed down on its verandas when the rush was particularly heavy. Well, with the opening of the Pago Pago Inter-Continental Hotel in late 1965, the Rainmaker became a bittersweet memory. And it gave way to one of the most imaginatively designed hotels in the entire Pacific. Built on the Goat Island promontory, whose one acre was enlarged to four by means of reclaiming land from the sea, it comprises twenty two-unit buildings, each of Samoan fale design, and sixty additional rooms in a pair of pavilions based on the traditional Polynesian long house. All rooms—with lahala matting on the floor and tapa cloth-decorated walls—are air conditioned and with private baths, and the plans of the gifted architect, Honolulu's George J. Wimberly, allow for a hundred-room expansion. I have described earlier in this chapter the important role the hotel plays in American Samoa's development program, how it is owned by twelve hundred Samoans, and how it was financed. Let me add only that nothing has been overlooked. The swimming pool is flanked by the Laumei Terrace and Snack Bar, with the design motif locally carved wooden turtles—a part of legendary Samoa —the cocktail lounge—called Fiafia (Samoan for "happy") overlooks the sea, and the handsome Rainmaker Restaurant faces the landmark mountain by that name. Palms on the grounds were brought from the various villages, and planted by each village's chief; youngsters strung the pods and shells for the beaded curtains used within. Naturally the hotel's regularly scheduled entertainment is Samoan, of the kind which was a hit at the Polynesian Pavilion at the New York World's Fair, where the fire dancers brought from Samoa were among the headliners. And there are, as well, duty-free and Samoan handicraft shops, sightseeing desk, airlines office, car-hire service—all adding up to a complete tourist center where for the first time in history the casual traveler can be truly comfortable in American Samoa. Rates run from $12 single, $15 double.

Away from the hotel, Pago Pago does not offer a great deal of after-dark diversion (there are no other recommended eating places). The private Goat Island Club welcomes visitors for dancing and drinks, and there are one or two honky-tonk-type "nightclubs"—the Island Moon (Friday floor shows), and the Seaside Club, where one can join the relaxing locals and see some incredible dancing. Liquor (aside from that sold at the duty-free shops to those departing from the territory) is available only to holders of permits, but tourists are, of course, served at the hotel and Goat Island Club bars. Beer, on the other hand, is available to anyone without a permit, and is sold in retail stores as well as taverns.

Tahiti

Entry requirements: A valid passport, a vaccination certificate, and proof of onward transportation (air or steamship ticket) are requisites. No visa is needed for in-transit travelers or for those whose stay will not exceed ten days. Visas *are* required, however, for stays longer than ten days, and may be obtained for $2.45 from French consulates; consulates in San Francisco and Los Angeles issue visas within twenty-four to forty-eight hours, but processing at other consulates may take longer. Upon exiting from Tahiti by air, be prepared to plunk down $4.59 "departure tax"; included in this amount is a baggage porterage fee. **Best times for a visit:** No Round-the-South-Pacific traveler in his right mind will omit Tahiti from his itinerary, no matter what time of year he's traveling. But be prepared for your share of torrential showers during the wet season, from October through March. And when I say rain, I mean rain. There's a consolation, though. The downpours can stop as suddenly as they begin, often after a relatively short period, and the sun (or stars) will stream through. But one must be prepared for precipitation in varying degrees, and not only during this period. The remaining months are dryer but not necessarily Sahara-like. Temperatures? During the cooler period (spring through fall in the Northern Hemisphere) temperatures average in the seventies, though they may drop to the sixties in the evenings. The rest of the year, the average is in the seventies, with few days seeing the thermometer exceed the mid-eighties. Year-round, humidity averages nearly 80 percent. Early morning and post-sunset are the pleasantest times of day, with evenings delightful. **Currency:** The French Pacific franc (CFP), of which there are 87 to the U.S. dollar,

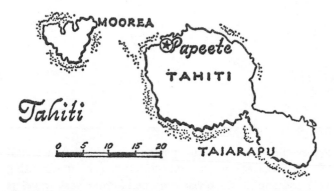

a franc, in other words, being worth a little more than a
cent (10 frs.=12 cents, 100 frs.=$1.15, 500 frs.=$5.75,
1000 frs.=$11.50). This money is legal tender only in
the islands of French Polynesia; it has the same value as
the currency of New Caledonia but is not acceptable there.
And banks in other countries are not at all disposed to
convert it into their currencies. You may reconvert your
francs into dollars before leaving, but you'll pay a small
commission when so doing. Cash traveler's checks, therefore, only as needed. The sole bank, the Banque de l'Indo-
Chine, the hotels, and the shops all cash traveler's checks
without difficulty. **Film availability:** There are both color
and black-and-white supplies in the shops, but prices are
a good deal higher than those in the United States, so take
plenty with you. Black-and-white processing is available.
Transportation: The jet age came to Tahiti in 1961, with
the opening of a splendid eleven-thousand-foot runway dramatically jutting into the sea at the international airport
known as Faaa (pronounced fa-ah-ah-ah). The new air
terminal is as impressive as the field, with lounge, bar-
cafe, duty-free shop, and a most attractive Franco-Polyne-
sian decor. Qantas flies in on its unique London–Bermuda–
Nassau–Mexico–Tahiti–Fiji–Australia route, on a nonstop
hop from Acapulco, and several other international lines
provide service. RAI (Reseau Aérien Interinsulaire) offers
DC-4 service to Bora Bora and Raiatea. Air Polynésie's
flying boats link Tahiti with Moorea. Moorea is also gained

by daily two-hour boat service; be warned that crossings can be rough, even in sunny weather. Small ships, hardly luxurious, connect with other islands in French Polynesia. There is regular passenger steamship service on ships of such lines as America's Matson, France's Messageries Maritimes, and New Zealand's Union Steamship Company. A number of other lines, including P & O Orient, Holland-America, and Swedish American, often include Tahiti in cruise itineraries. And passenger-carrying freighters call fairly often. A 120-mile road, most of it well paved, encircles the island, making it one of the easiest to see in the South Pacific, at least from the coast. There are few roads leading into the mountainous interior. Sightseeing is by means of self-drive cars (Hertz, Avis, and local firms are on the scene, one's home license is the only document needed, and the cost is about ten to fifteen dollars per day), organized tours, and taxis. Taxi rates both within Papeete and out of town, though not cheap, are fixed, but check in advance with the driver before setting off, and do not tip. Should you want to add to the already considerable in-town traffic bedlam, you may rent a motor scooter inexpensively, but I suggest that there are other ways of living dangerously. **Languages:** French is the official language, although Tahitian—a Polynesian tongue—is, of course, widely spoken. The substantial Chinese community still speaks Chinese, but the English-speaking visitor with nothing but his own language is rarely at a handicap. Most locals coming into contact with visitors speak English. Still, command of French, however minimal, can be most helpful. Few American visitors to Tahiti seem to speak it, and those who do are regarded as rare but most welcome characters. **Tipping:** Glory be! Tipping is *interdit, tabu,* forbidden. And no kidding, either; it's the law. The authorities, local residents, and your fellow tourists ask you to leave well enough alone, and express your thanks with a wide smile. **Clothes:** The high tourist influx has not, happily, had much effect on Tahiti's informality. It remains sensibly casual, and that includes the realm of *couture.* Ties are worn by the locals only on the most

solemn of occasions, and jackets only on coolish evenings
as a matter of comfort rather than custom. Men generally
wear sports shirts, shorts, and thongs or sandals during the
day; after dark the shorts may be replaced by long
trousers, although there's no need to substitute thongs or
sandals with shoes and socks. Visiting women wear shorts
or slacks (bikinis are popular for swimming), variations of
the Tahitian *pareu* and, particularly in town and in the
evenings, dresses. **Business hours:** This is early-bird territory; people are up with the roosters to take advantage
of coolish mornings. Most shops, places of business, and
offices are open from 7:30 A.M. to 11 or 11:30 A.M., close
for siesta until 2 P.M., and then resume until 5 P.M. Saturdays are generally half-days, 7:30 A.M. until 11 or 11:30
A.M. **Further Information:** Service du Tourisme de Tahiti,
Boîte Postale 65, Papeete, Tahiti; Qantas Airways, Papeete,
Tahiti; French Government Tourist Office, 610 Fifth Avenue,
New York; 18 South Michigan Avenue, Chicago; 323 Geary
Street, San Francisco; 9418 Wilshire Boulevard, Beverly
Hills, and 1170 Drummond Street, Montreal.

INTRODUCING TAHITI

Introducing *Tahiti?* No South Seas isle would appear to need
less introduction. Square mile by square mile (and there are but
402 of them) Tahiti must surely set some sort of global record
as the most glowingly and prolifically chronicled bit of earth on
our planet. Indeed, no island in the world has ever asked for less
—and received more—publicity. Until a very few years ago when
it was decided to replace the subsiding income of phosphate with
tourism, Tahiti had not even encouraged visitors. But they came.
   Cook, Bligh, Bouganville: Heavens, how they came! Ever since
the eighteenth-century visits of such captains as Cook and
Bligh, Tahiti has been the synonym par excellence for Paradise.

Indeed, America's consulate in Tahiti is located in a quarter by
that name. The mariners' accounts impelled the missionaries to
open up a South Pacific frontier that was to prove successful
beyond their dreams, and it was not long before writers and
painters captured the Tahitian scene, lured by earlier accounts.
"Scarcely a spot in the universe," Captain Cook wrote, "affords
a more luxurious prospect." And Cook had seen much of the
universe, so that he could make comparisons. The French explorer Bougainville compared Tahiti to the Garden of Eden.
Even Captain Bligh, not known for sentimentality, wrote that he
and his crew had "been treated with the utmost affection and
regard," during the five-month stay of the *Bounty*.

Later the writers arrived: Stevenson (who lived in Tahiti before
proceeding to Samoa) and Rupert Brooke, the French Pierre
Loti and Polish-born Joseph Conrad, Melville and Maugham,
and—more latterly—Nordhoff and Hall, Michener, and the musical stage's Rodgers and Hammerstein, whose *South Pacific* Bali
Hai might well have been (and in the movie version of their
musical *was*) the island of Moorea. What the writers did for
Tahiti with the printed word, painters—most particularly the
genius Paul Gauguin—did with brush and palette. Tahiti, in
consequence, is the collective South Seas dream of Americans
and Australians, Britons and Bulgarians, Hollanders and Hun-
garians. Even Hawaiians, those residents of our Polynesian-ac-
cented fiftieth state, are curious about their neighbors. Today,
there are those who say Tahiti will be the next Hawaii, that
within a generation—maybe two, maybe in even less time—
airborne tourists will have impelled the creation of a second
Waikiki. There is, to be sure, no doubt that, since the first jets
zoomed into Faaa Airport, Tahiti has seen more changes than
it had known in many, many decades.

The Tahitians' resilience: But the Tahitian must be given credit
for resilience. The skeptics must realize that Tahiti absorbs the
foreigner far more than the foreigner absorbs Tahiti. New Caledonia, the other major French Pacific isle, is today a bit of
France in the tropics, with a Melanesian accent, for the life

and culture of New Caledonians were not strong enough to dominate over the Europeans' ways. Tahiti, though, is something else again. The French influence, and most agreeable it is, is not of course to be discounted. But Tahiti—tourist hotels, jet runways, packaged sightseeing tours, French Foreign Legion base notwithstanding—remains essentially Tahitian.

Old hands who knew it "when" will not agree, of course. But they cannot deny that one need not even leave the streets of Papeete to see the Tahitians of Gauguin paintings. Nor that a few miles from the capital, the countryside is of the same outrigger-fringed, thatched hut-delineated blue lagoons of the old days. Nor that the Tahitian's outlook on life, his disdain for "security" in the ephemeral future, his love of the dance, the feast, music, indeed his love of love, are much as they have been. Nor that the Tahitian remains to this day the Polynesian at his (and her!) handsomest, most beguiling, most gracious—and, yes, most romantic.

Except for the unfortunate dietary deficiencies (now being corrected) which in recent years have induced partly toothless mouths among many maidens, no women in the world are more beautiful than those of Tahiti. And they need no twentieth-century Helena Rubenstein to enhance their loveliness. The age-old wrap-around pareu, a floral lei about the neck, a *couronne* of flowers over a head of long dark hair, or perhaps a single blossom behind the ear—and one encounters classic beauty, complemented by a natural background which is at once breathtaking, eye-filling, brilliant.

A backward glance: One look at Tahiti today (even with the noise of a stream of motor scooters chugging about Papeete) and the observer appreciates its centuries-old appeal. What is more difficult to perceive is that today's Tahiti, probably as happy with its French administration as any overseas territory flying the *tricoleur,* did not welcome French rule. As a matter of fact, it was adamantly against it. France quite literally forced its way into a Tahiti which, faced with European domination, had preference for the English.

It was, of course, an Englishman who is credited as the island's first European discoverer. Captain Samuel Wallis (for whom the French-controlled Wallis Islands are named) came across the island in 1767, charted it, and not only took possession of it for George III, but named it after that monarch. Only a year later, though, the French De Bougainville, presumably unaware of the Wallis claim, happened along and declared Tahiti French, with the name La Nouvelle Cythère.

Early hospitality: But then, in 1769, came the redoubtable Captain James Cook, in command of H.M.S. *Endeavour,* which had aboard a cargo of scientists commissioned by the British Royal Society to observe the transit of the planet Venus across the disc of the sun. The ship landed at Matavai Bay, and the locale of the scientists' work still is known as Point Venus. The Tahitians could not have been more hospitable, and before the *Endeavour*'s mission was completed Cook had visited Moorea, Bora Bora, Raiatea, and other islands, named them the Society Islands (after the British Royal Society, in case you were wondering *what* society), wrote about them with great enthusiasm, and revisited them on two subsequent trips, embracing a short period during which Spanish priests had set up (and disbanded) a Roman Catholic mission. (They called Tahiti Isle de Amat. It was the third foreign name given the island and it is an indication of the earlier-mentioned resilience of Tahiti that the island retains its own, original name; none of the others ever stuck. Cook is partially responsible for this, for he asked his hosts what the island was called upon arrival. They replied "O Tahiti" meaning "This is Tahiti." Cook and others after him accepted this and it was some time before the "O" was removed in European parlance.)

The Bounty's historic visit: Just a year after Cook's final visit, in 1788, Tahiti experienced a visit that, perhaps more than any other, was to put it on the maps and in history books. Captain William Bligh arrived on the *Bounty* to collect breadfruit plants on behalf of European settlers in the West Indies who wanted to cultivate them as a staple food crop for the slaves working their plantations. The *Bounty* and its crew stayed a bit over five months, and the story of the fate of the ship's master and crew has been told by Nordhoff and Hall, by other authors, and twice via the medium of motion pictures, so that it is more than familiar to readers.

The *Bounty*'s mutiny, led by Fletcher Christian, took place after the ship departed Tahiti, but that island continued to figure in the *Bounty* story, for the mutineers later returned there, and fourteen were later taken from there by the British. Others, though, had left, under Fletcher Christian, before the British arrived, and with Tahitian followers (a dozen women and six men) made off for uninhabited Pitcairn Island, which Christian had read about while on the *Bounty*. The party of twenty-seven arrived in 1790, and within two decades they gradually killed each other off—or almost. A sole survivor of the original group, and a number of their offspring, survived. In 1831 the British removed the little community from Pitcairn to Norfolk Island, off the coast of Australia. But some of *that* group, nostalgic for Pitcairn, later returned to it. The result is that today the part-European, part-Tahitian descendants of history's most dramatic mutiny live both on Pitcairn and Norfolk, as a direct result of an action which followed what might be called the overhappy stay of a ship's crew on Tahiti.

For there are historians who agree that dictatorial Captain Bligh was not the sole impetus for the mutiny. The easy life on Tahiti, attachments with Tahitian women, and the stark contrast between Tahiti and the rigid discipline on shipboard were also motivating factors in the rebellion. Captain Bligh, of course, was vindicated —indeed acclaimed—during his lifetime, as a result of the mutiny. He and that portion of the crew which was loyal to him were put to sea in one of the *Bounty*'s boats, and proceeded to make one of the most incredible open-craft voyages ever undertaken. They traveled some thirty-six hundred miles, ending in Java, from which Bligh departed for home on a proper sailing vessel. Tahiti entered in his life once again, though. He returned in the *Providence* in 1792 on still another breadfruit-collecting mission.

Kings and converts: All this while, Tahiti remained a lure. And it had still not been Christianized. The initial failure of the Spanish Catholics was not for long to prove a deterrent to succeeding missionaries. In 1797 the first London Missionary Society group appeared on the scene. They fled to Australia a decade or so later, but returned again, and by 1815 they had their first success. As missionaries were to learn later, in other South Pacific islands, the key convert is the top man. In this case it was the monarch, Pomare II. With his acceptance of the Cross, all of Tahiti—and its island neighbors—soon followed, and so Christian did it become that the first Christian missionaries to Fiji were not Europeans but Tahitians.

The aforementioned Pomare II was but one of a considerable line of rulers by that name, the most noted of which was a lady, Queen Pomare IV. It was she who was on the throne during the years when the British Protestant missionaries were effectively and successfully Christianizing Tahiti. Their work did not, of course, go unnoticed by the competition, and in 1836 a French Roman Catholic group attempted to establish itself, but to no avail. The English Protestant-oriented Tahitians would have none of them, and packed them off.

The French and Queen Pomare: In a rage, a French warship arrived to express official displeasure, and forced Queen Pomare to pay—in cash—for the inhospitality of her people. Later, still another French war vessel arrived and its commanding admiral threatened bombardment unless Her Majesty agreed to allow visits by the French, and their men of the cloth. The lady had no choice but to relent, and France had its foot in the door.

But that was just the beginning. In 1842 the same admiral was back. This time his claim was that the Tahitians were violating French rights. France would spare them, the absent Queen's ministers were told, only if they signed an agreement ceding Tahiti to France as a protectorate. In 1843, despite objections by Queen Pomare and efforts by her to void the document signed

by her ministers, the French declared her throne forfeited, and
took formal possession. The Tahitians appealed in vain to their
British friends for help. There were Tahitian-French skirmishes
on the island. The Queen was replaced by a French stooge of a
regent. But within a few years, she acquiesced, returned to her
throne, and the French proceeded to take over a good bit more
of Polynesia, with relatively little opposition.

Monarchy to colony: Queen Pomare outlived two consorts,
and reigned until she died in 1877. Her successor was King
Pomare V. He is known not only for the quantities of Benedictine he imbibed (his tomb is topped with a reproduction of a
Benedictine bottle) but as the last of the Tahitian monarchs. In
1880 he yielded to strong French pressure and brought an end
to the royal dynasty. His wife, half-European former Queen
Marau, lived until 1935. They had no children but other royal
relatives did, and some of them still are alive.

Tahiti, shorn of its monarchy and with self-imposed rulers in
control, ambled along. Not as interested in politics as some of
their Polynesian neighbors (the Samoans, for example) and for
the most part fairly content with their lot, they came to accept
their occupiers and good relations developed.

During World War I Papeete was partially bombed by two
German cruisers, and two French vessels in the harbor were sunk.
But the capital was rebuilt, and Tahiti's involvement in World
War II was not so unhappy. When the Germans took over France,
it, along with New Caledonia, opted to side with the Free French
and General de Gaulle, United States troops built a base on
Bora Bora (to this day the most English-speaking of the French
Polynesian islands), and the Allies helped Tahiti economically
until France was able to take over again at war's end.

Polynesian politics: Since that time, increasing self-government
has been given the Tahitians—although not, of course, without
pressure. With their fellow islanders in the rest of the far-flung
territory known as French Polynesia, they voted in the 1958
referendum (held in all French areas of the world) to remain a
French Overseas Territory, rather than become either independent

or a full-fledged Department of the mother country. Their Governor, therefore, continues to be appointed by Paris, but their legislature (Assemblée Territoriale) has a good deal of authority. Elections are held every five years. The last, in 1962, gave ex-members of the banned left-of-center Rassemblement Democratiques des Populations Tahitiennes party a majority. The pro-independence, anti-French RDPT was disbanded by law in 1963, but its supporters still are influential in the Assemblée Territoriale, its Social and Economic Commission, and the important policy-making Conseil du Gouvernement.

The people, by a two-thirds majority, voted to remain a French Overseas Territory in 1958, but as recently as late 1964 the RDPT created a crisis by proposing an income tax, which was met with a general strike. Tahiti is represented in the Parliament in Paris; it sends both a senator and a member of the Chamber of Deputies. At the local level, government is undertaken through two municipal councils, and nearly a hundred district councils which, Tahitian staffed, function both as lower courts and as legislative bodies. But Tahitians want more jobs in government, and the same rates of pay as French civil servants doing the same work. They struck in early 1965, just as a new Governor, Jean Securani, was arriving from Paris. He and the Conseil du Gouvernement agreed to boost salaries and the Assemblée Territoriale agreed.

Tahiti and its 109 neighbors: Tahiti, it should be made clear, is but one of the 110 islands of French Polynesia, with a land area of twenty-five hundred square miles scattered over a wide area. Its sole city, Papeete, is the capital of the entire territory. The town's population (some twenty thousand) is nearly half of that of the island of Tahiti (forty-five thousand) which is, in turn, more than half the population of all French Polynesia (about eighty thousand). French Polynesia breaks down into five principal groupings: The Society Islands, including Tahiti and Moorea in its windward subgroup, with Bora Bora in its leeward group; the Tuamotu Islands, the Austral Islands, the Gambier Islands, and the Marquesas Islands (five atolls of the Tuamotu-Gambier

group were selected as a nuclear testing area in 1963, despite
protests from neighbor nations, and local tourist interests as well).

The majority of Tahiti's residents are of course Polynesian, or
at least dominantly Polynesian, for there are relatively few pure-
bloods, there having been mixing and mingling between the races
since the days of the early European ships. The Polynesians are
believed to have migrated to the islands either from the mainland
of Southeast Asia (the dominant theory) or, if one accepts the
theory of *Kon-Tiki*'s Thor Heyerdahl and the expeditions of Dr.
Bengt Danielsson (now a Tahiti resident), from the coast of South
America. At any rate, it was from Tahiti (more accurately the
nearby island of Raiatea) that the migrations are believed to have
departed for such distant points as New Zealand and Hawaii.

Polyglot populace: But Tahiti is by no means all Tahitians.
There are, as would be expected, a sizable group of Europeans,
most of them French. (This group is kept from expanding by
the strict immigration controls of recent years; the government
quite wisely does its best to discourage beachcombers and dead-
heads who have for so long been attracted to Tahiti. Thus the
requirements that all visitors—even bona fide tourists—have air
or ship tickets with them, upon arrival, so that there'll be no
question about their having the wherewithal to leave when their
time is up.)

More of a surprise to the newcomer than the European is the
Chinese. There are probably about ten thousand in French Polynesia today, the overwhelming majority in Tahiti. Only about a
thousand of these are French citizens; the rest—even those born
in Tahiti and that includes most all—are citizens of the Republic
of China, and hold passports issued by the Chiang Kai-shek government in Taiwan; a consul of the Chiang regime is resident in
Papeete. The Chinese—about a thousand of them—first came to
Tahiti in the 1860s to work the new long defunct cotton plantations. Some went back to China but many stayed, and many new
immigrants arrived in the early years of this century, up through
the 1930s, when the doors were closed to them. Like overseas
Chinese communities everywhere they have stayed among them-

selves, married among themselves, lived among themselves, and been educated among themselves, retaining their own language and culture. In Tahiti they raise virtually all of the vegetables grown, as well as more than half the vanilla crop. And they are, as elsewhere, dominant in businesses of all sizes and types, and in white-collar jobs as well. Only recently have their young people begun to chafe at the bit, mix more with Tahitians, and join in the festive spirit of the island. With many, the all-work no-play maxims of their parents and grandparents are facing competition, at long last, from the Tahitian spirit of camaraderie. Indeed, if any group can get the hard-working Chinese to relax a bit, it would be the Tahitians!

Those Chinese who are breaking away from their traditional schools are mostly attracted to the schools operated by Roman Catholic missions. Generally, though, the Protestants—first to arrive on the scene—are dominant on the island, with the Presbyterians No. 1 and Mormons and Seventh-Day Adventists following. The religious denominations operate schools with government subsidies, and there are schools under direct government operation as well. Education is compulsory and in the government dayschools tuition is free. There is no university but there are government scholarships for universities in France. About a hundred Tahitians a year study abroad.

Phosphate and tourism: Tahiti, like most South Sea islands, is dominantly agricultural. More than 85 percent of the land remains Tahitian-owned. (Most of the Chinese farmers rent their plots.) And it is difficult for non-Tahitians to buy land. Still, the biggest income-producer for French Polynesia for some time has been phosphate, all of it on the island of Makatea. But the deposits are expected to be exhausted within a few years, and thus the official government encouragement of a new industry—tourism. The expensive new jet airport, financed by the Paris government, a spate of new hotels (with construction continuing), and a complete switch in visitor policy (from one of toleration to active encouragement) are expected to replace the phosphate income, and keep French Polynesia on its feet economically, supplemented by such revenue producers as copra, vanilla, and perhaps the most exotic industry of all: mother-of-pearl shell, fetched from the sea at a depth of twenty-five fathoms by skilled skin-divers in lagoons of the Tuamotu and Gambier islands.

Tomorrow's Tahiti: What will it all mean, this carefully planned development of an island group beloved precisely because it has for so long resisted the complexities—and the ensuing pressures— of the technologists of the West? No one can say for sure. Tahiti, I like to think, will never be a whit less lovely than it is now. But there is much skepticism in today's Tahiti. Fears are expressed over the nuclear test project, and the high-priced technicians and Foreign Legionnaires whose presence is tending to raise prices in an already overpriced economy. There is criticism, too, of get-rich-quick tendencies in the new tourist industry, with charges that only its promoters, and not the Tahitians, are profiting from it. I may be nothing more than a thoroughly cockeyed optimist—of the kind Mr. Rodgers and Mr. Hammerstein introduced to us in *South Pacific*. In which case you'd better come see for yourself, and know firsthand the reasons for the cries of alarm from the Old Tahitian hands.

YOUR VISIT TO TAHITI

At first glance Tahiti might seem almost frighteningly frenetic to the newcomer. And statistics might reinforce this initial impression. For there are, on this relatively small island containing but 120 miles of highway and but forty-five thousand human beings, something like twenty thousand vehicles—many of them far from silent motor scooters and motorized bikes, not to mention less terrifying (and much quieter) automobiles, taxis, trucks, and even some gloriously noiseless bicycles, propelled in the old-fashioned way by means of the driver's feet. Add to this overwhelming mass of mechanized transport an airport with giant jets buzzing in every day, and one might wonder if Times Square would be any less a strain.

But Tahiti deceives. Its capital has, to be sure, a contemporary bustle about it, but don't be fooled. This is by no means an ulcer-producing community. There's a one-word keynote to Tahitian life: relax. And I suggest you do just that, from the moment you pass through customs. There is—and the truth should be known straight off—a minimum to occupy one with conventional sightseeing. To savor Tahiti, one must get with it *dans le style tahitien,* or, roughly translated: Keep it casual. Be as utterly lazy and undisciplined as you like. Nap at midday siesta-time. Dine late, remembering this is French territory with none of the meal-hour rigidities of British or ex-British territories. Pub-crawl into the night, worrying not about a dining room appearance at breakfast. (Order a *café complet* delivered to your room or bungalow whenever you awaken.) Stroll the streets of Papeete at will, watch the sunset over Moorea at dusk, waste time over coffee or an apéritif at alfresco cafes on the harbor. Enjoy the camaraderie of the lounge, bar, pool, and/or beach of your hotel. Take time to fish and snorkel, to swim and sunbathe, to acquaint yourself with Tahitians as they feast, sing, dance, shop, worship—and (a favorite activity) gossip.

And when you've had an appreciable taste of the "big" island, hop over to Moorea and Bora Bora, both of which are even more beautiful, and even more detached from the cares and tensions of life as you know it at home. Allow for a long-enough stay to make relaxation possible. In as little time as a week (five days on a slam-bang schedule) one can take in the essentials of Tahiti, Moorea, and Bora Bora. But I should certainly stay longer, even with a crowded Round the Pacific itinerary. And I would, by no means, consider Moorea and Bora Bora as expendable extras. They are absolute requisites of a Tahitian visit. Skip them, and don't say you weren't warned!

Papeete is Tahitian for "basket of waters" and is so named because a veritable network of rivers flow from the mountains into its excellent harbor. One hears it called *Pap-eat* or *Pap-eatie* by many English-speaking people, and *Pa-pet* by many French. But it's properly pronounced *Pa-pay-AY-tay*. And not even its oldest residents would call it beautiful. With a population of about twenty thousand, it is a good bit smaller than New Caledonia's Nouméa, and it's less attractive than that city, with many fewer amenities.

To many, it's Major Disappointment No. 1 of a Tahitian visit. To others though, myself included, it's quite charming, eminently strollable, and most certainly *sympathique* in the true sense of that French term. One must simply resign oneself to its somewhat rustic façade. There have been new buildings in recent years, and new ones continue to rise, but the silhouette (I hesitate to use the word skyline) is anything but imposing. Papeete is ironroofed French Colonial houses, occasional steeples (none of them particularly inspiring), streets which turn into puddles at the slightest onset of precipitation, shops either massive and functional or small and inviting, a motley assortment of copra boats and giant liners in the harbor, the classic outline of Moorea's jagged peaks eleven miles across the water, and Tahiti's own verdant mountains—often cloud-enshrouded—as a backdrop. One must take Papeete on its own terms. Tourist industry or no, it makes no pretensions to be anything other than what it is—and has been for a good long while. No South Pacific capital is easier to walk about. Activity revolves about the waterfront, which is fringed by the Quai Bir-Hackeim (it takes on different names at its extremities—Quai Gallieni at one end, Quai de l'Uranie at the other), but it's from its central sector that one best orients oneself.

Using the Cafe Vaima as a guidepost, one can easily find the leading attractions—from Quinn's Bar, down a bit on the Quai du Commerce, to the nearby Public Market on Rue Bonnard (best seen *very* early Sunday mornings, when *very* late Saturday-nighters, produce vendors in from the countryside, and shoppers-in-general all converge to buy and gossip), the Museum of Papeete on Rue Bréa (smallish but packed with excellent bits of Polynesiana), the gardens of Government House, the Governor's official (and quaintly Pacific Colonial) residence, the modern post office, an imposing Mormon Temple (not unlike those on many South

Pacific islands), the elderly Assemblée Territoriale building, the Town Hall, the various churches (which one does well to take in, of a Sunday morning—the music and singing are lovely) and, as one would expect in France overseas, as well as in the mother-land—cafes, restaurants, bars, and shops (eminently worthy of inspection and described later on in this chapter).

Hotels? Only the smallish and elderly ones are in Papeete; the newer hostelries are along the coast, on either side of town, and they're dealt with in the Creature Comforts section of this chapter. Don't worry about getting lost in Papeete. Stop in at the Tourist Bureau for maps, directions, tips, and schedules of current events of interest. And feel free to ask in any shop or office —be it Qantas or a cafe—for directions. Tahiti is still not so tourist-infested that its people aren't interested in, and curious about, its visitors. They love to chat in any language that's mutually understood.

Touring the island: Tahiti is easy to visualize, geographically. It's shaped like an uneven "8" with the lower part by far the smaller. The larger and best-developed sector of the island is circular Tahiti-Nui with a splendidly mountainous interior and a plain-fringed coastline, around which winds a paved seventy-five-mile road, on which it's impossible to get lost; one simply drives around the circular highway and sooner or later is back where he started.

The interior of Tahiti, a primeval wonderland of peaks and gorges, falls and rivers, is virtually uninhabited and almost devoid of roads. Tahitians, while preferring to live near the lagoon (that portion of quiet water separated from the open sea by the barrier reef which fringes the island) enjoy the mountains for fishing, and bathing in the rivers. And the visitor does well to at least get a taste of the interior, whose highest peak, 7321-foot Orohena, was climbed by Europeans for the first time in 1953.

But first things first. A round-the-island circuit is easily and comfortably done in a day. I suggest going in the company of a Tahitian guide who knows the countryside and is bound to run across friends and family en route, making it possible to meet some locals while sightseeing. But one can rent a self-drive car or even a motor scooter and proceed independently. And there are always the local buses, loaded with Tahitians, pigs, and chickens, and lots of fun. They depart from the bus and taxi depot adjoining the market in Papeete.

Requisite stops? I should certainly include *Fautua Gorge,* about a mile and a half inland by road from the East Coast Highway, on the Fautua River. En route to the waterfalls one passes Pierre Loti Pool, named for the French author who wrote glowingly of Tahiti, and pleasant for a refreshing swim. Behind are the waterfalls, dropping hundreds of feet into a pool fringed in rich tropical growth. *Point Venus,* a few miles east of Papeete, brings back early European days in Tahiti. A marker designates the site where the Cook-transported scientists observed the transit of Venus in 1769. There is a monument, nearby, to the first London Missionary Society missionaries who came on the *Duff* in 1797, and a lighthouse—built more than a century ago—still functioning. Stop, too, at the Arahoho Blowhole on *Matavai Bay,* where Cook, Bligh, and other early captains anchored in the days before Papeete was established, and note in its general vicinity the earlier-mentioned memorial to Tahiti's last monarch, Pomare V, a Benedictine bottle reproduced at its top.

Even more historic (going back to ancient Tahitian times) are the partially restored ruins of what is believed to be a centuries-old temple at *Mahaiatea,* in the Papara district of the south coast. The *Tahiti-iti,* or *Taiarapu, peninsula* is charming and well worth driving through. Stops can be made at villages like *Taravao* and *Teahupoo,* where one can arrange for an outrigger canoe excursion to islets on the barrier reef. Tahiti-iti is the canoemaking center of Tahiti, and it was here, also, that Stevenson lived in 1888, and where he is believed to have written at least part of "The Master of Ballantree."

Tahiti is dotted with memories of other earlier residents of note. Rupert Brooke wrote "Tiare Tahiti" at *Mataiea,* now the site of the enormous Atimaono plantation, which produces citrus fruits and copra, and cattle as well (one sees cows wandering among the coconuts all about Tahiti and they appear strangely incongruous). Somerset Maugham wrote *The Moon and Sixpence* at *Mauu*. James Norman Hall (with Charles Nordhoff) wrote *Mutiny on the Bounty* at *Arue,* where his widow still lives. And the great Gauguin lived at Villa Ventura in *Punaauia,* now the wealthiest suburb of Papeete. (His son Émile lived in Papeete until quite recently and sold miniature fishtraps to tourists.) But it is not to Punaauia that one goes for Gauguiniana. Instead, there is the imaginatively designed new *Gauguin Museum,* beautifully situated in the Botanical Gardens (planted by M.I.T. Professor Harrison Smith) at *Papeari.* The museum, opened in late 1964, was endowed by the Paris-based Foundation Singer-Polignac, and its exhibits tell the moving story of Gauguin's tragic life by means of letters, newspaper clippings, other documents, and reproductions of the paintings which so splendidly captured the beauty of Tahiti—and of the Tahitians. We can all be indebted to the foundation for endowing and erecting the museum, but we must hope that somehow or other it will manage to secure at least a single *original* Gauguin. Surely a handsome museum on the island he helped immortalize deserves at least one of his paintings. Museum curators or trustees with Gauguins in your collections, please note!

Other Tahiti suggestions: *Good swimming,* if the truth be known, is limited. Most of the beaches are black volcanic sand and are not among the most beautiful in the South Pacific. There is a good white sand beach at the aforementioned suburb of Punaauia, which is probably the nicest destination for swimmers on the island. A number of the hotels have pools, and there are inviting swimming spots in the river and alongside the waterfalls of the mountain area. The earlier-mentioned Pierre Loti Pool (now with a new Olympic-size cement pool alongside it) is one such, and there are points on the Vaipopoo and Punaruu rivers. The black sand beach closest to Papeete, at Pirae, is shared by Hotel Taone guests and others in the neighborhood and leaves a great deal to be desired. There is virtually no shark problem on Tahiti beaches, but before you plunge into strange water, perhaps while on an island drive, ask about conditions from local people. The only other concern for swimmers is the nasty Nohu fish, which swims only in waters whose bottoms are coral-sur-faced, rather than of sand. In such places, and when walking about coral generally, wear tennis shoes. Tahiti's waters are azure blue, warm, clear, and full of fascinating marine life easily view-able by glass-bottomed boats (rentable at Papeete's main pier or through hotels) and by means of skin-diving, a skill which can be studied through the École de Plongée (office behind Vaima Cafe, Papeete), which also rents equipment. Water-skiing is popu-lar, too; one may either rent or buy equipment in Papeete.

Fishing is great in Tahiti. To be had are barracuda, tuna, swordfish, marlin, and a number of other salt-water species. And there are, in the streams and rivers of the interior, the local ver-sion of trout, known as *nato,* and shrimp as well. Best source of help for fishermen and would-be fishermen is the Haura Club, a local anglers' group which extends temporary membership to visi-tors and will help arrange boat and equipment rentals. Make con-tact with the club through your hotel.

Other sports popular in Tahiti include horse racing, with frequent meets at the track in Pirae and small-scale parimutuel betting; soccer, with matches usually held Saturday and Sunday at the Fautua Sports Stadium; cock fighting in the country vil-lages (sharp metal blades are not affixed to the cock's feet, as is the case in Bali and other cock fighting areas), and bicycle racing, with competitions held several times a year, the course being the streets of Papeete.

Mountaineering is, of course, for the rugged, and if you're in-terested, contact the Alpine Club through your hotel. But don't feel compelled to indulge in any of the foregoing strenuous ac-tivity. Many Tahiti visitors are content to take in the swaying palms, the hibiscus, frangipani, tiara Tahiti, and bougainvillea so evident at every turn. Or to watch the sun set over Moorea from the Papeete waterfront or the Taravao Plateau. Or, indeed, to size up the availability of Tahitians by noting the locations of the flowers decorating their ears. Pareu-clad men and women wear not only fragrant leis around their necks, and crowns (*couronnes*) of blooms on their heads, but flowers behind their ears. A blossom over the right ear means the wearer is taken, one behind the left ear indicates availability; and, over *both* ears—will consider the most desirable bid.

Nearby islands: *Moorea* is, as earlier indicated, one of the requisite splendors of any South Seas holiday; indeed, I would recommend no Pacific destination more highly, for this is an island with everything to recommend it to the visitor: easy accessibility (daily round-trip flying boat service in a few minutes, daily round-trip boat departures for a memorable—if conceivably rough —journey); two good hotels, one of them truly top rank; perhaps the finest singing, dancing, and feasting in the Tahiti area; fine swimming, snorkeling, and outrigger-canoeing on calm waters, and rides by bus over unbelievably rutty roads to vanilla plantations, tiny villages, white frame churches, and Chinese merchants' general stores, through what is just possibly the most beautiful island in the world.

Just eleven miles across the bay from Tahiti, Moorea—with a population of some three thousand and an area of but about fifty square miles—affords a spectacular natural skyline. The northern part of the island offers both Cook's Bay (also known as Paopao Bay) and Papetoai Bay, and separating them is the breathtakingly exquisite Mount Rotui, a needle-shaped spire extending more than twenty-nine hundred feet heavenward. The principal town, little Afareaitu, is on the east coast and it is fringed by rugged and jagged Mounts Muaputa and Tohivea, the latter nearly four thousand feet in elevation. Life on Moorea is extremely simple and about as uncomplicated as it can be. But for activity at the hotels on Cook's Bay, there is very little to occupy one. But who could ask for more? Even the first glimpse of the bay, as the boat turns into it from the coast, is alone worth a flight to Tahiti. A day's excursion is not to be despised, but stay for as long as possible. The mountains fringing the mirrorlike bay are at times misted in cloud, at times brilliantly emerald-hued, at others—as dusk approaches—somberly purple. Sound a little familiar? It

may be, if you saw the film *South Pacific;* its Bali Hai scenes
were filmed there.

Bora Bora, called Pora Pora before World War II, took on a
new appellation as a result of the U.S. troops pronouncing the
P's like B's. Bora Bora, 140 miles from Tahiti in contrast to
Moorea's eleven, has always been more isolated from the life of
the main island. Radio-telephone contact between the two was
not established until 1963—to give you an idea. And because it
is somewhat more expensive to reach (one must fly RAI's DC-4s
over) it sees fewer visitors. But those it does see—and I hope
the reader will be among them—it bowls over with its beauty.
Even getting to Bora Bora is delightful. The planes (which make
daily flights) stop en route at larger but less visited Raiatea
(now with a good hotel and worthy of an overnight stopover) and
then go on to Bora Bora. Its main island, with a twenty-three-
mile circumference, is reef-encircled, and from the air the vista
of jagged green peaks (Mounts Temauu and Pahia are both about
twenty-four hundred feet), azure waters, and the whitish fringe
of the reef makes a memorable panorama. Planes land at the
airport on the island of Motu Mate, in the reef, and from the
landing spot one goes by launch—an enjoyable forty-minute ride
—to the little harbor of Bora Bora's principal village, Vaitape,
headquarters of the administrator of the Society Islands' leeward
group. At the wharf, as one lands, local people are on hand selling shells and coral and shell jewelry. Heavy-duty truck-buses
pick up passengers and take them through the pretty little town
(competitions are held regularly for the most attractively decorated houses and gardens) either to the nearby Hotel Noa-Noa,
or to the very tip of the southwestern extremity of the island,
where, perched atop a cliff, giving one the impression of being on
a ship at sea, is the main building of the Hotel Bora Bora. I detail its amenities later on in this chapter, but let me say here
that there is no more superb swimming anywhere in the South
Pacific, nor can one so easily swim a few yards from the white
beach into a wonderland of marine life. One does not know
which is more beautiful: to look down at brilliant-hued fish, ex-

quisite coral formations, or up—at the hotel, with Bora Bora's superb peaks in the background. Other Bora Bora diversions: water-skiing, Tahitian feasts, journeys on giant Tahitian sailing canoes, bicycle (or motor, or ambulatory) ambles through the village, where there are, thanks to those World War II Yanks, occasional leftover Quonset huts (one is the island's sole cinema), and quantities of English-speaking residents—onetime students of World War II Yanks who continue to remember them fondly, and manifest their reminiscences by extreme cordiality toward visitors. If they don't yell "Hello" as you drive by, they'll say *"Iorana"*—welcome. And you will be.

Raiatea and Rangiroa are two undeveloped islands of exceptional charm, and both may be worked into Tahitian itineraries, for they are served by RAI Airlines. Raiatea, between Tahiti and Bora Bora, has a pleasant hotel (see Creature Comforts). Rangiroa, in the Tuamotu group, has only private houses for the occasional overnight visitor, but it can be taken in during half-day layovers on certain Tahiti–Bora Bora flights, when there's time for swimming, snorkeling, local entertainment at lunch, and a stroll through the welcoming village of Tiputa.

WHAT TO BUY

Tahiti is good for shopping and it's fun for shopping. It is not necessarily inexpensive, though. Best buys are French perfumes and colognes, at prices as much as half those of the United States, and the good-looking hand-blocked cotton fabric which is used to make the Tahitian pareus, and which serves also in Tahiti as the bases of men's sports shirts, women's dresses, draperies and curtains, bedspreads, place mats, napkins, furniture upholstery and slipcovers, pads for straight-backed chairs and, for all one knows, underwear. The traditional pareu cloth comes in white and a strong color—red, green, blue, or orange. The cotton itself is woven in Europe, but much of the printing and blocking is done in Tahiti. There are, besides the classic designs, contemporary motifs which are sometimes more subtle, rarely more attractive, and invariably more expensive. Women's pareus measure thirty-six by sixty-four inches, and may be worn breast length or (with a brassiere covered in the same material) waist length. Men's pareus, if they're to double as bathing suits, as is the case with the Tahitians, should be a yard and a half long. Traditional-design pareus can cost as little as a couple of dollars, and four or five times that in better quality or more original design. Most shops carry several qualities. Still other interesting articles? Well, there are *couronnes* (head pieces) of shell, designed much like those made of flowers. These are not to be found in most other South Seas destinations and, combined with shell leis, completely accessorize a pareu outfit. There are, as well, shell bracelets and earrings; grass skirts in both children's and adult sizes, and usually with an "embroidery" of shells, Tahitian style. There is a variety of woven pandanus-fiber material—hats, bags, place mats, and the like. There are wood-carved curios—war clubs and spears, *tikis* (reproductions of the ancient Tahitian idols, also in stone). There are shells and coral, recordings of Tahitian music, a variety of mother-of-pearl products, French-made merchandise ranging from skin-diving equipment to wood-block Christmas cards of Tahitian scenes, Chinese-style brocades and other orientalia, men's and women's clothing, both ready-made and custom-tailored, and original paintings and watercolors. Sources: For handicrafts, shells, coral, Christmas cards, shell jewelry, and the like, Manuia and René Pailloux appear to me to offer the best, most tasteful, and most interesting selections, often with one-of-a-kind originals. For perfumes Rose Marie and the Paris Perfumerie. Clothes: Any number of shops. Many are multi-function—selling ready-made clothes and accessories, for both men and women, pareu cloth by the meter (a meter is 39.37 inches), and custom tailoring, as well, often for men as well as women. In addition, most of these places carry curio sidelines, perfume, and accessories. The group includes Daniel Adam, Augustine, Marie Ah You, Charles, Tahiti Art and Les Tissus Beauté, Héloise, and Claire. The Caroline Baby Shop specializes in children's clothes, and Chao Léon Tailleur caters exclusively to men. Art galleries include Galerie Winkler, Wing Man Lung, and Photo Tahiti has Kodak film and black-and-white processing service. There is a duty-free shop at Faaa Airport, with liquor, cameras, and other luxury goods; the shop is a cooperative venture of a number of Papeete establishments. Bargaining is *not* the rule in shops, although I would certainly ask for a discount if you've made a substantial purchase. Better shops are usually happy to deliver to your hotel or ship, precluding the need to carry purchases with you as you make the rounds.

You'll want to browse through the cavernous interiors of one or two of the big general traders, typical of firms throughout the South Pacific, and usually dealing in just about everything, from automobiles to real estate, not excluding shipping, tourism, and general merchandise—which can run the gamut (particularly in Tahiti) from imported wines and cheeses to pareus and suntan lotion. These include Établissement Donald and Établissement Baldwin. The former are local agents for Matson Lines, the latter for American Express.

CREATURE COMFORTS

Bless them both: the Tahitians *and* the French. On no other South Pacific island are there happier combinations, at least insofar as the care, feeding, and well-being of the visitor are concerned. The French, to the delight of all of us Francophiles, take with them, wherever they settle, their glorious cuisine and wines, and their inimitable sense of style. The Tahitians, as you have surely surmised at this point, are by no means overrated in the departments of hospitality, charm, and pulchritude. And *their* sense of style is as much a South Pacific standout as is that of the French among Europeans. Add to this the influence of the Chinese, who at their best rank with the French as great cooks, and Tahiti, it would seem, has it made. It is not, to be sure, a bargain. The cost of living is high, far too high for the majority of Tahitians, who have a tough time making ends meet, and quite possibly too high for many prospective tourists, only a tiny handful of whom are millionaires—contrary to what appears to be a locally popular misconception. But tourism is still in its infancy in Tahiti, and one must hope that as it develops, a leveling-off period will follow as competition becomes more widespread. Meanwhile, the Pacific traveler does well to allot a disproportionately high chunk of his budget to Tahiti—and have a ball. There are consolations, the chief of them being that Tahiti's standards are high, that it is uniquely appealing, and that lower prices at other South Pacific destinations will compensate.

Hotels in Tahiti have been springing up with alacrity in recent years but there's nary a shoebox-type skyscraper among them, *merci le bon Dieu.* All blend in with the ambiance of the island —low-slung, Tahitian-bungalow style, Polynesian in decor, engagingly informal and, by and large, with delightful service that becomes increasingly efficient, thanks in large measure to the operation of a locally operated training school for hotel and restaurant personnel. As I have already indicated, the major hotels flank either side of Papeete, fringing the lagoon. One is offered a number of choices and there will be more to come, with the government and private groups undertaking a complex of three 150-room hotels at Punaauia. But currently the best all-round selection for most visitors is, in my book, the Hotel Tahiti, a mile and a half west of town. It is excellently managed, eminently comfortable, strikingly decorated, and still with an informally Tahitian air about it. The cool, high-ceilinged, and spacious lobby is the most attractive of any on the island, and there are as well an inviting cocktail lounge, a first-rate dining room which is Polynesia at its most tastefully elegant, swimming in a new garden pool (or off the reef) and a variety of accommodations, all of course with private bath. Take your choice of bungalows (all have bedrooms and veranda-sitting rooms, and the de luxe ones are about the most sumptuous in the South Pacific) or rooms in a pair of two-story plantation-style buildings. European plan rates: Bungalows rent for from $20 to $25 per day for single or double occupancy, plantation building rooms go from about $10 to $17 single, $12 to $20 double. American plan (all meals) and modified American plan (breakfast and lunch or dinner) rates are available. There's music, entertainment, and dancing nightly, and special Tahitian dance shows once a week, usually Saturday. And there are gift, barber, and beauty shops, sightseeing, and car rental desks. On the other side of Papeete, about two and a half miles east, is the Hotel Taone. It has a number of modern, functional rooms in its main building, but most accommodations are in the maze of bungalows strewn about its lovely gardens. All of the bungalows are spacious, with separate veranda-sitting room, bedroom, and bath. The dining room and cocktail lounge, both recently enlarged and redecorated, are in a separate building a good hike away from many of the bungalows and the main building, and facing the black sand beach of Pirae. The food is French and good, there's nightly music and dancing, and a once-a-week Tahitian dance presentation. My only reservation is that long trek to the dining room during rainy weather; should you be faced with this problem, be sure and have an umbrella—your own, or one the management will loan you if you smile sweetly and explain, as I did, that you don't enjoy dining while drenched. Swimming is limited to the disappointing black sand beach (there's no pool). There's no proper lobby-lounge. Bungalow rates go from $16 single, $18 double, rooms from $11 single and $12 double, European plan. Modified American plan is available, and there are reductions of 15 percent from October through January. The Te Puna Bel Air Hotel is a delightful place. All accommodation is in pleasantly furnished, well-equipped bungalows which flank either the logoon or the cleverly designed swimming pool which looks like a watering hole *au naturelle,* with a white sand beach. There is swimming, as well, in the lagoon just beyond. The spacious lobby, dining room, and cocktail lounge all are within the attractive main building. The location is at Punaauia, about five miles from Papeete, and the management is exceedingly cordial. Bungalow rates are European plan, including the use of a private car with unlimited mileage. They range from $21 to $25 per day for one or two persons. (Deduct $6 if you don't want the car.) Some have kitchens for which there's a moderate additional charge. The Matavai Hotel, about a mile from town in the Tipaerui Valley, embraces a substantial cluster of modern, self-contained bungalows, a fine swimming pool, and a popular restaurant-cocktail lounge-bar which attracts a lively clientele, and weekly Tahitian shows. The de luxe bungalows (which I suggest you aim for) go for about $13 single, $15 double, and there are some which are less expensive. The Tahiti Village at Punaauia, nine miles from Papeete, is a fairish distance from town, but a fine choice, particularly for the traveler who would enjoy a fine nine-hundred-foot *white* sand beach. A bungalow colony of some twelve acres, the "village" offers first-rank accommodation. De luxe beach bungalows go for $25 a single or double; those facing the garden, also de luxe, are $20, and there are still others for about half that rate, as well as some suites in the main building. Rates above are European plan, but American and modified American are available also. There's a charming cocktail lounge and bar-terrace facing the sea and Moorea, as well as an excellent dining room, entertainment, dancing, and regularly scheduled Tahitian shows. Even more distant from Papeete is the Hotel Faratea, at Taravao, about forty miles from town. It consists of half a dozen bungalows, a pleasant dining room and bar, and a beautiful coral garden in the reef just beyond its front door. The Faratea is a good bet as a lunch stop on day-long round-the-island tours, or an overnight headquarters for those taking longer to encircle the island. It's near the Tahiti-iti section of the island, and if your stay is an overnight one, I suggest you go over to Tautira and make an outrigger canoe excursion to Fenua Ino Island. European plan rates: $10 single, $12 double; more than double that for full American plan. **Moorea** offers two prime choices, and of them my favorite is the atmospheric Hotel Aimeo. It has a location nothing less than magnificent on Cook's Bay, and I can't think of anything closer to paradise than a stay in one of its de luxe bungalows, a few steps from the white sand beach, with those classic peaks just across the clear water. There's fine swimming and sunning, skin-diving, outrigger canoes, a bus designed to withstand the rugged unpaved roads for island tours, a bar, and a high-ceilinged restaurant which twice a week features superb Tahitian feasts, or *tamaaraas,* the entertainment portions of which take place after the meal is served, under the stars on the palm-fringed beach. The bungalows rent for $18 single or double, European plan, $21 American plan (single), and $29 American plan (double). Bedrooms in the main building are less ($10 single, $12 double, European plan) but do your best to get a bungalow; the difference in cost is well worthwhile. About a mile and a half from Cook's Bay, but with neither the setting nor the evocative decor of the Aimeo, is Hotel Bali Haì, American-owned and -managed, congenial, with comfortable bungalows (including some de luxe ones), dining room and bar, excellent swimming at a spacious white sand beach, skin-diving, deep-sea fishing, sightseeing, and tamaaraas as well. European plan rates range from about $10 to about $15 single, $11 to about $16 double; American plan tabs go from about $17 to $21 single, $24 to $33 double. Launches to both of these Moorea hotels go directly to their piers from Papeete, and both feature special one-day package tours, embracing round-trip transportation, lunch, sightseeing, and a tamaaraa which, of course, includes dinner. The tab at the Aimeo is $25, at the Bali Haì $18. **Bora Bora:** The Hotel Bora Bora is quite possibly the most expensive hotel in the South Pacific, but a stay, however brief, is worth every penny. The location, on a bluff at the very tip of the island, is inspired. There is nothing elaborate about the place, to be sure. It is simply, if stylishly, decorated *à la Polynésie.* The main building houses a lobby, bar-lounge, gift shop, and a circular dining room so situated that one feels quite at sea, in the best sense of that term. Paths lead down from the main building to clusters of excellently equipped bungalows, each with bedroom, bath, and lanai. Steps away is the white sand beach, and one need only go out a few yards into the crystal clear water to come in contact with all manner of marine life. The hotel provides, at no charge, glass-bottomed paddle boards, masks, flippers, and snorkels, so that one can take in the coral gardens in a variety of ways.

Outrigger canoes are also available, at no charge. There is, as well, a giant outrigger sailing canoe; excursions on it are reasonably priced, and one—a day tour of the island with a picnic lunch and swim stop at a tiny island on the reef—is particularly appealing. There are bus tours about the island, glass-bottomed boat tours of the lagoon, deep-sea fishing for tuna, bonito, and barracuda, motorbikes for rent, and absolutely swinging Saturday night entertainments, with performers from a trio of nearby villages, song, dance, and general merriment into the wee hours. (There's nightly dancing the rest of the week, too.) The ambiance, and that includes dress, is thoroughly informal, service of the caliber you'd expect in a private country villa, perfectly relaxed —and relaxing. Rates are American plan only, and the food is delicious as well it might be at these tabs: $35 single, $48 double, $61 triple. Newer, and just outside the village of Vaitape, is the sixty-room Hotel Noa Noa, with its bar and restaurant jutting into the lagoon, and a range of facilities and activities, aquatic and otherwise, including Tahitian entertainment. Rates (American plan only) are $19 single, $30 double. **Raiatea Island:** The Bali Hai Hotel, under the same management as Moorea's Bali Hai, has a lagoon setting for its bungalow accommodation, a dining room and bar, swimming, snorkeling, and canoeing, and sightseeing tours of this rarely visited but beautiful island, which is believed to have been the most sacred of ancient Tahitian isles, and from which the incredible Polynesian canoe-migrations presumably departed for New Zealand and Hawaii. Rates are identical with those of the mother house in Moorea.

Restaurants, Tahitian feasts, nightlife, et l'amour should not, possibly, be combined in one section of this chapter, but all are, as any visitor to Tahiti knows, of a piece. Let's start with the last-mentioned which is, after all, the most universally discussed feature of Tahitian life: Tahitian women *are* lovely, they are *friendly,* and the moral code of Tahiti is far less hypocritical than that of the West. It is, indeed, refreshingly realistic, and who is to condemn a society in which no stigma is attached either to unmarried mothers or illegitimate children, and in which there has never been an orphanage or any need for one? There is, of course, no color bar in Tahiti (although some of the more recently arrived French civil servants, out of Algeria, seem to have come to the South Pacific with the same racial prejudices in part responsible for France's demise in North Africa), so that it is easy to meet Tahitians at the bars, night spots, and hotel lounges. For the man who does not take the attitude that Tahitian womanhood has been breathlessly awaiting his arrival, dates are not difficult to arrange. The best maxims for Tahiti, as for any vacation locale: use common sense, and play it by ear. Tahiti for the single woman? Why not? Most enjoy themselves tremendously in Tahiti, there being a considerable bachelor population, particularly among the Europeans, who frequent the same after-dark spots as *les touristes*.

Reference has been made earlier in this chapter to the Tahitian feasts, or tamaaraas, and I suggest that you make it a point to work in at least one of these during your visit, bearing in mind that they are not to be confused with the pathetic hotel luaus you may have endured in Hawaii. The tamaaraa, even when experienced at the hotels in Tahiti, retains a ring of authenticity. Of course it is staged for visitors, but it's as close to the real thing as it could possibly be. And not only that: the indigenous Tahitian foods are tasty; you won't leave your banana leaf untouched, as many luau guests feel impelled to do in Hawaii. What's for dinner? Well, much of what you'll eat is cooked in a ground oven, known as a *himaa*. One eats with one's fingers, and the menu is likely to include baked suckling pig, baked breadfruit in coconut cream, curried chicken and/or shrimp, taro leaves and/or taro root, yams, poi (a kind of pudding of bananas and arrowroot), and possibly lobster. There's likely to be a course of raw fish marinated in lime juice and onions (not unlike the delicious Peruvian *ceviche*), a salad perhaps with avocado, and a variety of delicious fruit—mangoes, pineapple, green-skinned (and very tasty) oranges, papaya, guavas, and grapefruit. Take your choice of beverage—wine, the local beer, or coconut water from the shell. Try everything; you'll enjoy a good bit of what's offered. And arrive early, before the sun sets, to snap a photo or two of the colorfully attired chefs preparing the food at the himaa. After the repast comes entertainment, generally under the stars in a perfect, and perfectly natural, setting. The most noted Tahitian dance, called the *tamure,* makes the Hawaiian hula appear rather conventional in contrast, with its hip movements the feature to watch. One finds men dancers—graceful, lithe, athletic —at tamaaraas, and there are musicians—drummers and players of other instruments as well—in the background. Dance costumes are superb. Skirts are made of pandanus leaves or shredded bark, headgear is elaborate, and there are embellishments in the form of fresh floral decorations and seashell embroidery.

Tahitian specialties can be had, sans ceremony, at most restaurants and hotel dining rooms. A good introductory sampling is the platter known in French as a *repas tahitien*—baked breadfruit and butter, marinated raw fish, baked banana, taro, and a bowl of coconut cream in which all but the fish are dunked.

French dishes are much like those you've enjoyed elsewhere; you'll find the delicious crusty bread, cheeses, and wines from Metropolitan France, even imported delicacies like snails. Tahitian-brewed Hanano beer is cold and tasty, there are the usual soft drinks, and good daytime refreshers include fresh grapefruit juice (grapefruit is *pamplemousse* in French), and sugared lime juice with soda, known as *citron pressé.* Chinese food, often good, is not always authentically Chinese, the local Chinese having incorporated Tahitian and French innovations in many recipes, often with much success.

Where to dine? Here are some suggestions: A number of the hotels are wise choices, for either lunch or dinner. These include the Tahiti, the Taone, the Te Puna Bel Air, the Matavai, the Moana Nui, the Royal Tahitien, and the Tahiti Village. The Hotel Faratea, out on the island, is good for lunch on round-island tours, and so is a delightful little restaurant called Au Vieux Montmartre, near Punaauia. Other French restaurants, in or near Papeete: the Vaima for an apéritif, coffee, a soft drink, a snack, or a complete meal; the location is the center-of-town

Quai Bir-Hackeim, and all of Papeete congregates at Vaima, at one time or other, in the course of each twenty-four hours. Others in town are Chez Chapiteau, and Manava. Chinese restaurants include À la Soupe Chinoise, Liou Fong, and Dragon d'Or (air conditioned). The Pierre Roux Boulangerie-Patisserie-Salon de Thé is air conditioned and fine for French pastries, ice cream, espresso—and even pizza. Patisserie Guy Brault is at once a bakery, pastry shop, soda fountain, hamburger bar, and coffee shop—and it's also air conditioned.

Cocktails and after dark: The Hotel Tahiti's handsome bar-lounge offers nightly music, dancing, entertainment, and a congenial crowd—a good place to meet people and strike up acquaintanceships; tamaaraas are held in conjunction with the Tahiti Village Hotel; Tahitian shows, usually on Saturdays. The Hotel Taone bar is bouncy and there's nightly dancing, and a midweek Tahitian show. The Matavai Hotel has local presentations too, and adds tea-dancing Sunday afternoons. The Te Puna Bel Air Hotel is pleasantly quiet during the week, but with dances on weekends. Leaving the hotels, one gets into the more, shall we say, traditional atmosphere of Tahiti: the bars in town. These include the Bar Lea, the Zizou, Whisky à Gogo—each worthy of a drink, and there are—last but hardly least—the most renowned duo between San Francisco and Sydney: Quinn's and the Lafayette. Quinn's remains as wild, raucous, and distinctively Tahitian as ever, with a *really* swinging band perched on a platform behind the bar, a dance floor jammed with *vahines,* both Tahitian and *popaa* (white), and with a male clientele running a wide gamut—Tahitians, French Foreign Legionnaires (generally potted and anxious to sing you native folk songs of their country, which appears, most often, to be Germany); local Frenchies, tourists of all ages and many nationalities, and sailors with backgrounds quite as diverse. The noise, particularly on a Saturday, is deafening, the alcohol quotient is high, everybody is everybody's buddy, the facilities are coeducational, and the Tahitian equivalent of "Time, Gentlemen!" is eleven-thirty at which time nine out of ten occupants make a beeline for the out-of-town Lafayette, where the revelry—often faster-pitched and -paced—continues until something like three in the morning. Miss this duo and you miss a juicy slice of Tahiti—a bit raw, perhaps, but undeniably flavorful. Other attractions: The Office du Tourisme publishes a bilingual calendar of events weekly; copies go to all hotels. There are, despite the relatively small populace, three daily papers: *Le Journal, La Dépêche, Les Nouvelles,* and a number of weekly newspapers, one of which (*Échos de Polynésie*) has an English-language news section. Others include *Ici Tahiti, Tahiti Presse,* and *Le Canard Tahitien*—which, like the noted Paris journal similarly named, is mainly political. All are illustrated, so that even with minimal French they help fill in the Tahitian picture.

Tonga

Entry requirements: A valid passport, a visa (for which there is a charge of $2.07) obtainable at British consulates or British visa offices, and a valid smallpox certificate. **Best times for a visit:** The coolest, dryest months are May through November, and this is when Tonga is at its most pleasant. Humidity is relatively low, and the temperature rarely is higher than eighty. The wet season, from December through April, sees rain, of course, but it is by no means incessant and with luck one might hit a goodish dry spell. Temperatures go as high as ninety, and the humidity increases as well. But even at this time of year, evenings are generally comfortable, particularly along the sea. There can be occasional hurricanes during the wet months, but by and large they occur in the little-visited northern islands. **Currency:** The Tongan pound has been at par with the now-defunct Australian pound, and equals U.S. $2.24. It is divided into twenty shillings, each worth about twelve cents. Currency notes are Tonga's own (ranging from £5 to 5/) but coins are of an elderly Australian vintage, so quaintly archaic that leftovers taken to Australia prove to be excellent conversation pieces, for most Australians know virtually nothing about Tonga, let alone that their coins, circa George V, are in use there. Important note: Tonga is expected to follow Australia from the pound-shilling-pence system to decimal coinage, and when it does, chances are that the new currency, at par with the new Australian dollar (£1=$1.12 U.S.), will succeed the pound. There is a government savings bank in Tonga but no proper trading bank. Traveler's checks can be cashed at the hotel, at leading business establishments, and at the Royal Treasury.

Tonga issued its first gold coins in 1963 but don't count on seeing any in circulation; they were the first issued by any Pacific territory. So unique were they that they sold like hotcakes, and are now collectors' items. The Crown Agents, in London, where the coins were minted, sold them to collectors around the world and were oversubscribed to the point of upsetting all known records. **Film availability:** The big trading establishments maintain some stocks, but I should not count on finding what I wanted; take along plenty. There is no local processing, even for black-and-white. **Languages:** Tongan, a Polynesian tongue, and English are the official languages. All students study English although Tongan is the medium of instruction in the primary schools. You'll have no difficulty in making yourself understood, although the English you'll hear varies tremendously, and ofttimes delightfully, in fluency. Vocabulary and accent are influenced, in varying degrees, by the proximity of Australia and New Zealand—and of the United States, via the Silver Screen. The accents of visiting live Americans—relatively rare—are frequently greeted with whoops of joy, particularly in the case of younger Tongans. **Transportation:** Scheduled air transport to Tonga is a modern innovation. There still are no jets, let alone any truly substantial piston aircraft. Frequency of service, though, is improving regularly. One may fly from Nadi and Suva in Fiji, via Fiji Airways' modern four-engine craft—the most frequent service—and from Apia, Western Samoa, via Polynesian Airlines' DC-3s. The international airport, at Fuaamotu, is a lovely fourteen-mile drive from the capital, and its terminal consists of a tiny Immigrations

and Customs shed, just big enough for the inspector and
a passenger or two at a time; a waiting room shed (furnished with a table but no chairs, when I last saw it,
and with space enough for half a dozen passengers—if
they sat on the table), and a Quonset hut entrance hall
with a ticket and weighing-in counter. Formalities are
friendly, informal, and lightning-like, and the airlines provide inexpensive transportation into town. Access by sea
is principally by the Union Steamship Company of New
Zealand's *Tofua,* which has a regular service from Auckland and calls at both Nukualofa, the capital, on Tongatapu
Island, and at the northerly island of Vavau. Getting about
in Nukualofa is by means of inexpensive taxi (set the
price in advance, no tipping), and via foot in the central
portions of the town. Sightseeing tours are arranged at the
hotel; through H. Lipoi Tupou (telephone 320 and 214),
a firm of general merchants which has a fleet of half a
dozen cars that double as taxis and sightseeing vehicles;
or simply through the driver of the car who takes you
from airport to hotel and who is bound to solicit your
patronage while so doing. There is no air service between
Tongatapu and the other islands of the Tonga group.
Ships, on which the principal cargo is freight rather than
passengers, ply between the islands on fairly (only fairly)
regular schedules, the exception being the above-mentioned
Tofua, between Nukualofa and Vavau. There also is ship
service between Tonga and Fjii, but it is not recommended.
Tipping: Tourism is such an infant industry (if indeed it
can be called that) in Tonga that organized tipping has
not intruded upon its way of life. Still, tips made to those
who have looked after one during a visit can be offered.
Gracious smiles and warm expressions of thanks are always
valued, however. **Business hours:** Shops are open six days
a week, government offices five days (Monday through
Friday). As for Sunday, I quote the Constitution of the
Kingdom of Tonga: "The Sabbath Day shall be sacred in
Tonga forever and it shall not be lawful to do work or
play games or trade on the Sabbath. And any agreement

made or documents witnessed on this day shall be counted void and not recognized by the Government." **Clothes:** By and large, Tonga dresses most informally. Daytime wear, for the visitor, need consist only of shorts, thong-sandals, and sports shirts, for men; simple cottons, slacks, or shorts for the women. Ties and jackets, even after dark, are not generally necessary, although women prefer dresses for dinner. Government and palace receptions, certain events at the private clubs and in private homes do call for ties, jackets, and dressier dresses, however, and one does well to inquire in this regard upon receipt of an invitation, should it not specify. Tongan men, incidentally, wear lava-lava suits for dressy occasions. Jackets are made of tropical worsted or flannel, to match the tailored lava-lava skirts, and are worn with shirts, ties, leather sandals, and no socks. Except for high socks and other accessories, the outfits are not too unlike the Scot in his dress kilts. **Further information:** Office of the Premier, Nukualofa, Tonga; Tonga Travel Bureau, Nukualofa, Tonga; Fiji Airways (E. M. Jones Company, Agents for Tonga), Nukualofa, Tonga; Fiji Airways, Suva, Fiji; Qantas Airways, Suva, Fiji.

INTRODUCING TONGA

Tonga is an anachronism—a quite marvelous anachronism—that works. The odds, one might think, would be so stacked against it that long ago it would have been absorbed by more powerful neighbors. But here it is today—our planet's sole Polynesian kingdom, a realm of some two hundred islands, most of them uninhabited, with a population of but seventy thousand, a total area of less than 260 square miles, a tortoise brought by Captain Cook some two hundred years ago still wandering about in the heart of the capital, and shrimp-eating pigs which waddle through coastal waters (not far from where the *Bounty* crew mutinied) quarrying their prey.

Neighbors' influence: A few air minutes away is Fiji, the multiracial British colony working toward independence with verve and bustle—and a veritable giant in contrast to Tonga. Quite as close is American Samoa, much smaller in area and populace, but with jets zooming into its new airport and TV receivers piping education into the remotest village schools. Western Samoa, the Pacific's newest entirely independent state, is a neighbor, too— making a go of going it alone. Tonga is by no means unaffected by all of this neighborhood activity, but at the same time is moving at its own pace—far more rapidly than Captain Cook's beloved tortoise, to be sure, but with nothing like harelike agility. Heavily influenced by the missionaries (Tonga and Tahiti have known Christianity longer than any other Pacific islands), under British protection since the turn of the twentieth century, with many of its principal civil servants New Zealanders, with its coins (and policemen's slouch-hats) Australian, Tonga manages to remain Tongan, and few of its citizens would have it otherwise. For there is probably no Pacific people more innately conservative, more conscious of, and devoted to, tradition.

An ancient monarchy: Tonga, in the centuries preceding European penetration, had not one but a pair of sovereigns, each with well-defined powers—the one temporal, the other spiritual—and apparently with influence that spread over much of Polynesia. The co-King system remained as late as the mid-nineteenth century, when the temporal monarch took over. But today's Royal Family is descended from the ancient spiritual ruler, known as the Tui Tonga.

Tonga comprises a trio of island groupings—Vavau in the north, which is beautifully mountainous, Haapai in the center (low-slung coral formations), and the southerly Tongatapu cluster of which lush but flattish Tongatapu is the principal island, the most populous, and the site of the capital and only town of substance. The northern islands were the first to be visited by Europeans— Dutch navigators who came upon them in 1616. Later, in 1643,

Abel Tasman (after he discovered Dutch-named New Zealand and the Australian island-state which now bears his own name) visited Tongatapu and a couple of other islands which he promptly named Amsterdam, Rotterdam, and Middleburgh, in the manner of the period. His appellations did not, of course, stick. He liked what he saw, though—an industrious, peaceable, amiable people —but no one in Europe paid much attention. There was not a visit of consequence until more than a century later when (you have guessed by now, I am sure) Captain Cook went ashore. Two decades later, Captain Alejandro Malaspina annexed the northern island of Vavau in the name of his Spanish sovereign— but Spain could not have cared less, and ignored the matter.

Distinguished callers: Cook, meanwhile, had returned in 1777 for a three-month sojourn and, like Tasman, was enthusiastic. It was he who named Tonga "The Friendly Islands," even though he and his crew are believed to have narrowly escaped murder toward the end of their stay. Tonga had still another distinguished visitor during this period—none other than Captain William Bligh of *Bounty* (and cinema) fame, who paid a call in 1789. (Indeed, it was off the Haapi group of islands that his crew mutinied.) Bligh had less trepidation about going ashore in Tonga (thanks to its reputation for friendliness) than he did in Fiji, whose islands he sailed past, thanks to their already notorious reputation for cannibalism.

But not long after the Cook-Bligh visitations, Tonga itself entered its unhappiest and most unfriendly period. Tongans had heard about the Fijians' great war canoes, the biggest and most beautiful in the area. Some paddled over to procure the boats, and the Fijians, as a condition of sale, got them to disrupt the peace at home, the idea being to weaken Tonga and ripen it for Fijian conquest. The result was a rather ghastly era of civil warfare, complicated by the arrival of the first missionaries (a London Missionary Society party of nine laymen) in 1797. This prime effort at evangelization was anything but a success. Disreputable ex-convicts from Australia came upon the scene to make life miserable for the Londoners, the Tongans appeared interested only in the missionaries' iron tools which they made away with, and during the civil war three missionaries were killed.

Understandably, a quarter of a century elapsed before another attempt was made to Christianize Tonga. This time it was a Wesleyan (Methodist) from London who gave up after a frustrating year and four months. But then in 1828 came the third attempt, also Wesleyan, which was anything but a strikeout. The missionaries' zeal impressed itself upon a leading chief, Taufaahau. His influence helped turn his realm, the Haapai islands group, 100 percent Christian. And by 1845, when he became the first ruler of a united Tonga, embracing all three major island clusters, the realm was one of Christendom's proudest domains—and so it has remained.

A united, Christian Tonga: Taufaahau became King George Tupou I (the present King is his great-great-great grandson) and promptly proceeded to organize his realm along the lines of a modern constitutional monarchy with all of the requisite trappings: parliament, privy council, cabinet. With the aid of a remarkably forceful, persuasive, and politically minded British Wesleyan missionary, the Reverend Shirley Baker—who managed to become Premier—George Tupou, most of his chiefs, and many of his people broke away from the established Wesleyan Church and established the Baker-inspired Wesleyan Free Church of Tonga. Although independent of the parent body in the United Kingdom it retains its theology and forms of worship and remains Tonga's major denomination. Other schisms followed as a result of some rather bizarre intrigues in which Mr. Baker ("Misi Beika" to the Tongans) involved himself with the Tongans, with the Germans (who were trying to move into Tonga), and with the British, who at one point had him banished from Tonga.

"Misi Beika's" influence: The Baker influence had two lasting effects. Through his counsel, the monarchy modernized itself, and while so doing became strong and effective. At the same time, the interrelationship between church and state, a Baker innovation, has remained, and in no country is it more powerful. Tonga is almost unique, with its constitutional provision (quoted earlier in this chapter) forbidding Sunday work and play. The dove in its official coat of arms represents "Christianity and peace," the laurel leaves represent "the submission of the Sovereign to the Divine will," and the cross is dominant in the design of the national flag (rarely seen outside of Tonga) because, as King George Tupou I stated: "It is my wish that our flag should have the cross of Jesus, for we are saved because of the sacrifice made by Jesus on the Cross at Calvary. Every Tongan should remember the Cross and the flag should be red in color to represent the blood shed on the Cross for our salvation."

The towns and villages of virtually every South Pacific island are dotted with churches, but no more so than in Tonga. After the various Wesleyan groups, the Roman Catholics and the Mormons are the most popular denominations, with modern churches of the latter—thanks to the heavy outlay it budgets for missionary activity in the Pacific—all over the kingdom, to the extent that a bit of local resentment has developed over the largess of the rich Mormon Yankees.

A copra economy: All the while developing in the area of church and state, Tonga rather limped along economically. Today it remains a completely agricultural state, with but one factory— a copra processing plant. Copra, of course, is the equivalent of the old American South's cotton, as king. And bananas follow. They are now marketed by efficient government-sponsored co-operatives—the Tonga Copra Board and the Tonga Produce Board. And on neighboring American Samoa, the Tonga Government owns 40 percent of the new Coconut Processing Corporation, to which it plans to ship some nine million coconuts a year. (Tongan-U. S. Samoan ties have been particularly close and cordial since Rex Lee assumed the governorship in Pago Pago.)

Every male Tongan—if he wants, and many town-dwelling Tongans do not—is entitled to a Crown Grant of eight and a quarter acres of land in the country, and two-fifths of an acre for his village home. The grants take effect when youths become sixteen—and taxpayers, with the annual land tax coming to less than the equivalent of two U.S. dollars. All land in the kingdom is the property of the Crown, even though great parcels of it are divided among the major nobles, and in turn leased to peasants in the nobles' districts.

Royalty's role: The role of the monarchy is indeed everywhere apparent. Even though Tonga is nominally under British "protection," it does today conduct a great deal of its own business, and one has the feeling that in no other British protectorate is there less influence exerted by London or its representatives on the scene. (The British Protectorate has been in effect since 1900; in 1958 a new Anglo-Tongan treaty was ratified and now the British Commissioner and Consul's chief role is as an adviser on finance and foreign affairs. British diplomatic and consular missions represent Tonga abroad, and Tonga is under the aegis of the British Governor of Fiji, who appoints the Commissioner and Consul resident in Nukualofa.) I suspect the British tread so lightly because the Tongan Government is in capable hands. There is, to be sure, some important duplication of roles, for the Premier of this Graustarkia-in-the-Pacific also happens to be the Crown Prince—H.R.H. Tuipelehake, the broad-girthed, personable, younger son of the late Queen Salote, and of Regent Tungi, who himself had been Premier until his death in 1941. He studied agriculture at Gatton College in Queensland, Australia, and his wife is Crown Princess Melenaite Tupou-Moheofo; they have six children. Tonga's King is the Crown Prince's elder brother, Tupou IV, the former Crown Prince Tungi, who studied at Newington College in Sydney, and later was graduated with an honors degree in jurisprudence from the University of Sydney. He is, appropiately enough, Tonga's best-educated citizen, widely traveled in Europe, America, and the Pacific, and a Knight of the British Empire as well. He and his wife, the Queen, have four children. Before ascending the throne, and while Premier, he held down the cabinet portfolios of Foreign Affairs, Agriculture, and Broadcasting (ZCI—"The Voice of the Friendly Isles"—is one of the South Pacific's most modern and powerful stations), and he was chairman of the important Tonga Copra and Produce boards. Modern-minded and articulate, King Tupou's interests are as broad as his girth—he told me that he weighs 365 pounds. He himself introduced the sport of surfing to Tonga only recently (his board was made to order in Hawaii), and it is he whom the tourist must thank for the construction of the island's first proper hotel, and for the increasing frequency of air service.

Beloved Queen Salote: But it was, of course, the late Queen Salote who was Tonga's most beloved—and most internationally famed—personality. Salote, born in 1900, ascended to the throne at the age of eighteen, a year after she had married. A tall (six feet three), erect, and strikingly good-looking woman, she first became known to the world at large when she appeared in the procession at the coronation of Queen Elizabeth II, in June 1953. Later that same year Elizabeth paid Salote a call, and was an overnight guest at the Tonga Royal Palace with Prince Philip. Twice decorated by the British Government, Salote presided as head of the Privy Council, traveled throughout the islands of her kingdom, and spent several months of each year at a private residence in Auckland, New Zealand, which the Tongan government owns and operates as both a royal retreat and hostel for Tongans studying in New Zealand. It was in Auckland that she died, of cancer and diabetes, on December 15, 1965. Fifty thousand Tongans donned black to mourn at her funeral in Nukualofa, sitting for nearly three hours in the rain to bid farewell to their Queen. The rain was the first in months and many Tongans interpreted it as a sign that the skies were weeping for their sovereign. Salote's coffin rested on a two-foot-thick pile of hand-woven fine-mats. More than a hundred pallbearers carried the coffin from the Royal Chapel to the Royal Burial Grounds, a quarter-mile distant.

Perhaps because of its proximity to Tonga (it is closer than Sydney and the other major Australian centers), New Zealand's ties with Tonga appear even closer than those with Britain. Even though it is a British protectorate, with a Briton resident in Nukualofa as Commissioner and Consul, the bulk of European civil servants in Tonga are New Zealanders—"seconded" (under the employ of) the Tongan Government. None has position of Cabinet rank; they are mostly in technical posts (the Broadcasting Commission, the tiny Defense Force, schools, hospitals) which are gradually being turned over to properly qualified Tongans.

Today's Tonga: The kingdom still is poor. There still are not enough schools (there is, of course, no university, but Tonga College, Tonga High School, and the Mormons' ultramodern high school are pre-university level), nor enough well-qualified teachers; hospital facilities need to be modernized and expanded, still additional new ships could well supplement those now plying between the Tonga islands and neighbor islands. Liquor laws still discriminate against poor Tongans. Roads need paving, sanitation in the villages wants more attention. Indeed, Tonga has many of the problems common to developing Pacific countries.

But it is way ahead of many because of the deep pride and *esprit* of its people. They *know* they are Tongans. They're *glad* to be Tongans. The frustration, the confused identity, the unhappy fusion of Pacific and Western cultures elsewhere is less evident in Tonga than in any of the other principal Pacific islands. It may all change, of course, with the advent of tourism, with more air service, with increased education. One hopes for material progress, of course, but one wants Tonga to remain itself—gay and gracious, spontaneously hospitable, and as at peace with the world as any land could ever hope to be in the era of the bomb.

YOUR VISIT TO TONGA

Tonga (at least the principal island of Tongatapu, the only easily accessible one of the kingdom) is not, I must admit at the outset, endowed with great natural beauty, and Nukualofa, the capital and sole town of importance, is by no stretch of the imagination of any aesthetic distinction. It is reason enough to visit Tonga simply to meet the Tongans and to observe their minuscule kingdom. Unless one's mission is of a commercial or professional nature, or unless it develops that transport should be available to other islands of the kingdom, a visit need not be long.

Indeed, within a week, one can have gotten about reasonably well, and I should not hesitate to go for an even shorter stay if the demands of an itinerary so dictate.

It is well to remember, though, that even though Tonga saw a good many thousand American troops a generation ago, during World War II, it is only just beginning to encourage casual tourism. Aside from its new hotel, it has very little to offer in the way of modern facilities. One must take it on its own terms. And its own terms are not at all difficult, for there are no more attractive, friendly, or hospitable people in the vast Pacific. One's principal equipment for getting to know the locals is the smile. No one is ever in a hurry, so there is always time to pass the time of day, even amongst the relatively tiny European community. And one need not leave the confines of the capital to come across this spontaneous camaraderie. Just amble about at will, whenever the spirit moves you, and see if you regret your Tonga visit!

Nukualofa: Quite possibly the world's least-known capital, certainly not an easy name to roll off one's lips, and with fewer pretensions toward grandeur than any seat of government I know of, save possibly Asunción, Paraguay, Nukualofa fronts the northern coast of Tongatapu. The sea is at its front door and a quiet lagoon is its back yard. With some thirteen thousand residents, Nukualofa is long, low, and rectangular. Its reef-protected harbor is calm, thanks to protection from an outer reef, and there is little enough commercial activity in it so that it is fine for swimming, with no record of itinerant sharks to mar the fun—or the swimmer.

Geographically, no South Pacific capital is easier to know. A thoroughfare, more or less paved and rather grandly known as Beach Road, fronts the waterfront, and two wharves protrude from it. One, substantial and a good city block in length, still is known as the "American" wharf, and is. the sole remainder of Uncle Sam's largess during what must have been a rather frightful World War II period when U.S. troops were on the island. Before the construction of the new hotel, with its swimming pool, it was the place for an in-town swim or sunbath. And very pleasant it was, too. The heart of Nukualofa extends on either side of the pier. In one direction, facing the sea, is the Royal Palace and Chapel—white frame Victorian buildings surrounded by a capacious lawn and what is possibly the lowest wall to enclose any royal residence. The palace is not open to the public, but there are frequent services in the Royal Chapel which visitors are welcome to attend. Coronations (the coronation chair is a chief feature), royal weddings, and other royal events of note take place there. The chapel was prefabricated in New Zealand in 1882. The principal occupant of the garden is the earlier-mentioned tortoise, given to an ancestor of Queen Salote's by Captain Cook in 1772, and now nearly two centuries old. The tortoise, known as Tuimalila, has been blind for some time as a result of a bush fire, and its back is rather severely dented, the consequence of a collision with a car. But it is as spry as ever, and when it strays beyond the grounds it's always returned by whoever spots it. Its keeper, stationed near the wall, will be glad to pick it up so that you can have a good look, and a photo. (He'll also attempt to sell you some local souvenirs.)

The palace proper has passed the century mark, having been built by New Zealand contractors in 1865 (some additions were made in 1882). During the visit of Queen Elizabeth II and Prince Philip in 1953, it was guarded throughout the night by a hundred torch-bearing Tongans, and the royal couple awoke in the morning to the tunes of Tongan nose flutes, in the grounds below their suite.

Closer to the center of town is a cluster of public buildings: the post office, where visitors beeline to pick up sets of the noted Tongan stamps; a little park with a memorial to Tonga's war dead; the minuscule headquarters of the minuscule Tonga Defense Force; a tiny white frame building, like a country frame church without a steeple with the national coat of arms over its door, which is the Parliament of Tonga; and—going inland— the public market, principal shops, cinemas, *kava* bars, and quite pleasant residential streets, along which are interspersed schools and churches. There are no proper sidewalks, but there is really no great need for them, vehicular traffic being almost minimal despite the presence of smartly uniformed policemen mounted on wooden pedestals directing—with great precision—the occasional car or truck that passes by.

Excursions from Nukualofa: Away from the town center—and most certainly worth a look—is the ultramodern headquarters of ZCI, the Tonga Broadcasting Commission, whose programs, broadcast in Tongan, English, and Samoan (including commercials!) are heard throughout the area. ZCI, the new hotel, and (two miles from town) the *Copra Board* complex are Tonga at its most modern. To be seen, too, are the *Tombs of the Kings,* the royal burial grounds since 1893; the splendid coastal *blowholes,* where water gushes heavenward from exposed coral reef to a height of as much as seventy feet; the remains of the ancient fortified village of *Houma,* and, in a pair of enormous trees in the village of Kolavai, the thousands—literally thousands—of black *flying foxes* hanging head downward, apparently for time immemorial; the *lagis* (stone terraces) at *Mua,* where the sacred kings or *tui-tonga* of old are buried; and the nearly sixteen-foot-high coral arch, or *Haamonga-a-Maui,* each slab of which weighs more than thirty tons, and which is believed by tradition to have been a royal archway, built some seven centuries ago.

All of the foregoing can be taken in in a solid half-day's drive. But I would suggest enough time for a fairly leisurely journey, for all about are the squarish thatched-hut villages of this island which, though flat, is green, lush, and not at all difficult on the eye. Rural Tongans—women in longish, shapeless dresses in vivid prints; men in lava-lavas with the distinctively Tongan woven-mat sashes, or *tao'vala,* around their waists—are delighted to see strangers in their midst, and the youngsters will congregate en masse before a stopped car within seconds, their faces smiling, their rudimentary English being put to the test of conversation, their parents looking on amicably. When the road follows the coast, look toward the sea for those rare creatures, Tongan hogs. They slouch about in the shallow offshore waters in search of succulent shrimp and other marine morsels, and I've not seen their like anywhere else in the world. The American visitor cannot help but be interested in the prevalence throughout the island of modern-design Mormon churches. All of them, on this island as elsewhere in the Pacific, are of the same standard design with steeples not unlike—and I mean no disrespect—the newer of the Howard Johnson restaurants on the U. S. East Coast.

Vavau, in the northern group of Tongan islands, is a port of call (along with Nukualofa) for the lucky passengers aboard the Union Steamship Company's ships out of Auckland, and shore visits are generally organized for the day spent ashore. There is, usually, a launch trip to the splendid Swallows' Cave, with its remarkable hundred-foot-high interior chamber, and boats usually pass by Bell Rock (so named because of the odd tinkle which it ensues after being struck). *Neiafu,* the little port town of Vavau, is perched at the tip of a ten-mile-long sound, and the trip to it, from the open sea, is one of the loveliest in the Pacific.

WHAT TO BUY

Tongans are expert at the manufacture of tapa cloth (there are innumerable designs but the most popular are those featuring the Tongan coat of arms), and they weave fine-mats, baskets, fans, bags, and hats beautifully. Other articles to be found include hand-carved miniature outrigger canoes, sandals of the kind worn locally, shells and coral, duty-free Dutch and Japanese transistor radios (which the government buys to sell to Tongans, so that they can listen in to ZCI at little expense, but which are also available to visitors), and the famed Tongan postage stamps. Now, about the stamps. You may have heard about, or seen, the unique laminated gold-foil stamps—two issues of them—which were produced in the last few years. Well, don't plan on buying them in the post office! They were, like the earlier-mentioned Tongan gold coins, overnight sellouts. You will, however, find occasional private individuals—taxi drivers, guides, waiters or waitresses—with sets they've managed to get hold of, and which they'll part with at steep prices. If you're a collector, they're well worth bargaining for. Regular-issue stamps, obtainable in the post office, are hardly to be despised even if easily come by. They come in fourteen denominations and may be purchased in sets or individually.

Sources of handicrafts are the government-sponsored Handicraft Store opposite the post office, the Dateline Hotel shops, and the leading general merchandise stores. These include Burns Philp, Morris Hedstrom, E. M. Jones, Riechelmann Brothers, O. C. Sanft, and H. Lipoi Tupou. Don't count on finding quantities of handicrafts in all stores at all times; a lot depends on local production and delivery. The same, as a matter of fact, goes for postcards, which may warrant a store-by-store search. The aforementioned duty-free transistor radios are on sale at the Government Store. The only printed newspaper in the kingdom, *The Chronicle,* a weekly, goes on sale each Friday morning at the counter of the Government Printing Office.

CREATURE COMFORTS

Tonga's first attempt at mass hospitality was in August 1964, when it played host to two hundred representatives of a dozen countries for the Pan-Pacific and South East Asia Women's Association Conference. It billeted most of them in private homes, its sole and much-beloved boarding establishment, Beach House, not being able to accommodate more than a dozen-odd. Well, times have changed, with the opening of the kingdom's first proper hostelry, the Dateline Hotel. Facing the waterfront, it is a three-story building affording a sea view from all rooms, with a swimming pool, tennis courts, restaurant, bar, shops and private facilities in each of its fifty bedrooms and suites, many of which are air conditioned. Rates in air-conditioned rooms average about $8, doubles about $12. Facilities include dining room, a cocktail lounge, and pool. There are shops, as well, Tongan entertainment at least once weekly and such diversions as surfing, skin-diving, boating, and canoeing. The staff, aside from the New Zealand manager, and chef, consists entirely of specially trained Tongans. The hotel's name, I was told by King Tupou, was first suggested by Queen Salote, to emphasize the country's dateline-straddling position. (I had hoped it would be called after the Queen herself, who was, after all, the leading symbol of Tonga abroad.) The hotel's eating facilities are *it* in Nukualofa, although visitors may obtain guest privileges for the little Yacht Club (and its bar). There are two members-only clubs, British Colonial Pukka-Sahib style—the Nukualofa and the Tonga clubs. Most of their members are New Zealand government employees, and if you have introductions to members you'll be taken over for a beer or two, or possibly to one of the clubs' social events. Otherwise there are the movies, and whatever special events for visitors scheduled by the hotel. Liquor by the bottle may be purchased only by permit holders. Permits are not difficult to obtain for Europeans or upper-class Tongans, but the mass of the populace still must resort to brewing its own. Kava, the non-alcoholic beverage common to islands in this region, is something of a substitute.

Acknowledgments

To acknowledge the kindness of a great many people of—and associated with—the South Pacific in the preparation of this book is a formidable task, but I should like to make the effort, at least partially. I am most particularly indebted to Miss Joyce C. Chivers, Qantas Airways' pert, petite charmer of a public relations officer for North America, who, I hope, will not regret that this book was her idea, and who has been of invaluable help ever since I took her up on the suggestion. Many of her Qantas colleagues have been of great assistance, too: N. H. Powell, general manager for North America, in San Francisco; John S. Rowe, head of the New York branch, and John Weeks, Barry Connor, and Barbara Keller, also of that office. I thank, also, Qantas' Captain Hugh M. Birch, D.F.C., commercial manager (marketing), and John A. Ulm, the airline's chief press information officer, both headquartered in Sydney, and Ward Washington of the Honolulu office. The first-rate Australian National Travel Association has been of inestimable aid, and I offer kudos to Basil Atkinson, the general manager, L. R. "Doc" Watson, the genial, never-flustered information manager, and his crack assistant Ian Kennedy, all in Melbourne headquarters; John R. Elliott, the Sydney manager, and his ball-of-fire colleague, Douglas R. Hayman; and the ever-congenial, never-too-busy-to-help New York staff—Manager William J. Walker and his assistant, Nancy J. Cochrane.

Many other Australians were of help in the course of my travels: Lillian Roxon of the Sydney *Morning Herald,* Robert Hatherley of J. Walter Thompson in Sydney, and Keith M. Johns of the Western Australian Government Tourist Bureau, in Perth, were but a few. In American Samoa, Governor H. Rex Lee and Mrs. Lee were both hospitable and helpful, and I am most appreciative. Across the water, in Western Samoa, I recall with pleasure the assistance and hospitality of His Highness Malietoa Tanumafili II, the Head of State, and of Alan Ripine, the excellent public relations officer in the office of the Government Secretary, Ash Leveston. In Tonga, I am much indebted to His Majesty King Tupou IV, who was Crown Prince Tungi during my visit, and His Royal Highness, Crown Prince Tuipelehake, the Premier, as well as Uliti Palu of Radio Tonga. Donald I. Lane, then Executive Secretary of the Fiji Visitors Bureau, was of great help to me, as were his assistant, Herb Marlow; R. K. Wightman, Assistant Manager of Fiji Airways, and Glen J. Durbin, manager of Nadi's Mocambo Hotel. In Tahiti, I am grateful for the courteous aid and counsel of Gerard Gilloteaux, gifted *chef du service du tourisme,* his equally skilled counterpart in New Caledonia, Louis P. Eschembrenner, and their representatives in New York, René Bardy, director-general, and Myron Clement, public relations director, French Government Tourist Office. Maurice Schneider, of Nouméa's Établissement Ballarde, was also of great help in New Caledonia, as was M. Duvernois, Nouméa manager of UTA French Airlines, and his North American counterpart, my friend from *Africa A to Z* days, Hans J. Winter. Neil S. Munro, former New Zealand Government Travel Commissioner in New York and now back at headquarters in Wellington, paved my way in New Zealand with skill and charm, and was most ably aided and abetted by Donald Welsh, his successor in New York, and by John P. Campbell, public relations officer of the New Zealand Government Tourist Department in Wellington. Paul Gabites, New Zealand's Consul-General in New York, was also most kind. Many thanks, too, to Jack P. Gabriel, ace publicity director of the Pacific Area Travel Association in San Francisco, who came to my aid with this book as he did in the case of *Asia A to Z;* to Shirley Fockler, astute editor of PATA's excellent journal, *Pacific Travel News;* to Pan Am's Paul Kendall, always a good, helpful, and hospitable friend of every writer, in Honolulu and the Pacific; to Genie Hotaling, of Pacific Pathways; to Richard E. Webb, Reference and Library Director at British Information Services, New York, who cordially assisted on this as with previous *A to Z* books, and—it should go without saying but I won't let it—to Senior Editor Clara Claasen and Copy Editor William D. Drennan of Doubleday, and my literary agent, Anita Diamant: no writer could ask for better. It should go without saying, also, that whatever errors crop up, in a compendium as comprehensive as this, are mine—as are the opinions expressed.

R.S.K.

Index

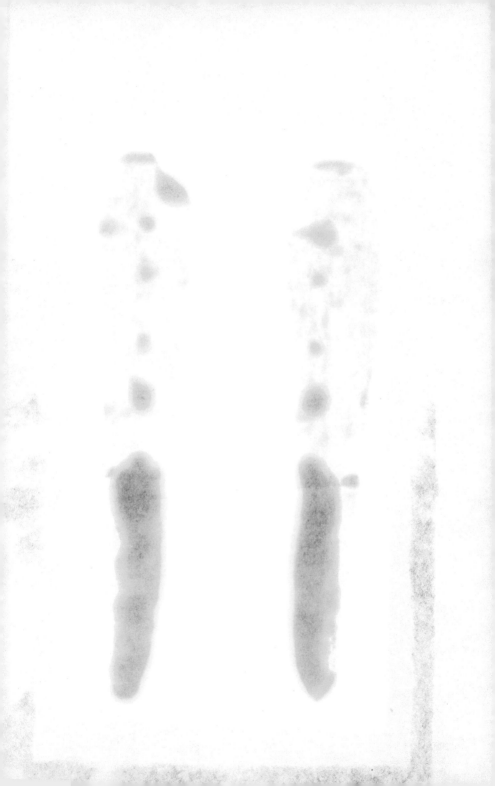

51564

DU
15
K3

KANE, ROBERT
SOUTH PACIFIC A TO Z.

DATE DUE

JUL 17 1995	

11/10/66

Parke Inside

Korea
Seoul

Japan

China

Shanghai

Taiwan

RYUKYU ISLANDS

Hong Kong

NORTH

South China Sea

Philippines

Sarawak

Borneo

Celebes

INDONESIA

Sunda Islands

MARIANA
ISLANDS

Guam

Truk

CAROLINE ISLANDS

Ponapé

Wake

MARSHALL
ISLAND

ADMIRALTY
ISLANDS

New Guinea
Papua

Arafura Sea

Darwin

NORTHERN
TERRITORY

Port Moresby

GREAT BARRIER REEF

Coral Sea

Solomon
Islands

GILBERT
ISLANDS

ELLI

New
Hebrides

Fiji
Isl

New
Caledonia

Australia

WESTERN
AUSTRALIA

SOUTH
AUSTRALIA

QUEENSLAND

Brisbane

SOUTH   P

Norfolk
Island

Perth

NEW
SOUTH WALES

Sydney
Canberra

Adelaide

Melbourne

Indian Ocean

Tasman Sea

New Zealand

Wel

SOUTH